SAMUEL BARBER

ROUTLEDGE MUSIC BIBLIOGRAPHIES
Brad Eden, *Series Editor*

ISAAC ALBÉNIZ by Walter A. Clark
C. P. E. BACH by Doris Powers
SAMUEL BARBER by Wayne C. Wentzel
BÉLA BARTÓK by Elliot Antokoletz
ALBAN BERG by Bryan R. Simms
LEONARD BERNSTEIN by Paul Laird
BENJAMIN BRITTEN by Peter J. Hodgson
ELLIOTT CARTER by John F. Link
CENTRAL EUROPEAN FOLK MUSIC by Philip V. Bohlman
CARLOS CHÁVEZ by Robert L. Parker
FRÉDÉRIC CHOPIN by William Smialek
CHORAL MUSIC by Avery T. Sharp and John Michael Floyd
AARON COPLAND by Marta Robertson and Robin Armstrong
GAETANO DONIZETTI by James P. Cassaro
EDWARD ELGAR by Christopher Kent
GABRIEL FAURÉ by Edward R. Phillips
SCOTT JOPLIN by Nancy R. Ping-Robbins
JAZZ RESEARCH AND PERFORMANCE MATERIALS, 2ND EDITION by Eddie S. Meadows
ZOLTÁN KODÁLY by Michael Houlahan and Philip Tacka
GUILLAUME DE MACHAUT by Lawrence Earp
FELIX MENDELSSOHN BARTHOLDY by John Michael Cooper
NORTH AMERICAN INDIAN MUSIC by Richard Keeling
OPERA, 2ND EDITION by Guy Marco
GIOVANNI PIERLUIGI DA PALESTRINA by Clara Marvin
GIACOMO PUCCINI by Linda B. Fairtile
ALESSANDRO AND DOMENICO SCARLATTI by Carole F. Vidali
SERIAL MUSIC AND SERIALISM by John D. Vander Weg
JEAN SIBELIUS by Glenda Dawn Goss
GIUSEPPE VERDI by Gregory W. Harwood
TOMÁS LUIS DE VICTORIA by Eugene Casjen Cramer
RICHARD WAGNER by Michael Saffle

SAMUEL BARBER
A GUIDE TO RESEARCH

WAYNE C. WENTZEL

Routledge Music Bibliographies

ROUTLEDGE
NEW YORK AND LONDON

Published in 2001 by
Routledge
29 West 35th Street
New York, NY 10001

Published in Great Britain by
Routledge
11 New Fetter Lane
London EC4P 4EE

Routledge is an imprint of the Taylor & Francis Group.

Printed on acid-free, 250-year-life paper.
Manufactured in the United States of America.

10 9 8 7 6 5 4 3 2 1

Library of Congress Cataloging-in-Publication Data

Wentzel, Wayne C. (Wayne Clifford), 1942-
       Samuel Barber : a guide to research / Wayne C. Wentzel.
       p. cm. - (Composer resource manuals; v. 55)
       Includes bibliographical references and indexes.
       ISBN 0-8153-3496-6 (alk. paper)
       1. Barber, Samuel, 1910-Bibliography. I. Title. II. Series.

ML134.B175 W46 2001
016.78'092-dc21   00-066506

Contents

Acknowledgments

There are many people I would like to acknowledge for helping me assemble this book. I would like to thank the committee on Academic Grants at Butler University for helping fund my first summer of research on the project. The grant allowed me to get the project off to a productive start. I extend thanks to the entire staff at Butler University's Irwin Library, particularly Amber D. Blackwell of the interlibrary loan department who was able to track down and obtain, often at considerable effort, most of the dissertations and theses that I requested. I am also grateful to the many colleges and universities that granted those interlibrary loan requests. I would like to thank Sheridan Stormes, the music and fine arts librarian, who greatly assisted me in many ways, especially by tracking down information through various internet programs. I made good use of the resources at the Music Library of the School of Music at nearby Indiana University, where the staff always helped me find the materials that I needed.

In New York City, Karen Rose Gonon, the Director of Fellowship Programs at the American Academy in Rome, provided all the documentation on Barber's association with the academy, including letters related to his activities there. Kathy Kienholz, the archivist at the American Academy and Institute of the Arts, allowed me complete access to the many documents related to Barber's activities at that institution, particularly correspondences involving his committee work and the nominations and seconds of new members. I'd also like to thank the staff at the New York Public Library for their assistance, both at the main branch where I consulted their many newspaper files, and at the performing arts division where they had to cope with the less-than-ideal circumstances of their temporary headquarters. Nevertheless, they were able to provide quick access to both the clippings files on Barber and the many files of letters between him and several of his colleagues, including William Schuman, Edith Evans Braun, and Walter Damrosch.

In Washington, D.C., the staff at the Music Division of the Library of Congress was very accommodating in their retrieval of many documents, including the files of letters between Barber and those associated with the library, such as

Elizabeth Sprague Coolidge, Oliver Strunk, and Harold D. Spivacke. The staff also provided access to letters from Barber in the Copland and Bernstein collections. I would particularly like to thank Kevin Lavine for getting my research started in the right direction. The library was also the main source for Barber manuscripts.

At Georgetown University Nicholas Scheetz, the manuscript librarian in the Special Collections Division, provided me access to a well-ordered file of letters in the Francis and Katherine Biddle papers. The fact that this material was waiting for me when I arrived made me able to accomplish the research task easily and quickly.

Librarians at other universities also provided valuable service in my pursuit of letters and manuscripts. My thanks goes to Kendall Crilly, Richard Boursy, and Suzanne Eggleston for expediting my study of letters in the archival papers collections at Yale University. I would like to thank the staff at the University of Pennsylvania's Van Pelt Library, particularly John Pollack at the Walter H. Lemore Annenberg Rare Book and Manuscript Library for his assistance in providing access to the letters in their Eugene Ormandy collection and in showing me the library's holdings of Barber's scores in both the Ormandy and Marian Anderson collections. I would also like to thank the staffs of the libraries at Kent State University, Bowling Green University, and Ohio State University for their assistance. I am also grateful for the assistance of librarians at the University of Illinois at Champaign-Urbana, Northwestern University, the Chicago Public Library, and the Free Library of Philadelphia.

I also extend my sincerest thanks to David Peter Coppin, the rare books librarian at the Eastman School of Music's Sibley Library and to Susan Feder, vice president at G. Schirmer, for allowing me access to many Barber manuscripts owned by Schirmer but on loan to Eastman. This is a very rich resource of material.

I would like to thank other Barber scholars for their support in this project. To Jean Kreiling, who allowed me to use and modify her inventory of Barber manuscripts at the Chester County Historical Society and in answering various questions I had concerning that collection. My very sincere thanks goes to Barbara Heyman, who has cordially replied to my requests for information and has generously and graciously supported my efforts at various stages of this book. I am also very grateful to Guy Marco and Richard Carlin at Routledge for their very meticulous scrutiny of my manuscript submissions, and to Julie Ho for overseeing the production of this book. It is through their diligence that the work has proceeded from the rough draft stage to a readable final product. Finally my thanks goes to friends and colleagues who have encouraged me throughout the research and writing stages of this project.

Introduction. The State of Barber Research

Serious studies of Samuel Barber and his music are not numerous. There are two biographies, one from the early 1950s (Broder; Item 254), which is obviously out of date, and another from the early 1980s (Heyman; Item 258). Heyman's study, written after Barber's death, is both more inclusive and more scholarly than Broder's Work. Heyman refers to many documents and letters. Most of the articles about Barber, in both popular newspapers and magazines, are general. There are very few scholarly articles, and two of them (by Dressler; Item 411 and Kreiling; Item 423) were refashioned from parts of the authors' dissertations. Barber is not represented in any of the twentieth-century music periodicals such as *American Music* or *Perspectives of New Music* (his music is probably not "new" enough), where you might expect to find research on him. Yet his name is constantly mentioned wherever American music is discussed, although often along with a list of other composers, or as a footnote. It is clear that more scholarly research is necessary if we are to understand Barber's music and compositional style.

Even if the world of musical scholarship has not focused on Barber's music, college campuses have a growing interest around the country in his works. Students are performing Barber's music (see the website WorldCat, see page 26, which often lists recent recitals that include his music), and many graduate students are increasingly writing theses and dissertations on his specific pieces and works in general. While a few of these documents discuss Barber's operas, many focus on his choral, vocal, and instrumental works, particularly for piano. There are at least eight documents dealing with his choral works in general and one each on *The Lovers, Prayers of Kierkegaard,* and *Reincarnations.* Individual theses concern his songs op. 10, op. 45, *Mélodies passagères,* and *Despite and Still.* The most popular of his vocal works are the *Hermit Songs* and *Knoxville: Summer of 1915,* with eight theses on each of them.

Barber's chamber music does not fair as well. There is one thesis on these works in general, one on the Cello Sonata, and one on *Summer Music.* Of Barber's orchestral works, the Piano Concerto is the most popular subject with nine different theses. There are three theses on the violin concerto. Only two theses concern the first symphony, while only one deals with the *Adagio for Strings.* It seems odd that this work, clearly Barber's most popular with the public, should have so little written about it.

Barber's piano music is discussed more than any other part of his repertoire. There are six works on this music in general, one on the *Ballade*, one on the *Nocturne,* and 13 on the piano sonata. While the quality of scholarship obviously varies from one thesis to another, the writers clearly love Barber's music and try to explain how themes and forms constitute his work. Sadly lacking are works that discuss *Music for a Scene from Shelley;* the orchestral Essays; *Dover Beach;* the *Capricorn Concerto;* and the Cello Concerto. Perhaps future graduate students will tackle these pieces.

Another encouraging sign was the international symposium on Barber's music held at Virginia Commonwealth University in the spring of 2001. Papers from this meeting may result in scholarly articles.

BARBER IN HIS OWN WORDS

Unlike Copland or Bernstein, who wrote extensively about their music and music in general, Barber is reticent to a fault. He wrote only two articles, "Birth Pangs of an Opera" and "On Waiting for a Libretto." There are, however, several articles in which he is interviewed: e.g. Ardoin (Item 259), Henahan (271), Kozinn (275–76) Gruen (291), Klein (294), Coleman (306), and Ramey (389). These valuable articles not only record Barber's opinions and relate pertinent information about some of his compositions, but also make us aware that he is just as much a "composer of words" as he is of music. His way of verbal phrasing can reveal insights into his character and wry sense of humor. For example

- Barber says he gave up conducting because, "I had about as much projection as a baby skunk."[1]
- "Sometimes I get tired of hearing the *Adagio for Strings.* But I amuse myself during performances because I know there's going to be a mistake somewhere. Happens everytime."[2]
- Should composers write for themselves or the public? "I write for myself and Helen Carter"; "Mrs. Carter once proclaimed that all American composers are dead except for Elliot. Well, she's the judge."[3]
- When asked, what is the future for today's composers, he replied, "Ask the musicologists. They know everything."[4]

[1]Kozinn (Item 275), 46.
[2]Ibid., 66.
[3]Ibid., 65.
[4]Ibid.

- "I love quoting deceased critics—the more the merrier."[5]
- From a letter to his mother when he was young: "I was meant to be a composer . . . Don't ask me to try to forget this unpleasant thing and go and play football."[6]
- "Francis [Poulenc] was a darling man, but he was enamored only with his own songs."[7]
- When Aaron Copland announced, " 'Here in Tanglewood we have decided that Charles Ives is a great composer!' I backed my car out onto Route 183 and drove away without comment."[8]
- Stravinsky's pieces are so short that George Balanchine "has to have one played three times in one sitting to dance a ballet to it."[9]
- Louise Homer [Barber's aunt] had a voice that was so "sharp, of such richness, that recalcitrant angels might have melted."[10]

To read Barber's words is one thing, but to see and hear him speak is another, and for that you need to go to New York or Washington, D.C., to view the TV program from *Camera Three,* "Happy Birthday, Samuel Barber" (Item 600). It is well worth the effort to hear him comment about himself and his music, as well as having the chance to see him play the piano. We can also hear a tape of his *Dover Beach* recording, which was out of print until just recently.

CURRENT STATE OF RECORDINGS

If a scarcity of books and articles about Barber indicates a lack of interest on the part of scholars, then the abundance of recordings surely indicates that the listener still likes to hear Barber's music. The number of columns in recent *Schwann* catalogues listing his recordings (c. 5 1/2) is large for an American composer, and only somewhat less than Copland (c. 6 1/2), although both are still far behind Gershwin (c. 8). Yet the number of recordings of *Adagio for Strings* (37) far exceeds that of any other American work, other than Gershwin's main orchestral works (e.g. *Rhapsody in Blue* at 81). In contrast, there are only 31 recordings of Copland's *Appalachian Spring* (12 complete, 19 of the suite) and 19 of *Rodeo.* Most of Barber's works are now available on CD, including both new performances and many "classic" recordings, except for *Toccata Festiva* and the original string quartet version of *Serenade.* Even these are likely to appear in the next record catalogues.

---

[5]Kozinn (Item 276), 49.
[6]Ramey (Item 389), 18.
[7]Ibid., 19.
[8]Ibid.
[9]Klein (Item 394), 109.
[10]Ibid.

The music of Samuel Barber has regained much of its original popularity. It is, in the words of Terry Teachout, "Samuel Barber's revenge" (see Item 284). After years of being accused of "conservatism" and "neo-romanticism," and being out of touch with contemporary sounds, he now seems to have gained stature in the musical world. The record-buying public and those attending concerts never really abandoned him. Now that the possible excesses of the musical avant-garde appear to have subsided, we can look back on the twentieth century and regard Barber as one of its finest composers.

CONTENTS OF THE BOOK

This book is a survey of available research on the life and works of Samuel Barber, and like the other volumes in this Composer Resource Manuals series it is necessarily selective in scope. Because a simple list of Barber's published works is easily obtainable (in various editions of the *Grove Dictionary*, the Schirmer website, etc.), the list in this book adds a brief reference to various manuscript sources (primarily in the Library of Congress). Also listed but not annotated are one or two reviews of the score (when available). This is followed by the first one or two performances of each work, giving performers, dates, and places, and a short list of reviews (cited but not annotated) to allow the reader to consult critics' and audiences' reactions to the music.

The bibliography section starts with general material on the composer and his music, including books, dissertations, and general articles. The remainder of the chapter proceeds by individual compositions, divided into genre categories. This section does not list popular articles such as those from *Time* or *Life* magazines, but does include somewhat general articles. It also excludes liner notes even though such information can sometimes be useful and interesting. Dissertations and masters theses are also included because they contain much of the most analytical discussions of Barber's music. These sources show what research has already been accomplished and provide a practical guide for future students, scholars, and performers.

The discography section is even more selective. It contains listings of "classic" recordings, primarily those that were issued shortly after the date of composition, especially those already reissued on compact disc. Also included are brief references to record reviews (without annotations) both from representative magazines and the *New York Times*.

These first chapters are primarily an updating and reorganization of the *Bio-Bibliography* of Barber compiled by Don Hennessee in the late 1970s (see Item 256). In his book, however, Hennessee puts together rather diverse sources in the same location. It is often difficult to sort out scholarly articles and dissertations from performance and recording reviews. Moreover, he seldom evaluates his sources, relying on quotations that are relevant to the subject or musical composition under consideration. However, because these quotations are still significant and can indeed inform the reader about the general content of the source, I have decided to include a "Hennessee number" in brackets along with my own citations and annotations when applicable.

The next chapters go beyond the scope of Hennessee's book. Chapter 5 is a listing of most of Barber's manuscripts, at least those that are within reasonable access of the scholar. The list does not include sources that are in private hands. Very few people have worked on Barber's manuscripts. Heyman has included some discussion in both her book and dissertation, providing good opportunities to compare and contrast manuscript versions of many pieces with their final published scores. When facsimiles of some of this material appear in published sources, I have included page references to them. Unfortunately, many manuscripts of Barber's unpublished works lay hidden and uncatalogued in the recesses of the Library of Congress. I have included a selective list of these works with a general description. Diligent researchers may have luck in obtaining a look at these some day. Manuscripts of other unpublished works are housed in the Chester County Historical Society, which usually allows researchers access to them.

Finally, chapter 6 is devoted to the correspondence between Barber and other twentieth-century music figures, including composers, conductors, and friends. These letters have not yet been published, although Heyman plans to publish selected letters in the near future. Only those letters that are generally accessible to the public have been included, not those still in private hands. In this chapter I have listed the letters, the name of the correspondents, dates (when known), and a brief annotation of their contents. When some of these letters are quoted, whole or in part, in published books, these references are included with the annotations.

Chapter 1. Basic Information

DICTIONARIES AND ENCYCLOPEDIAS

There are many ways to begin biographical research. A good place to start is to find fairly general Barber biographies in dictionaries and encyclopedias. These provide concise summaries of his life and music and brief bibliographies at the end often point the way to more specific sources.

1. Bull, Storm. *Index to Biographies of Contemporary Composers.* In three vols. Vol. 1, Metuchen, NJ: Scarecrow, 1964. ML 105 .B9; Vol. 2, 1974, ISBN 8108-0734-3; Vol. 3, 1987, ISBN 0-8108-1930-9.

    The first volume lists 13 sources of then current Barber biographies, including the first *ASCAP Biographical Dictionary of Composers.* The two later volumes add many other sources, including those in foreign language publications and the numerous citations in *The Music Index.*

2. Slonimksy, Nicolas. In "Barber, Samuel." *Baker's Biographical Dictionary of Musicians,* 8th ed. NY: Schirmer, 1992. ISBN 0-0287-2415-1 ML 105 .B16

    The article is divided into the categories of life and works. There are only four items in the bibliography.

3. Slonimksy, Nicolas. "Barber, Samuel." In *Baker's Biographical Dictionary of Twentieth-Century Music.* ed. Laura Kuhn. NY: Schirmer, 1997. ISBN 0-0287-1271-4 ML 105 .S612

    Written somewhat later than the article in the main Baker's dictionary, this one is more extensive with ten items in the bibliography. At the end is a list of works, by genre, with performers and dates of performance.

4. Randall, Don, ed. *Harvard Biographical Dictionary.* Boston, MA: Harvard University Press, 1996.

This short article contains a list of Barber's teachers and compositions. It has only two items in the bibliography: Hennessee (Item 256) and Heyman (Item 258).

5.   Blume, Friedrich, ed. *Die Musik in Geschichte und Gegenwart.* Basel: Bären-reiter, 1949-1967. 17 v.

The article on Barber by Karl Wörner was issued in Vol. 1 in 1949 and is less than a column long, covering Barber's life and works up through op. 27.

6.   *Die Musik in Geschichte und Gegenwart.* 2nd. ed. Kassel: Bärenreiter, "Personenteil" Series, Vol. 2. ISBN 3-7618-1110-1 ML 100 .M92 1994

The updated version of this encyclopedia is now split into two components: the "Sachteil" which is by subject and is now complete, and the "Personenteil" which contains the biographical material that was interspersed with subjects in the original version. This series currently has only two volumes, up through "Bi." Because Barber's name is so early in the alphabet, it is included in the second volume, with an entirely new biography by Barbara Heyman. She now devotes three columns to the composer, updating both his life and list of compositions. She also includes a longer bibliography.

7.   Sadie, Stanley, ed. *The New Grove Dictionary of Music and Musicians.* London: MacMillan, 1980. ISBN 0-333-2311-2 ML 100 .N48 Reprinted in *The New Grove Twentieth-Century American Masters.* NY: W. W. Norton, 1988. ISBN 0-9438-1836-2 ML 390 .N469

This concise biography, written by Richard Jackson shortly before Barber's death, is divided into two sections: career and style. The works are listed by genre, and by opus number within that genre. The date of composition is given along with the date of the first performance, if known. He lists only a few unpublished works. A newer biography is likely to appear when the 2nd edition of *The New Grove Dictionary* comes out shortly.

While Peggy Glanville-Hick's article on Barber in the earlier, 5th edition of *Grove* (1954) is clearly out of date, it is still worth reading because of her own insights and relevant comments.

8.   Hitchcock, H. Wiley, and Stanley Sadie, eds. *The New Grove Dictionary of American Music.* London: Macmillan, 1986. ISBN 0-943-81836-2 ML 101 .U6 N48

This biography, published after Barber's death, is basically a reprint of the one above, but Jackson now includes the composer's death date, and a few minor additions. The list of works, this time compiled by Barbara Heyman, is organized somewhat differently from Jackson's list, but maintains a similar order by genre and chronology. Heyman also includes the names of the performers in the premieres and a list of unpublished works. The bibliography is very extensive, with 26 listings as opposed to only 4 in the earlier article.

A BARBER CHRONOLOGY

The following chart shows the date in Barber's life, one or two significant events in that year, and the works he composed. Opus numbers are given for those works eventually published by G. Schirmer. The genres are given for unpublished works.

Dates	Events in life	Musical compositions
March 9, 1910	Barber's birth	
1916	began to study piano with William Hatton Green; attends Met performance of *Aida,* with his aunt Louise Homer as Amneris	
1917		**Piano**: "Melody in F"; "Sadness" **Song**: "Sometime"; "Why Not?"
1918		**Piano**: "Largo"; "War Song" **Song**: "In the Firelight"
1919		**Piano**: "At Twilight"; "Lullaby" **Song**: "Isabel"
1920	played "At Twilight" and "Lullaby" at First Presbyterian Church, West Chester, PA.	**One act of an opera:** "The Rose Tree" **Song**: "The Wanderer"; begins "Nursery Songs"
1921		**Song**: "Prayer"; "An Old Song"; "Hunting Song"
c. 1922	Organist at Westminster Church, West Chester	**Song:** "Thy Will Be Done"
c. 1923	Sara Barber sings "Nursery Songs" and selections from "Rose Tree" at First Presbyterian Church	**Piano**: "Themes"; Two of *Three Sketches*—"Love Song" & "To My Steinway" **Song**: "October-Weather"
1923–24		**Piano**: Third of *Three Sketches*— "Minuet"
1924	Becomes charter student at Curtis Institute of Music; studies piano with George Boyle, voice with Emilio de Gogorza, and music theory and composition with Rosario Scalero	**Piano**: Untitled; "Petite Berceuse" "Fantasie for two pianos" **Choral**: "Christmas Eve" **Song**: "Dere Two Fella Joe"; My Fairyland"; "Summer is Coming"; "Little Children of the Wind"; "Longing"

Dates	Events in life	Musical compositions
1925		**Organ**: "To Longwood Gardens" **Piano**: "Fresh from West Chester (Some Jazzings)"; "Poison Ivy" and "Country Dance" **Song**: "A Slumber Song of the Madonna"; "Fantasy in Purple"; "Lady, When I Behold the Roses"; "La Nuit"; "I never thought that youth would go"; "Invocation to Youth"
1926	Graduates from West Chester High School; program of songs presented at the Barber home.	**Piano**: "Fresh from West Chester"— "Let's Sit it Out, I'd Rather Watch"; "Three Essays;" "To Aunt Mamie on Her Birthday"; "Main Street" **Organ**: "Chorale for a New Organ" **Song**: "An Earnest Suit to His Unkind Mistress"; "Ask Me to Rest"; "Au clair de lune"; "He Nonny No"; "Man"; "Music, When Soft Voices Die"; "Thy Love"; "Watchers"
1927		**Song**: "Dance" (lost); "Mother, I Cannot Mind My Wheel"; "Only Of Me and Thee"; "Rounds for Three Voices"; "There's Nae Lark"
1927–28	Louise Homer performs "Only of Me," "Longing," "Summer is coming," and "Slumber Song."	"The Daisies," Op. 2, no. 1 **Organ**: "Three Chorale Preludes"; "Partita" **Piano**: "Two- and three-voice fugues"
1928	Wins Bearns prize of $1200; meets Gian Carlo Menotti; travels to Europe	*Serenade for String Quartet,* Op. 1 "With Rue My Heart is Laden," Op. 2, no. 2 Sonata for Violin (lost) **Song**: "The Shepherd to his Love"; "The Nymph's Reply"
1930		Piano Concerto (lost) **Choral**: "Motetto"
1930–31		*Pieces for Carillon: Round, Legend, Dirge*
1931	Wins second Bearns prize	*Dover Beach,* Op. 3 Overture to *The School for Scandal,* Op. 5
1931–32		**Piano**: "Two Interludes"
1932	Travels in Europe; Cello Sonata earns him American Prix de Rome	Cello Sonata, Op. 6 *Suite for Carillon*

Dates	Events in life	Musical compositions
1933		*Music for a Scene from Shelley,* Op. 7
1934	Conducting debut (of works by Corelli, Vivaldi, Menotti, etc.)	"Bessie Bobtail," Op. 2, no. 3 **Song:** "Song of Enitharmon"; "Love at the Door"; "Serenader"
1935	All-Barber radio program on NBC; G. Schirmer begins publication of Barber works; awarded first Pulitzer traveling scholarship; in Rome at American Academy; meets Toscanini in Italy	*The Virgin Martyrs,* Op. 8, no. 1 "Rain has fallen," Op. 10, no. 1 "Sleep now," Op. 10, no. 2 Incidental music for "One Day of Spring" **Song:** "Love's Caution"; "Night Wanderers"; "Peace"; "Stopping By Woods on a Snowy Evening"; "Of that so sweet imprisonment"; "Strings in the earth and air"; "Who carries corn and crown"
1936	Receives second Pulitzer traveling fellowship	"Let down the bars, O death," Op. 8, No. 2 Symphony in One Movement, Op. 9 String Quartet, Op. 11 "I hear an army," Op. 10, No. 3 **Song:** "Beggar's Song" **Choral:** "Mary Ruane"; "Peggy Mitchell"
1937		*Essay for Orchestra* (No. 1), Op. 12 "Mary Hynes," Op. 16, no. 1 "A Nun Takes the Veil," Op. 13, no. 1 **Song:** "In the Dark Pinewood"
1938		*Adagio for Strings* (arr. of SQ, 2nd movement) **Song:** "The Secrets of the Old," Op. 13, no. 2; "Sure on this shining night," Op. 13, no. 3 *God's Grandeur*
1939	Briefly joined the faculty of The Curtis Institute of Music	Violin Concerto, Op. 14 **Song:** "O the mind, the mind has mountains"
1940		"Anthony O'Daly," Op. 16, no. 2 "The Coolin," Op. 16, no. 3 *A Stopwatch and an Ordnance Map,* Op. 15 "Nocturne" (song) Op. 13, no. 4 "Ave Maria" (after Josquin)

Dates	Events in life	Musical compositions
1941		"Commemorative March"; "Song for a New House"
1942		Begins *Excursions,* Op. 20 "The queen's face on a summery coin," Op. 18, no. 2 *Second Essay for Orchestra,* Op. 17 **Song**: "Between Dark and Dark"
1943	Inducted into the army; purchase of Capricorn	*Commando March* **Band**: "Funeral March"; "Ad bibinum" "Monks and Raisins," Op. 18, no. 2
1944		Second Symphony, Op. 19 *Capricorn Concerto,* Op. 21 *Serenade for String Orchestra* (arr. from SQ) **Choral**: "Long Live Louise and Sidney Homer"
1945	Completed military service; traveled to Europe; gives commencement address at Curtis	Cello Concerto, Op. 22 *Horizon* (unpubl.)
1946		*Serpent Heart* (Medea), Op. 23
1947	Death of Barber's father	*Nuvoletta,* Op. 25
1948	Travel in Europe	*Knoxville: Summer of 1915,* Op. 24
1949	Travel in Europe	Piano Sonata, Op. 26 String Quartet, slow movement
1950	Conducted his own works in Europe	"Puisque tous passe," Op. 27, no. 1 "Le clocher chant," Op. 27, no. 4 "Départ," Op. 27, no. 5
1951		"Un cygne," Op. 27, no. 2 "Tombeau dans un parc," Op. 27, no. 3 *Souvenirs* (piano, four hands) Op. 28
1952	Appointed to executive board of International Music Council	*Souvenirs* (arr. for orchestra) "At St. Patrick's Purgatory," Op. 29, no. 1 "Church Bell at Night," Op. 29, no. 2 "The Heavenly Banquet," Op. 29, no. 4 "The Crucifixion," Op. 29, no. 5
1953	Death of his uncle Sidney Homer	"St. Ita's Vision," Op. 29, no. 3 "Sea-snatch," Op. 29, no. 6 "Promiscuity," Op. 29, no. 7 "The Monk and His Cat," Op. 29, no. 8 "The Praises of God," Op. 29, no. 9 "The Desire for Hermitage," Op. 29, no. 10

Dates	Events in life	Musical compositions
1954		*Adventure* *Prayers of Kierkegaard*, Op. 30
1955		*Summer Music* for woodwind quintet, Op. 31
1957		*Vanessa*, Op. 32
1958		*Wondrous Love: Variations*, Op. 34
1959		*Nocturne*, Op. 33 *A Hand of Bridge*, Op. 35
1960		*Toccata Festiva*, Op. 36 *Die Natali*, Op. 37
1961	Addresses the Congress of Soviet Composers in Moscow	
1962		Piano Concerto, Op. 38
1964		Chorale for Ascension Day
1966		*Antony and Cleopatra*, Op. 40
1967	Death of Barber's mother	*Mutations from Bach*
1968		"Twelfth Night," Op. 42, no. 1 "To Be sung on the Water," Op. 42, no. 2
1971		*The Lovers*, Op. 43 *Fadograph of a Yestern Scene*, Op. 44
1973	Sale of Capricorn	
1977		*Ballade*, Op. 46
1978		*Third Essay for Orchestra*, Op. 47 *Canzonetta for Oboe and String Orchestra*, Op. 48
1981	Death at age 71; memorial service at St.Bartholomew's Church (NY)	

AWARDS, PRIZES, AND HONORS

1929   Joseph A. Bearns Prize of Columbia University

($1200) for Violin Sonata "for musical compositions in the larger forms" (Heyman, p. 61.) It was announced (or verified) in a letter from Frank Fackenthal to Barber, May 11, 1929, Columbia University Archives.

1933   Joseph A. Bearns Prize of Columbia University

9.   "Composer Wins Again." *New York Times,* April 12, 1933, p. 24. [Henn
     BG20]

     Frank Fackenthal announced that Samuel Barber has won the Joseph A.
Bearns prize of $1200 "for the second time in five years," for his Overture to the
School for Scandal. The prize is conferred annually to "encourage young American composers." Verified in letter from Frank Fackenthal to Barber, April, 6,
1933, Columbia University Archives.

1935   Pulitzer Traveling Scholarship

The award for $1500 was announced on May 6.

1935   Prix de Rome

An award given to "the most talented and deserving student of music in America."
In this case it went to Barber for Sonata for Violoncello and Piano, Op. 6 and
Music for a Scene from Shelley, Op. 7. The award was announced on NBC Radio
May 9 as part of a concert of his music where both works were played (Heyman,
p. 123).

10.   S., M. L. "Prix de Rome Winner Prepared for Work." *Musical Courier,* Dec.
      7, 1935.

      The author of this article mentions the award and Barber's years as a student
at Curtis. He also mentions that all of Barber's works have been accepted by "a
prominent New York publisher" (i.e. G. Schirmer).

11.   Pleasants, Henry. "Samuel Barber Wins Two Musical Awards." *Philadel-
      phia Bulletin,* May 25, 1935.

      An announcement of Barber's winning both the Pulitzer traveling award and
the Prix de Rome.

12.   "Samuel Barber Wins Another Prize." *New York Times,* May 10, 1935, p. 24.
      [Henn BG122]

      The prize mentioned in the title is the "Prix de Rome" for which Barber sub-
mitted his Sonata for Violoncello and Piano and his *Music for a Scene From Shelley.* The jury consisted of Deems Taylor, Carl Engel, Leo Sowerby, and Walter
Damrosch.

13. "Samuel Barber Wins Two Musical Awards: Pulitzer Prize and Prix de Rome Come to Young Composer During Single Week." *Musical America* 55 (May 25, 1935): 27.

Both awards go to Samuel Barber to enable him to continue his studies in Europe. [What is called a "prize" in the title is not the kind of award designated as such in other disciplines and the kind later awarded for music, as was the case for *Vanessa* and the Piano Concerto. It is a "traveling" award.]

14. "Samuel Barber Wins New Prize." *West Chester Daily Local News*, May 7, 1935. Article is cited without page number in Broder, p. 29 and Heyman, p. 134.

1936   Second Pulitzer Traveling Scholarship

The announcement is more like a renewal of the first award (Heyman, p. 142).

1940   Nomination to National Institute of Arts and Letters

See proposal of his nomination by Walter Damrosch, Letters of the Academy [Acad 1].

1945, 1947, 1949   Guggenheim Fellowships

May 12, 1945   Honorary Doctorate from the Curtis School of Music

According to Viles's dissertation (see Item 502), both Barber and Menotti received honorary degrees at the commencement exercises that year. Barber was also the speaker. For a brief excerpt, see Heyman, p. 4.

June 27, 1946   Prize of Music Critics Circle of New York

For his Concerto for Violoncello and Orchestra

15. "Barber Concerto gets Critics Prize." *New York Times,* June 28, 1946, p. 16, col. 5. [Henn B67a]

Miles Kastendieck announced that Samuel Barber has received the fifth annual award from the Music Critics Circle of New York for "the work of an American composer considered exceptional among the orchestral compositions performed for the first time in this city during the season."

1958   Pulitzer Prize for *Vanessa*

16.   Christ, Judith. "Agee Novel, Wolfe Play earn '57 Pulitzers." *New York Herald-Tribune,* May 6, 1958, p. 1, and "These are the Pulitzer Prize Winners," p. 15.

The article mentions that Barber received $500 and the Pulitzer prize in music for his opera *Vanessa.* In the short biography, she mentions his student days at Curtis and that many of his works have been performed by major orchestras. While *Vanessa* may not "strictly reflect the American scene," it does reflect the stature of an American composer today. [It is not clear whether Christ wrote the information on both pages 1 and 15.]

17.   "Sketches of the Pulitzer Prize Winners for 1958 in Letters, Music and Journalism." *New York Times,* May 6, 1958, p. 8. [Henn BG133]

The author mentions that Samuel Barber's music seems to grow "more conservative over the years." He has maintained a "strong melodic gift" ("decidedly easy listening"), and an aptitude for "successful firsts." He stands midway between the extreme radicals and the conservatives of contemporary American music. The article includes a brief biography, a picture, and a plot summary for *Vanessa.*

1958   May 18, 1958   Philadelphia Contemporary Composer Award

The award is given for "original works by contemporary composers played by the Philadelphia Orchestra during the 1957-58 season, selected by first chair men of the orchestra but given by an anonymous donor."

18.   "Composers Honored." *New York Times,* May 18, 1958, p. 23. [Henn B66f]

Selected for the two awards were Samuel Barber, for his Violin Concerto ($3000) and Arthur Honegger for his Second Symphony (the equivalent of $1500 in francs). Honegger's widow accepted his award.

19.   "Notes on the News!" *International Musician* 57 (July 1958): 18. [Henn B66nn]

A brief mention that Barber received $3000 for his Violin Concerto, which was played by the Philadelphia Orchestra during its 1957–1958 season.

May 20, 1958   Henry Hadley Medal of the National Association for American Composers and Conductors.

Awarded for exceptional service to American music. See Heyman, p. 394.

20.   "Barber Receives Hadley Medal." *New York Herald Tribune,* May, 21, 1958.

The Hadley Medals for exceptional service were announced by the association's president, Paul Creston, last night at the Waldorf Astoria Hotel. Other recipients included Rosina Lhévine, Thor Johnson, and Julius Rudel.

21. "Samuel Barber Cited." *New York Times,* May 21, 1958, p. 40. [Henn BG119]

At the awards presentation at the Waldorf Astoria Hotel on the previous night, several people were awarded the Henry Hadley Medal, including Samuel Barber, Van Cliburn, Randall Thompson, and Guillermo Espinoza.

1958   Barber Elected to the American Academy of Arts and Letters

See the letters of proposal [Acad 2, 3,], election [Acad 4], notice of induction ceremony [Acad 5], and notice of the medallion of membership [Acad 6].

22. "American Academy of Arts and Letters Elects Four." *New York Times,* December 6, 1958, p. 18. [Henn BG3]

Membership is limited to fifty who are chosen for special distinction from the 250 members of the Academy's parent organization, The National Institute of Arts and Letters. For speech read by Allan Nevins at induction, but written by Douglas Moore, see Heyman, p. 394. The other three elected were Charles Burchfield, water color painter; the Reverend Reinhold Niebuhr, writer and theologian; and the poet, William Carlos Williams.

1959   Honorary Doctor of Music Degree from Harvard University

23. Fenton, John H. "Dillon Urges Aid to Needy Nations." *New York Times,* June 12, 1959, p. 3. [Henn BG49]

Acting secretary of state, Douglas Dillon, gets the headline because of the speech he gave at the annual ceremony of Harvard alumni in the Harvard Yard "outdoor theatre." Barber's honorary degree, one of thirteen given that day, has the citation that reads: "Samuel Barber, composer of orchestral and choral music. His music lends strength and grace to the culture of our time."

March 9, 1960   Curtis Honors Barber Birthday

24. "Samuel Barber Cited: Composer Honored on 50th Birthday by Curtis Institute." *New York Times,* March 10, 1960, p. 37. [Henn BG120]

A special "invitation," all-Barber concert was presented at Curtis Hall Auditorium for an audience of 250, including Barber and his mother, Marguerite. On the program were: *Dover Beach, Souvenirs,* the Cello Sonata and the Piano Sonata. (See also, letters Miller [2], [3], [4], and [5].)

October 14, 1960   New York Philharmonic Honors Barber's Birthday

25.   K., R. "Philharmonic Honors Schuman and Barber." *Musical Courier* 162 (Dec. 1960): 16.

The New York Philharmonic, directed by Leonard Bernstein, honored Samuel Barber and William Schuman at a concert that performed Schuman's Symphony No. 3 and Barber's Violin Concerto with Aaron Rosand, violinist. The Violin Concerto is a "movingly melodious score."

26.   Schonberg, Harold C. "Music: a Birthday Party." *New York Times,* October 15, 1960, p. 27. [Henn B66ss]

Leonard Bernstein and the New York Philharmonic observed the fiftieth birthdays of the American composers, Samuel Barber and William Schuman, by performing Schuman's Symphony No. 3 and Barber's Violin Concerto. At the end both composers took bows.

1960   Orchestra of America Honors Barber's 50th Birthday

27.   Parmenter, Ross. "Music: Orchestra of America Opens 2nd Season." *New York Times,* November 17, 1960, p. 45. [Henn BG103]

The Orchestra of America is dedicated exclusively to the performance of American music. Under the direction of Richard Korn, the orchestra performed Barber's *Second Essay for Orchestra*, a work that has entered the standard repertory. The orchestra also observed Walllingford Riegger's seventy fifth birthday by playing his *Sinfonietta*, and Copland's sixtieth with his Clarinet Concerto. Both of the latter composers were present but no mention was made as to whether Barber attended the program.

1963   Pulitzer Prize in Music for Barber's Concerto for Piano and Orchestra, Op. 38

28.   "Biographies of 15 Selected to Receive the 1963 Pulitzer Prize." *New York Times,* May 7, 1963, p. 35.

This is the announcement of Barber winning his second Pulitzer prize, for his Piano Concerto "No. 1." A basic biography of Barber is given, including the mention of his 1958 Pulitzer prize for *Vanessa*. He is among fifteen to be given the prize in 1963. Winners in other areas included Barbara Tuchman, William Faulkner, and William Carlos Williams.

1964   New York Music Critics Circle Award for Concerto for Piano and Orchestra

29.   "Britten Honored by Music Critics." *New York Times,* May 20, 1964, p. 37. [Henn B65c]

The Music Critics award for an orchestral composition for both musical seasons 1962–1963 and 1963–1964 goes to Barber's Piano Concerto. Two seasons are involved because of the newspaper strike of the '62–'63 season. Britten receives the article title because of his awards for both his choral work, *War Requiem,* and the opera, *Midsummer Night's Dream.* Also selected were Milton Babbitt's *Philomel* and Lukas Foss's *Echoi.*

30.   "Britten, Barber Win Music Awards." *New York Post,* May 20, 1964. Not examined.

December 17, 1970   Birthday Concert (60th) by New York Philharmonic

31.   Henahan, Donal. "Birthday Concert (Not Beethoven)." *New York Times,* December 19, 1970, p. 18. [Henn BG67]

Stanislaw Skrowaczewski conducted *Medea's Dance of Vengeance,* Op. 23a. in honor of Barber's sixtieth birthday (actually the previous March). The program honored both Barber and his fellow composer and friend William Schuman, whose *Song of Orpheus* was also performed. Henahan notes that while the orchestra performed "ably," neither work "struck any real spark," nor was the conductor quite the right person to make the most of Medea's "dark ecstasies."

1971   Certificate of Special Achievement in the Arts

32.   Webster, Daniel. "Cantata by Barber Premiers at Concert." *Philadelphia Inquirer,* September 23, 1971, p. 1, 8.

The certificate was presented to Barber by Milton J. Shapp, the governor of Pennsylvania, at the premiere performance of *The Lovers,* September 21, 1971. (See Item 103 for a list of reviews of the concert.)

1976   Gold Medal (in Music) of the Academy of Arts and Letters

Several documents at the Academy relate to the gold medal: letters of notification of guest list [Acad 6, 7], a request for an acceptance speech [Acad 8], the brief acceptance speech itself [Acad 9], and an insurance statement about the gold medal [Acad 10, 11]. William Schuman's tribute to Barber can be found in Heyman, p. 509 and in the Proceedings of the American Academy and Institute of Arts and Letters, 1977, p. 26.

1976   National Music Award

American Music Conference

August 24, 1980   MacDowell Colony Medal

33.   "Mr. Schuman on Mr. Barber's Behalf." *Colony Newsletter,* The MacDowell
      Colony, Inc. 10 (Fall 1980): 37.

An account of the ceremony honoring Barber with the MacDowell Medal
and of Schuman's reading of Barber's acceptance speech. Not examined.

34.   Rockwell, John. "Samuel Barber Honored with MacDowell Medal." *New
      York Times,* August 26, 1980, p. 8.

In a gathering of 400 guests, Samuel Barber was awarded the MacDowell
Medal, the 21st recipient. It is a "peer award" that is, an award given by a
select panel drawn from "artists of comparable distinction." The panelists who
clearly fit this description were: Aaron Copland, Virgil Thomson, William
Schuman, David del Tredici, Lester Trimble, and Francis Thorne. Barber
was too ill to attend, recuperating at Menotti's home in Scotland. After
some remarks by Charles Wadsworth (see also Item 35), Schuman read
Barber's brief acceptance speech, relating a typically bizarre anecdote about
his encounter with Dame Edith Sitwell. The text is included in the article,
and can also be found at the American Academy and Institute of the Arts
in New York City, because it is exactly the same speech he used at the Academy's Gold Medal ceremony in 1976 (See [Acad 10]). A program then followed featuring a flute arrangement of the main theme from the quintet of
Vanessa, and a performance of *Summer Music* by winds from the Monadnock
Music Center.

35.   Wadsworth, Charles. "Charles Wadsworth on Samuel Barber." *Colony
      Newsletter,* The MacDowell Colony, Inc. 10 (Fall 1980): 2–3.

Wadsworth, the director of the Chamber Music Society of Lincoln Center,
remarked that Barber has always "demonstrated total disdain for trend and fashion in the music world." Other composers "go this way and that, joining and dropping from various cliques, while Sam continues a straight path." He is among
those rare composers who can write music that is both complex but still easy to
understand.
    See also: letters between Barber and William Schuman (Schu [41] and [42]),
where Barber says that he is too ill to attend the ceremony. Schuman hopes that
Barber will send a written response that he (Schuman) can read. This is indeed the
way it was handled.

March 9, 1980   Curtis Institute Tribute to Barber (on his 70th birthday).

36.   Ericson, Raymond. "Notes: Reviving the L. A. Chamber Orchestra." *New York Times,* February 24, 1980, sect. 2, p. 19, 25.

The author describes plans for the Curtis Institute's tribute to Barber on his seventieth birthday, including two concerts on March 9. One will feature Rose Bampton singing *Dover Beach* (the original performer) and Ruth Laredo playing the Piano Sonata, and the other will feature the Curtis Symphony performing an all-Barber program.

37.   Felton, James. "A Moving Tribute to Barber." *Bulletin* (Philadelphia), March 10, 1980. [Henn BG 48]

Efrem Zimbalist Jr. paid tribute to Barber saying that "Sam was born with a song in his heart . . . With lifted glass let us proclaim 'Happy Birthday, Sam!' " Zimbalist's stepmother was Mary Curtis Bok, who had encouraged Barber through much of his early career. See Viles's dissertation, Item 510.

38.   Webster, Daniel. "Curtis Institute Concerts Salute Barber's 70th Birthday." *Philadelphia Inquirer,* March 10, 1980. [Henn BG150]

The author notes that Barber's music did not "open the door on the 21st century any more than it closed the door on all that had happened before" his op. 1.

39.   Webster, Daniel. "Debuts and Reappearances: Curtis Institute: Barber Tribute." *High Fidelity/Musical America* 30 (July 1980): 36–37 (of the *Musical America* section). [Henn BG151]

Webster describes the ceremony honoring Barber on his seventieth birthday. Efrem Zimbalist Jr. (see Item 37) and Gian Carlo Menotti both spoke and the first of two concerts was given, devoted to solo and chamber works, including *Dover Beach,* the Cello Sonata and the Piano Sonata. Barber could not attend this ceremony because his cancer treatments were debilitating and kept him confined to his New York apartment. However, he was able to hear the N.P.R. radio broadcast of the evening concert, which featured the Curtis Orchestra and the Academy of Music performing his Overture to *The School for Scandal,* the Violin Concerto, *Knoxville: Summer of 1915,* and the *Second Essay.* Webster sums up Barber's position in twentieth-century music: none of Barber's forms "pointed to a future transfiguration, but to a present fulfillment. Each is a model of urbane expression of a personal eclecticism."

March 11, 1980   Wolf Trap Award

40.   Ericson, Raymond. "Notes: Reviving the L. A. Chamber Orchestra." *New York Times,* February 24, 1980, sect. 2, p. 19, 25. [Henn BG38]

Barber will be in Washington, D.C. to accept the Wolf Trap Award, which will be presented by Roslyn Carter on March 11 in a ceremony at the White House. Later that evening the National Symphony Orchestra, under the direction of Antal Dorati, will perform Barber's Piano Concerto, with soloist, James Tocco.

For a review of Tocco's performance see Paul Hume, "Dorati and the NSO." *Washington Post,* March 12, 1980, sect. D, p. 8.

1997   Postage Stamp

41.   Dobrin, Peter. "Postal Service Delivers Honors to Three Philadelphians of Note." *Philadelphia Inquirer,* March 12, 1997, section D, p. 1.

The Postal Service plans to issue a series of stamps honoring classical composers and conductors, including Leopold Stokowski, Eugene Ormandy, and Samuel Barber. Photographs are included. (Visit www.schirmer.com to see the stamp.)

OBITUARIES AND TRIBUTES

42.   "Acclaimed Composer Samuel Barber Dies." *Chicago Tribune,* January 24, 1981. Sect. 2, p. 13. [Henn BG1]

Barber died in his Fifth Avenue apartment after a long illness. He was 70. His acclaim has been "early, persistent, and long-lasting." This seems to be an uncredited version of Henahan's obituary for the Los Angeles *Herald Examiner* (see Item 47).

43.   "Closing Chord: Samuel Barber." *High Fidelity/Musical America* (June, 1981): MA 22.

The anonymous author mentions Barber's studies at the Curtis Institute, his various honors and prizes, and says of his compositions that "many are still heard in the repertoire of major orchestras."

44.   Dickinson, Peter. "Obituary." *Musical Times* 122 (March 1981): 193. [Henn BG32]

The author considers Barber to be "one of the most widely performed American composers of this century." His gift for creating a musical atmosphere is finely expressed in his many songs. Yet his lyrical style also comes off well in the concerto medium.

45.   "Final Bar." *Downbeat* 48 (May 1981): 13. [Henn BG50]

Barber's music is well known for its "careful craftsmanship" and "long-limbed neo-romantic melodies."

46.   Heinsheimer, Hans W. "Adagio for Sam." *Opera News* 45 (March 4, 1981): 30-31. [Henn BG64]

While Barber has written no film scores, no TV shows, and no Broadway musicals, his work has carved out a dominant position in American Arts and Letters. His secluded existence allowed him the opportunity to compose art songs, orchestral works, choral works, chamber music, and operas.

47.   Henahan, Donal. "American Composer Samuel Barber, 70, Dies." *Herald Examiner* (Los Angeles), January 24, 1981. [Henn BG66]

Barber's acclaim has been "early, persistent, and long-lasting." See "Acclaimed" (Item 42).

48.   Henahan, Donal. "Samuel Barber, Composer, Dead; Twice winner of Pulitzer Prize." *New York Times,* January 24, 1981, p. 1, 16. [Henn BG69]

Barber's "deep-seated conservatism" was something audiences could find congenial often at first hearing. Amidst some dissonance and complex rhythms, there was a lyricism that established him as a neo-romantic composer. He did not use the 12-tone technique nor did he "dabble" in chance or electronic music.

49.   Hume, Paul. "Honored American Composer Samuel Barber, 70, Dies in New York." *Washington Post,* January 25, 1981, section B, p. 6. [Henn BG 73]

Barber was equally comfortable writing for small and large ensembles, and for voices "in various idioms." His music is likely to "win enthusiastic admirers for years to come" and will probably find a "permanent place among the finest music of this century."

50.   Hume, Paul. "The Musical Legacy of Samuel Barber." *Washington Post,* February 1, 1981, section K, p. 1. [Henn BG74]

As a follow-up to his obituary (see Item 49), Hume notes that Barber may not have been particularly prolific as a composer, but he did have the remarkable attribute of possessing "equal mastery of both vocal and instrumental writing, a dual gift not common to his other American colleagues."

51.   "Milestones." *Time* 117 (February 2, 1981): 81. [Henn BG92]

The article describes Barber as a composer whose "lyrical music won him international popularity. It mentions his Pulitzer prizes and the "rare failure" of his opera, *Antony and Cleopatra*. He "loved and understood the human voice," and "stood apart from avant-garde trends."

52.   "Names, Dates and Places." *Opera News* 30 (February 19, 1981): 5. [Henn BG96]

Barber left about 35 percent of his million dollar estate to Gian Carlo Menotti, plus his books, tapes, memorabilia and lifetime use of his home in Santa Christina, Italy.

53.   "Nunc Dimittis." *Diapason* 72 (April 1981): 3. [Henn BG98]

Four paragraphs long, the obituary mentions several works. Because this publication is designated primarily for organists, it singles out Strickland's arrangement of *Adagio for Strings*, the composer's own arrangement of "Silent Night" (from *Die Natali,* Op. 37), the "Wondrous Love" variations, and the *Toccata Festiva* for organ and orchestra. It also mentions the January 25 funeral service at St. Bartholomew's Church in New York City.

54.   "Obituaries." *Gramophone* 58 (March 1981): 1148. [Henn BG101]

This is a short paragraph about the death of Barber, citing his awards and accomplishments, and specifically mentions *Dover Beach* as one of his most significant works. His music is essentially "elegant and conservatively melodic," perhaps more European in character than American.

55.   "Obituary: Mr. Samuel Barber." *The Times* (London) January 26, 1981, p. 14. [Henn BG100]

The article notes Barber's tendency toward the lyrical and romantic temperament instead of the "neo-classical" and the "many experimental trends in modern composition." Always expressive, he developed a "highly individual style."

56.   "Obituary: Samuel Barber." *The Strad* 91, no. 1092 (April 1981): 895.

This brief anonymous obituary mentions some of Barber's works and concludes that his music was part of the "lyrical and Romantic tradition." The composer remained unaffected by "contemporary developments and the avant-garde."

57.   "Samuel Barber." *Clavier* 20, no. 3 (1981): 16.

Three paragraphs about Barber's accomplishments: the Prix de Rome in 1935, a Guggenheim fellowship in 1946, an honorary degree from Harvard University, and two Pulitzer prizes, one for *Vanessa* and the other for the Piano Concerto.

58. "Samuel Barber." *Variety* 301 (January 28, 1981): 94. [Henn BG117]

The writer gives a brief biography of the composer and lists many of his works and notes that almost every piece of music by Barber was introduced by an "internationally known orchestra or artist." While he was successful with almost every composition, his "most lasting works" are his opera, *Vanessa,* and his *Adagio for Strings.*

59. Schillaci, Daniel. "For the Record." *New West* 6 (April 1981): 118. [Henn BG127]

The author laments that more press coverage was given to the death of Maria Callas's husband than to Samuel Barber, who died the same day. Barber's music is "far too attractive, one suspects, to become insignificant." Certainly no one who is touched by his music "need worry about the precious few who will no doubt always scoff" at it.

60. Shawe-Taylor, Desmond. "Music." *Times* (London) January 25, 1981. [Henn BG129]

The author notes Barber's death and gives a brief summary of his life and works.

ELECTRONIC INFORMATION RETRIEVAL

Websites

You can find many items on Netscape by typing in "Samuel Barber" or other more specific references. Most of these are very general and seem to be of rather limited usefulness. The sheer number of them is often daunting. For instance, Google claims to have more than 25,000 items. One valuable source (usually appearing near the beginning of various lists) is the Schirmer home page (www.schirmer.com) which contains a short biography, a very short discography (not recently updated), and a list of works that is virtually the same as the printed source by Norman D. Ryan (see item 286). Also included is a listing from *Schirmer News* that shows the postage stamp mentioned in item 41. The Look Smart search contains a list of recent articles (often record reviews) relating to Samual Barber. One word of caution: many lists will include other men with the name of Samuel Barber.

BIOGRAPHICAL INFORMATION

Biographical Resource Center

An entry of the name "Barber Samuel" will result in a page listing:

1. Thumbnail Biographies: at the moment the only entry is from Merriam-Webster's *Biographical Dictionary.*

2. Narrative Biographies: currently containing three entries
   [a] from Contemporary Authors On-line (actually an obituary);

   [b] from *Encyclopedia of World Biography*, divided into sections on biographical essay, early works, operas, major themes and techniques, and further reading.

   [c] from *International Dictionary of Opera*, including a biographical essay, personal information, a listing of his operas, and further reading.

3. Magazine and Newspaper Articles.

   This section currently contains only 18 articles, mainly recent reviews of performances and recordings (See IIMP for a larger selection.)

4. Additional Resources.

   While all the above items are "full text" citations, this section is merely a listing of biographical sources. There are currently 83 items listed, including several editions of *Baker's, Biography Index, Who's Who in America,* and many others.

Biography and Genealogy Master Index

The items under all these lists are very much the same as those cited above in the "additional resources" section of Biographical Resource Center, but there are some additional ones. None have full texts.

BOOKS, ARTICLES, AND THESES

Two of the most important sources of recent Barber material are: WorldCat and RILM. These sources list various types of print material from articles to theses and dissertations. The ordering of listings, however, is somewhat haphazard, but the most recent items are usually given at the beginning.

WorldCat

The search: "Subject= Barber, Samuel," will list over 1600 items, many of which are recording reviews and often a mention of Barber works being performed on doctoral recitals around the country. Since reviewing such a list is time-consuming and often frustrating, a narrow search may be necessary.

RILM (Répertoire International de Littérature Musicale)

This is a better source for "non-performance" information, including, books, articles, theses, and dissertations. Some libraries still have a print copy of this series, going back to 1967; but the indexing of these volumes is extremely cumbersome. The computer version is much more "user friendly."

MLA Bibliography

At the time of this book, this site contained nine items on Barber, mainly articles in non-musical periodicals, items that would go unnoticed if you relied only on RILM.

Newspaper Articles

Shortly after the publication of this book, more information concerning Barber and his works will naturally become available. For the most up-to-date information, the best resources are available on various computer search engines. The following are recommended.

1. Netscape

2. Academic Universe (Lexus-Nexus): Document list under the heading: "Arts and Sports."

By typing in the keyword search: "Barber, Samuel," you will see a listing of many recent newspaper articles, mainly reviews of performances of the last decade. They are listed in reverse chronology, going back to July of 1980. Most of these are reviews of important performances in major cities as printed in The *New York Times, San Francisco Chronicle, Houston Chronicle,* and the *Boston Globe.*

PERIODICALS

The most important site devoted strictly to periodical literature is **IIMP:**

International Index to Music Periodicals

This source has many items arranged in reverse chronology from May 2000 back to 1993.

Chapter 2. Published Works, with First Performances and Reviews

This list of Barber's works is similar to the list compiled by Norman D. Ryan for G. Schirmer's catalogue (see Wittke, Item 286, but updated in May 1996). The Schirmer catalogue numbers are included. The vocal and choral works also include the name of the author of the text, the title of the poem, and the first line if it is different from the title. For those poems that were originally in a foreign language, the translation that Barber used is also included. Holograph copies of full scores, reductions, and sketches are listed when known. Fuller descriptions can be found in the annotated list in chapter 5.

The list also includes the date of the first performance (when known), including the place (city, hall, etc.) and the performers. Also included are performances given shortly thereafter, especially if the work was premiered outside of the main metropolitan areas of New York, Boston, etc. The most important reviews are then listed (in short reference form, i.e., only author and newspaper or periodical date and page). Particularly significant are the critiques appearing in the *New York Times,* often written by Olin Downes or Harold Schonberg. Some citations, especially reviews from the *New York Journal American* and *New York Post,* are sometimes hard to find in their original newspaper format. Many can be consulted in the "clippings" file folders at the New York Public Library, which often contain the article, cut out and pasted onto a larger sheet, but unfortunately, without the page number attached, and sometimes without author or other source information. The periodical, *New Music,* is also an extremely valuable resource for many of these early performances. Citation numbers are included from Hennessee's book, where the reader will find quotations of many of these reviews, and of many later performances as well. For more recent performances (mainly after 1980), see the Lexus-Nexus website on Academic Universe.

For the following citations, Barber's works are grouped into categories, such as opera and ballet, orchestral music, etc. with individual items listed alphabetically within the category. Occasionally a work may be suitable for more than one category; e.g. is *Andromache's Farewell* an orchestral work or a vocal work?

When that situation occurs the piece should be in at least one logical place. (For this list, *Andromache's Farewell* has been placed arbitrarily in the vocal category.) Usually various arrangements are saved for the end of the list (e.g. *Adagio for Strings* for clarinet ensemble), unless two versions of a work are equally well-known (e.g. *Adagio for Strings* and the String Quartet or the original piano version of *Souvenirs* and the orchestral version for ballet.) In that case it is listed in both categories. On the other hand, if a work was created as an independent piece but has been used consequently as a score for a dance production (e.g. *Adagio for Strings),* the choreographed version is simply added after the original score. Because the music is unlikely to be different, the score number will not change. The only thing affected will be first additional performances and reviews.

OPERA AND BALLET

61.   *Antony and Cleopatra,* Op. 40

Opera in Three Acts
Libretto: by Franco Zeffirelli and Barber, after William Shakespeare's *Antony and Cleopatra.*
Commissioned for the opening of the new Metropolitan Opera House at Lincoln Center by a grant from the Ford Foundation.
Dedicated to Orazio Orlando.
Score, vocal score (English) 50338440; libretto (English) 50481516

Holographs

LOC: Music 1907
        item 56: short score
        item 57: full score, act 1
        item 58: full score, acts 2 and 3
        item 59: misc.
        item 60: "Give me some music," concert version, full score
NYPL: Toscanini Memorial Archive
        JPB 86-2 R.S. A. 4: reproduced from holograph;
        JPB 96-1: another copy, "recording, editing, mixing score"

Review of piano-vocal score

Ringo, James. "From Schirmer, Barber's Antony and Cleopatra," *American Record Guide* 35 (May 1967): 871–872. [Henn B1rr]

First performance: September 16, 1966 (original version)

New York, Metropolitan Opera House
Cast: Cleopatra: Leontyne Price, soprano; Antony: Justino Diaz, baritone; Stage director/designer: Franco Zeffirelli; Metropolitan Orchestra and Chorus, conductor: Thomas Schippers. See *Annals of the Metropolitan Opera: The Complete Chronicle of Performances and Artists.* Edited by Gerald Fitzgerald, et al. Boston: G. K. Hall, 1989, vol. 1: Chronology 1883–1985, p. 773; and vol 2: Tables 1883–1985, p. 1A, 1. ISBN 0-816-18903-x ML 1711 .8 .N52 M38

Reviews

Edwards, Sydney. *Music and Musicians* 15 (November 1966): 20–21, 57. [Henn B11]

Gelatt, Roland. *Reporter* 35 (November 17, 1966): 57.   [Henn B1p]

Johnson, Harriet. *New York Post,* September 17, 1966, p. 6.

Kastendieck, Miles. *New York World-Journal-Tribune,* September 17, 1966.

Kolodin, Irving. *Saturday Review* 49 (October 1, 1966): 35–36.   [Henn B1dd]

Mercer, Ruby. *Opera Canada* 7 (December 1966): 16–19.   [Henn B1ii]

Mordden, Ethan C. *Opera News* 40 (August 1975): 16–21.   [Henn B1mm]

"Opening Night." *Opera News* 31 (October 15, 1966): 12–17.   [Henn B1nn]

Sargeant, Winthrop. *New Yorker* 42 (September 24, 1966): 114.   [Henn B1vv]

Schonberg, Harold C. *New York Times,* September 17, 1966, p. 16.   [Henn B1xx]

Strongin, Theodore. *New York Times,* May 7, 1964, p. 39   [Henn B1aaa]

"Tony and Cleo." *Newsweek* 68 (September 26, 1966): 98.   [Henn B1bbb]

62.   **Walter McGowan Upchurch Papers, Duke University**

This unprocessed collection contains 4,616 items, some of which are related to the world premiere of *Antony and Cleopatra* at Lincoln Center, September 16, 1966. Included are invitations, commemorative programs and booklets, and the opera libretto.

There are, however, no indication of any holographs or facsimiles.

63.   *Antony and Cleopatra:* **Revised Version**

Libretto: changes from the original Zeffirelli were made by Gian Carlo Menotti.

First performance: February 6, 1975

New York, Juilliard School of Music, American Opera Center
Cleopatra: Esther Hinds, soprano; Antony: Ronald Hedlund, bass; stage director:
Gian Carlo Menotti; conductor, James Conlon.

Reviews

Jacobson, Robert. *Opera News* 39 (April 5, 1975): 36–37.   [Henn B1aa]

Oppens, Kurt. *Opern Welt* 16 (May 1975): 49–51.   [Henn B1oo]

Porter, Andrew. *New Yorker* 51 (February 6, 1975): 123–144.   [Henn B1pp]

"Sam Barber Rep." *Variety* 278 (February 12, 1975): 81.   [Henn B1tt]

Smith, Patrick J. "*High Fidelity/Musical America* 25 (May 1975): 25–26.
[Henn B1zz]

64. *A Hand of Bridge,* Op. 35

Opera in One Act
Libretto: Gian Carlo Menotti commissioned by Spoleto Festival of Two Worlds/
Vocal Score (English) 50338130

Holographs

LOC: Music 1907
        item 72: sketches
        item 73: short score
        item 74: full score

Review of score

Yellin, Victor. *Notes* 18 (September 1961): 641.   [Henn B5i]

First performance: June 17, 1959

Spoleto, Italy; Festival of Two Worlds, Teatro Caio Melisso.
Geraldine: Patricia Neway, soprano; Sally: Ellen Miville, contralto; Bill: William
Lewis, tenor; David: René Miville, baritone; settings and costumes, Jac Venza;
Robert Feist, conductor.

U.S. Premiere: April 6, 1960

New York, Mannes College of Music, Fashion Institute of Technology Auditorium. Cast: David: John Fiorito; Geraldine: Donna Murray Porteous; Bill: Stanley Storch; Sally: Jean Stawski; Opera Production workshops and Orchestra of the Mannes College of Music; Carl Bamberger, conductor.

Reviews

Ardoin, John. *Musical America* 80 (May 1960): 39–40.   [Henn B5a]

Lang, Paul Henry. *New York Herald Tribune,* April 7, 1960, p. 18.

Taubman, Howard. *New York Times,* April 7, 1960.   [Henn B5h]

65.   *Medea,* Op. 23

Commissioned by Martha Graham through the Alice M. Ditson Fund of Columbia University.
Dedicated to Martha Graham.
Score (chamber version) 50048144467

Holograph

Pierpont Morgan Library, Mary Flagler Cary Music Collection: sketches for *Medea,* 4 pages.

First performance as *The Serpent Heart:* May 10, 1946

New York, Columbia University, MacMillan Theatre; Martha Graham Dance Co. (Chamber version).
Cast: "One like Medea": Martha Graham; "One like Jason": Erick Hawkins; the Princess: Yuriko [Yuriko Kimura]; "the chorus": May O'Donnell.

Reviews

Fuller, Donald. *Modern Music* 23 (Summer 1946): 200.   [Henn B71h]

Martin, John. *New York Times,* May 11, 1946, p. 24.

Sabich, Robert. *Dance Observer* (June–July, 1946): 73.

First performance; now called *Cave of the Heart:* February 27, 1947

New York, Ziegfeld Theatre; Martha Graham Dance Co.
Cast is the same as above, but the characters are now called "sorceress" (Graham), "adventurer" (Hawkins), and "victim" (Yuriko).

Review

Martin, John. *New York Times,* February 28, 1947, p. 26.   [Henn B71j]

66.   *Medea: Ballet Suite* Op. 23

(No score number listed.)

Holograph

LOC: Music 1907
       item 12: full score

Review of score

Donovan, Richard, *Notes* 7, no. 2 (March 1950): 431.   [Henn B71d]

First performance: December 5, 1947

Philadelphia, Academy of Music; Philadelphia Orchestra, Eugene Ormandy, conductor.

Review

Johnson, Harriet. *New York Post,* December 10, 1947, p. 56.

67.   *Medea's Meditation and Dance of Vengeance* Op. 23a

Score 50339360

Holograph

LOC: Music 1907
       item 13: full score

Review of score

"Reviews of New Music." *Musical Opinion* 80 (January 1957): 221. [Henn B72l]

First performance: February 2, 1956

New York, Carnegie Hall; New York Philharmonic-Symphony Orchestra, Dimitri Mitropoulos, conductor.

Reviews

Kastendieck, Miles. *New York Journal American,* February 3, 1956.

Kolodin, Irving. *Saturday Review* 39 (February 18, 1956): 27.   [Henn B72h]

Levinger, Henry W. *Musical Courier* 153 (March 1, 1956): 14.   [HennB72i]

"Medea by Barber," *Time* 67 (February 13, 1956): 42.   [Henn B72j]

Sabin, Robert. *Musical America* 76 (February 15, 1956), p. 223.   [Henn B72n]

68. *Souvenirs,* Op. 28

Ballet in One Act

Commissioned by Lincoln Kirstein for the New York City Ballet Society.
Dedicated to Charles Turner.
Orchestral Score 50341561

Holograph

LOC: Music 1907
          item 29: (a) sketch and (b) full score

Review of score

Morton, Lawrence. "Samuel Barber: *Souvenirs." Notes* 12, no. 3 (June 1955): 483.

First performance: November 15, 1955

New York, City Center; New York City Ballet; libretto and choreography by Todd
Bolender; sets and costumes by Rouben Ter-Arutunian; lighting by Jean Rosen-
thal. Cast: Todd Bolender: leading role; Jillana [Jill Zimmerman]: prima balle-
rina, and Irene Larson: the "Vamp."

Reviews

Herridge, Francis. *New York Post,* November 17, 1955.

Sabin, Robert. *Musical America* 75 (December 1, 1955): p. 5.   [Henn B78o]

69. *A Blue Rose*

Ballet using *Souvenirs* as score

First performance: December 26, 1957

London, Covent Garden; The Junior Company of the Royal Ballet.

Review

Rutland, Harold. *Musical Times* 99 (February 1958): 92.   [Henn B63a]

First performance as orchestral suite: November 12, 1953

Chicago; Chicago Symphony Orchestra, Fritz Reiner, conductor.

70.   *Vanessa,* **Op. 32**

Opera in Three Acts
Libretto: Gian Carlo Menotti Commissioned by the Metropolitan Opera Co.
Vocal score 50338080; libretto 50340390

Holographs

LOC: Music 1907
          item 44: sketches
          item 45: short score
          item 46: copyist's short score
          item 47: first draft of libretto
          item 48: full score
NYPL: Toscanini Memorial Archive, ZBT 227
          first page of "To leave, to break,"
          microfilm of holograph page.

Review of score

Hitchcock, H. Wiley. *Notes* 16, no. 1 (December 1959): 139–140.

First performance: January 15, 1958

New York: Metropolitan Opera
Vanessa: Eleanor Steber, soprano; Erika: Rosiland Elias, mezzo-soprano;
grandmother: Regina Resnik, mezzo-soprano; Anatol: Nicolai Gedda, tenor;
Doctor: Giorgio Tozzi, bass-baritone; stage director: Gian Carlo Menotti; Sets
and costumes: Cecil Beaton; Metropolitan Opera Orchestra, Dimitri Mitropoulos, conductor.

See *Annals of the Metropolitan Opera: The Complete Chronicle of Performances and Artists.* Edited by Gerald Fitzgerald, et al. Boston: G. K. Hall and Co., 1989, vol. 1: Chronology 1883–1985, p. 671; and vol 2: Tables 1883–1985, p. 1A, 12.

Reviews

"American Masterpiece." *Newsweek* 51 (January 27, 1958): 62–63.   [Henn B7b]

"Barber at the Met." *Time* 71 (January 27, 1958): 59–60.   [Henn B7g]

Biancolli, Louis. *New York World-Telegram and Sun,* January 16, 1958.

Blanks, Henry. *Canon: Australian Music Journal* 11 (March–April 1958): 284–285.   [Henn B7i]

Broder, Nathan. *Musical Quarterly* 44 (April 1958): 235–237.   [Henn B7m]

Coleman, Emily. *Theatre Arts* 42 (March 1958): 66–68.   [Henn B7q]

Evett, Robert. *New Republic* 138 (January 27, 1958): 18–19.   [Henn B7y]

Eyer, Ronald. *Opera* (London) 9 (March 1958): 165.   [Henn B7z]

Eyer, Ronald. *Musical America* 78 (February 1958): 5.   [Henn B7aa]

Johnson, Harriet. *New York Post,* January 16, 1958, p. 28.

Kastendieck, Miles. *New York Journal-American*, January 16, 1958.

Kolodin, Irving. *Saturday Review* 41 (January 25, 1958): 41.   [Henn B7xx]

Landry, Robert J. *Variety* 209 (January 22, 1958): 309–312.   [Henn B7ccc]

Landry, Robert J. *Variety* 213 (January 14, 1959): 2.   [Henn B7ddd]

Lang, Paul Henry. *New York Herald Tribune,* January 16, 1958, p. 1, 12.   [Henn B7eee]

"Mr. S. Barber's *Vanessa*." *Times* (London), January 18, 1958, p. 36.   [Henn B7ooo]

Noble, Jeremy. "*Opera* (London) 10 (April 1959): 214.   [Henn B7ppp]

Reisfeld, Bert. *Musica* 12 (April 1958): 218–219.   [Henn B7xxx]

Sargeant, Winthrop. *New Yorker* 33 (January 25, 1958): 100.   [Henn B7bbbb]

Stoddard, Hope. *International Musician* 56 (March 1958): 36.   [Henn B7gggg]

Taubman, Howard. *New York Times,* January 16, 1958, p. 33.   [Henn B7jjjj]

"The Test of *Vanessa*." *New York Times,* May 21, 1958, p. 32.   [Henn B7mmmm]

Trimble, Lester. *Nation* 186 (February 1, 1958): 106.   [Henn B7qqqq]

Walldrop, Gid W. *Musical Courier* 157 (February 1958): 10.   [Henn B7aaaaa]

71.   *Vanessa:* **Intermezzo**

Score 50353810

First performance: March 15, 1958

New York, Carnegie Hall; New York Philharmonic Symphony Orchestra, André
Kostelanetz, conductor.

Review

"Score by Barber Heard." *New York Times,* March 17, 1958, p. 21.   [Henn B9c]

ORCHESTRAL MUSIC

72.   *Adagio for Strings,* **Op. 11**

Arranged by Barber for string orchestra from the slow movement of String Quar-
tet, Op. 11. An earlier title is "Essay for Strings," dedicated to Henry-Louis de La
Grange
Score 50341440 and set 50341430

Holographs

LOC: Music 1907
               item 20: score, now called, Adagio for Strings
Eastman: Box 1, M2A 1, 4-2, 3
               Folder 1/6: ink copy
Pierpont Morgan Library, Mary Flagler Cary Music Collection
               Holograph, version entitled "Essay for Strings."

First performance: November 5, 1938

New York, NBC Symphony Orchestra, Arturo Toscanini, conductor.

Reviews

Downes, Olin. *New York Times*, November 6, 1938, p. 48.   [Henn B61m]
Lieberson, Goddard. *Modern Music* 16 (November–December 1938): 65–69.
"U. S. Composer . . ." *New York Times,* Oct 27, 1938, p. 26.   [Henn B61zz]

73. *Through the Edge* [**Dance choreographed to** *Adagio for Strings*]

First Performed: March 29, 1967

New York, City Center; National Ballet of Washington; Michael Lopuszanski, choreographer.

Review

Barnes, Clive. *New York Times,* March 30, 1967, p. 53.   [Henn B61b]

74. *Youth* [**Dance choreographed to** *Adagio for Strings*]

First Performed: November 7, 1967

New York, Broadway Theater; Harkness Ballet; Richard Wagner, choreographer; dancers: Lone Isaksen and Lawrence Rhodes.

Review

McDonagh, Don. *New York Times,* November 8, 1967, p. 57.   [Henn B61ee]

See also: *The Maryinsky Ballet St. Petersburg Mixed Bill,* 1991 (Item 605).

75. *Adventure* (**no opus number**) (**1954**)

Commissioned by CBS Television and the Museum of Natural History.

Holograph

LOC: Music 1907
        item 2: full score

First performance: November 28, 1954

For the CBS television program "Adventure"
CBS Symphony Orchestra, with various "non-western" musical instruments; Alfredo Antonini, conductor.

76. *Canzonetta,* **Op. 48**

for oboe and string orchestra
Orchestrated by Charles Turner.
Score (piano reduction) 50481827

Review of score

Friedheim, Philip. *Notes* 22, no. 1 (Fall 1965): 813.

First performance: December 17, 1981

New York, Avery Fisher Hall; New York Philharmonic, Harold Gomberg, oboe; Zubin Mehta, conductor.

Reviews

Johnson, Harriet. *New York Post,* December 18, 1981.

Porter, Andrew. *New Yorker* 57 (January 18, 1982): 112.   [Henn B64b]

Rockwell, John. *New York Times,* December 20, 1981, p. 74.   [Henn B64c]

77.   *Capricorn Concerto* **Op. 21**

for flute, oboe, trumpet, and string orchestra
Named after Barber's (and Menotti's) home in Mt. Kisco, New York.
Score 50339000

Holograph

LOC: Music 1907
       item 4: score

Reviews of score

Beeson, Jack. *Notes* (1946): 99.

Berger, Arthur. *Modern Music* 23 (Winter 1946): 66.   [Henn B85c]

Harrison, Lou. *Modern Music* 22 (November 1944): 31–32.   [Henn B85h]

First performance: October 8, 1944

New York, Town Hall; John Wummer, flute; Mitchell [Mitch] Miller, oboe; Harry Freistadt, trumpet; Saidenberg Little Symphony; Daniel Saidenberg, conductor.

Reviews

Mills, Charles. *Modern Music* 23 (Winter 1946): 74.   [Henn B85j]

P. *Musical America* 64 (October 1944): 24.   [Henn B85k]

Strauss, Noel. *New York Times,* October 9, 1944, p. 17.   [Henn B85q]

78.   **Concerto for Piano Op. 38**

for piano and orchestra
Commissioned by G. Schirmer, Inc. for their 100th anniversary
Dedicated to Manfred Ibel.
Score 50339520; piano reduction 50289380

Holographs

LOC: Music 1907
      item 49: sketches
      item 50: short score
      item 51: full score

First performance: September 24, 1962

New York, Philharmonic Hall; John Browning, piano; Boston Symphony Orchestra, Erich Leinsdorf, conductor.

Reviews

Broder, Nathan. *Musical Quarterly* 49 (January 1963): 94–97.   [Henn B65d]

Helm, Everett. *Musical America* 82 (November 1962): 18–19.   [Henn B65u]

Kastendieck, Miles. *New York Journal-American,* September 25, 1962, p. 20.

"New Sound in Manhattan." *Time* (October 5, 1962): 39.

Lang, Paul Henry. *New York Herald Tribune,* September 25, 1962, p. 16.

Schonberg, Harold C. *New York Times,* September 25, 1962, sect. 2, p. 32. [Henn B65ll]

79.   *Configurations* **[Dance choreographed to Concerto for Piano]**

First performance: October 9, 1981

Washington D. C., Lisner Auditorium.
Ballet, choreographed by Choo San Goh, to the Barber Piano Concerto, with Mikhail Baryshnikov and Marianna Tcherkassky and the National Ballet of Washington. (See *South Bank Show,* Items 598 and 607.)

Review

Kriegsman, Alan M. *Washington Post,* October 10, 1981, sec. 1, pp. 1, 9.   [Henn B65bb]

80. *Poeme*

First performance: November 22, 1969

New York, Brooklyn Academy of Music; Alvin Ailey Dance Co.
Ballet choreographed by Pauline Koner; soloists: George Faison and Linda Kent;
choreographed to the second movement of the Barber Piano Concerto. Costumes
by Christina Gianini.

Review

Barnes, Clive. *New York Times,* November 24, 1969, p. 62.   [Henn B65b]

81. **Concerto for Violin, Op. 14**

for violin and orchestra
Commissioned by Samuel Fels for violinist, Iso Briselli.
Score 50339370; piano reduction 50337010

Holograph

LOC: Music 1907
            item 34: full score
Eastman: Box 1, M2A 1, 4-2, 3
            Folder 1/24: photocopy of piano reduction

Reviews of score

"Music Reviews." *Strad* 60 (October 1949): 186.   [Henn B66ll]
"Music Reviews." *Strad* 61 (January 1951): 338.   [Henn B66mm]

First performance: February 7, 1941

Philadelphia, Academy of Music; Albert Spalding, violin; Philadelphia Orchestra,
Eugene Ormandy, conductor.

Reviews

Bronson, Arthur. *Philadelphia Record,* February 8, 1941, p. 11.
Fuller, Donald. *Modern Music* 18 (March–April 1941): 168.   [Henn B66t]
Martin, Linton. *Philadelphia Inquirer,* February 8, 1941, p. 12.
Pleasants, Henry. *Modern Music* 18 (March–April 1941): 181.   [Henn B66oo]
Pleasants, Henry. *Philadelphia Bulletin,* February 8, 1941, sect. E, p. 4.

New York Premiere: February 11, 1941

New York, Carnegie Hall; same performers

Reviews

Downes, Olin. *New York Times*, February 12, 1941, p. 25.   [Henn B66k]

Thomson, Virgil. *New York Herald Tribune,* February 12, 1941, p. 17.

Tanglewood Premiere: August 14, 1941

Berkshire Music Festival performance

Tanglewood, Boston Symphony Orchestra; Ruth Posselt, violinist; Serge Koussevitzky, conductor.

Review

Taubman, Howard. *New York Times,* August 18, 1941, p. 16.

82.   Concerto for Violoncello and Orchestra, Op. 22

for violoncello and orchestra
Commissioned by Raya Garbousova, with funding from John Nicholas Brown.
Dedicated to John and Anne Brown
Score 50339240; piano reduction 50284730

Holograph

LOC: Music 1907
          item 5: full score
Eastman: Box 1, M2A 1, 4-2, 3
          Folder 1/8: piano reduction

Reviews of the score

Finney, Ross Lee. *Notes* 11, no. 1 (December 1953): 146–147.   [Henn B67k]

Klenz, William. *Notes* 8, no. 2 (March 1951): 392.   [Henn B67q]

Sabin, Robert. *Musical America* 71 (August 1951): 30.   [Henn B67x]

First performance: April 5, 1946

Boston, Symphony Hall; Raya Garbousova, cello; Boston Symphony Orchestra, Serge Koussevitzky, conductor.

Reviews

Downes, Olin. *New York Times,* April 14, 1946, sect. 1, p. 46.   [Henn B67g]

Durgin, Cyrus W. *Boston Globe,* April 6, 1946.

Fine, Irving. *Modern Music* 23 (Summer 1946): 210.   [Henn B67j]

Smith, Warren K. *Boston Post,* April 6, 1946.

Thomson, Virgil. *New York Herald Tribune,* April 14, 1946.

83.   *Die Natali:* Chorale Preludes for Christmas, Op. 37

for orchestra
Commissioned by the Koussevitzky Music Foundation.
Dedicated to the memory of Serge and Natalie Koussevitzky.
Score 50339500

Holographs

LOC: Music 1907
    item 15: first draft sketches
LOC: Music 1811
    item 2: full score

Review of score

Kroeger, Karl. *Notes* 20, no. 2 (Spring 1963): 317.

First performance: December 22, 1960

Boston, Symphony Hall; Boston Symphony Orchestra, Charles Munch, conductor.

Reviews

Ardoin, John. *Musical America* 81 (February 1961): 43–44.   [Henn B74a]

Durgin, Cyrus W. *Musical America* 81 (February 1961): 16.   [Henn B74e]

Lewando, Ralph. *Musical Courier* 163 (February 1961): 13.   [Henn B74f]

"Music." *Time* 77 (January 13, 1961): 42.   [Henn B74g]

Sargeant, Winthrop. *New Yorker* 36 (January 14, 1961): 106.   [Henn B74k]

Schonberg, Harold C. *New York Times,* January 5, 1961, p. 28.   [Henn B74l]

84.   *Fadograph of a Yestern Scene,* Op. 44

for orchestra
Commissioned by the Alcoa Foundation for the opening of Heinz Hall, Pittsburgh Pa.
(no score listed)

Holograph

LOC: uncatalogued

First performance: September 10, 1971

Pittsburgh, Heinz Hall for the Performing Arts; Pittsburgh Symphony Orchestra,
William Steinberg, conductor.

Reviews

Apone, Carl. *High Fidelity/Musical America* 22 (January 1972): 25–26.   [Henn
B69a]

Hughes, Allen. *New York Times,* September 12, 1971, p. 94.

New York Premiere: November 5, 1971

New York, Carnegie Hall, same performers.

Reviews

Ericson, Raymond. *New York Times*, November 7, 1971, sect. 1, p. 83.   [Henn
B69b]

Niemann, Suzanne. *Music Journal* 30 (January 1972): 74.   [Henn B69c]

85.   *Essay for Orchestra,* Op. 12

for orchestra
Dedicated to C[arl] E[ngel].
Score 50341770 and set 50341760

Holograph

LOC: Music 1907
         item 43: sketches

Review of score

B., F. *Musical Times* 82 (December 1941): 430.   [Henn B68a]

McPhee, Colin. *Modern Music* 19 (November–December, 1941): 47.

"Review of *First Essay,*" *Music Review* 3 (1942): 74.

First performance: November 5, 1938

New York; NBC Symphony Orchestra, Arturo Toscanini, conductor.

Reviews

Downes, Olin. *New York Times*, November 6, 1938, p. 48.   [Henn B68d]

Lieberson, Goddard. *Modern Music* 16 (November–December 1938): 65–66. [Henn B68i]

Thomson, Virgil. "Superficially Warlike." *The Musical Scene,* New York: Alfred A. Knopf, 1945, p. 125 (reprint from *New York Herald Tribune*).   ML 60 .T5 [Henn B61l]

86.   *Music for a Scene from Shelley,* **Op. 7**

for orchestra
Score 50338850

Holograph

LOC: Music 1907
              item 43: sketch
Curtis: score

Review of score

Copland, Aaron. *Modern Music* 14 (January–February 1937): 100.   [Henn B73c]

First performance: March 24, 1935

New York, Carnegie Hall; New York Philharmonic, Werner Janssen, conductor.

Reviews

Downes, Olin. *New York Times,* March 25, 1935, p. 13.   [Henn B73d]

E. *Musical America* 55 (April 10, 1935): 14.   [Henn B73e]

Gilbert, Gama. *Philadelphia Evening Bulletin*, March 24, 1935.

Henderson, Walter J. *New York Sun,* March 25, 1935.

Perkins, Francis D. *New York Herald Tribune,* March 25, 1935, p. 10.

87. *Night Flight,* Op. 19a

(Revised version of the Second movement of Symphony No. 2)
Score 50339590

Holograph

LOC: Music 1907
    item 42: short score

First performance: October 8, 1964

Cleveland, Severance Hall; The Cleveland Orchestra, George Szell, conductor.

88. Overture to *The School for Scandal,* Op. 5

for orchestra
Score 50338930

Review of score

McPhee, Colin. *Modern Music* 19 (November–December, 1941): 47.

First performance: August 30, 1933

Philadelphia, Robin Hood Dell; Philadelphia Orchestra, Alexander Smallens, conductor.

Review

Martin, Linton. *Philadelphia Inquirer,* August 31, 1933.

New York Premiere: March 30, 1938

New York, Carnegie Hall; New York Philharmonic-Symphony Orchestra, John Barbirolli, conductor.

Reviews

Downes, Olin. *New York Times,* March 31, 1938, p. 14.　　[Henn B76f]

"Music Fame at 28 . . ." *Newsweek*, April 11, 1938, p. 24.

89.　*Second Essay for Orchestra,* Op. 17

for orchestra
Commissioned by Bruno Walter for the centennial of the New York Philharmonic-
Symphony Orchestra.
Dedicated to Robert Horan.
Score 50481360

Holograph

LOC: Music 1907
　　　　item 41: short score
　　　　item 43: sketches

Reviews of score

Berger, Arthur. *Modern Music* 23 (Winter 1946): 66.　　[Henn B77b]

Carner, Mosco. *Music Review* 7 (February 1946): 52.

Thomson, Virgil. *Notes* 2, no. 3 (June 1945): 175–176.

Ward, Robert. *Notes* 3, no. 1 (March 1946): 181.

First performance: April 16, 1942

New York, Carnegie Hall; New York Philharmonic-Symphony Orchestra, Bruno
Walter, conductor.

Reviews

Bohm, Jerome D. *New York Herald Tribune,* April 17, 1942, p. 15.

Fuller, Donald. *Modern Music* 19 (May–June 1942): 254.　　[Henn B77h]

Taubman, Howard. *New York Times,* April 17, 1942, p. 20.　　[Henn B77r]

90.　*Serenade*

for string orchestra, arranged from Serenade for String Quartet Op. 1
Score 50341561

Holograph

LOC: Music 1907
  item 36: full score

First performance: 1943

New York, Mutual Radio Network Broadcast; Symphonic Strings, Alfred Wallenstein, conductor.

Review

Mills, Charles. *Modern Music* 20 (March–April 1943), p. 213.   [Henn B88h]

91. **Symphony No. 1 in One Movement, Op. 9**

for orchestra
Dedicated to Gian Carlo Menotti.

Holograph

LOC: Music 1907
  item 61: full score
  item 43: sketches
NYPL: Edith Evans Braun collection
  Series S: Box 1: MAI 20074 Holograph sketches
  "discarded pages" from the score

First performance: December 13, 1936

Rome, Adriano Theatre; Augusteo Orchestra, Bernadino Molinari, conductor.

Reviews

"Barber Symphony Approved in Rome." *New York Times*, December 14, 1936, p. 28.   [Henn B79a]
"New Symphony . . ." *New York Herald Tribune*, December 14, 1936, p. 14.

U.S. Premiere: January 21, 1937

Cleveland, Severance Hall; The Cleveland Orchestra, Rudolf Ringwall, conductor (substituting for Artur Rodzinsky).

New York Premiere: March 24, 1937

New York, Carnegie Hall: New York Philharmonic-Symphony Orchestra, Artur Rodzinsky, conductor.

Reviews

"Music: Rodzinsky's Audience Acclaims Barber's Latest Work." *Newsweek* 9 (April 3, 1937): 28.   [Henn B79t]

Perkins, Francis D. *New York Herald Tribune,* March 26, 1937, p. 13.

92.   **Symphony No. 1 in One Movement (Revised version)**

Score 50338970

Review of score

Mann, William S. *Music Review* 13 (August 1952): 246.   [Henn B79s]

First performance: February 18, 1944

New York, Carnegie Hall; New York Philharmonic-Symphony Orchestra, Bruno Walter, conductor.

Reviews

Biancolli, Louis. *New York World Telegram and Sun,* March 9, 1944.

S[traus], N[oel]. *New York Times,* March 9, 1944, p. 15.   [Henn B79aa]

93.   **Second Symphony, Op. 19**

for orchestra
Originally entitled: *Symphony Dedicated to the Army Air Forces;* also referred to as *Flight Symphony.*
Commissioned by the U.S. Air Forces.
No published score of first version

Holograph

LOC: Music 1907
        item 31: full score

First performance: March 3, 1944

Boston, Symphony Hall; Boston Symphony Orchestra, Serge Koussevitzky, conductor.

Reviews

"The Case of Samuel Barber." *Newsweek* 23 (March 13, 1944): 94. [Henn B80b]

Downes, Olin. *New York Times,* March 10, 1944, p. 21. [Henn B80d]

Elie, Rudolph Jr. *New York Herald Tribune,* March 4, 1944.

Haddock, Laura. *Christian Science Monitor,* March 3, 1944.

Sloper, L. A. *Christian Science Monitor,* March 4, 1944.

Smith, Moses. *Modern Music* 21 (May–June 1944): 252. [Henn B80y]

New York Premiere: March 9, 1944

New York, Carnegie Hall, same performers

Reviews

Harrison, Lou. *Modern Music* 21 (May–June 1944): 233–234. [Henn B80i]

Thomson, Virgil. *New York Herald Tribune*, March 10, 1944.

94. Second Symphony, revised version, 1947

Score 50481096

Review of score

Keys, Ivor. *Music and Letters* 33 (January 1952): 89. [Henn B80m]

"New Publications in Review." *Musical Courier* 142 (December 1, 1950): 42. [Henn B80q]

"Reviews of New Music." *Musical Opinion* 73 (July 1950): 583. [Henn B80t]

"Reviews of New Music." *Musical Opinion* 74 (Aug 1951): 589. [Henn B80u]

American Premiere: January 5, 1949

Philadelphia, Academy of Music; Curtis (Institute of Music) Symphony Orchestra, Alexander Hilsberg, conductor.

January 21, 1949

Philadelphia Orchestra, Alexander Hilsberg, conductor.

Reviews

Persichetti, Vincent. *Musical Quarterly* 35 (April 1949): 296.   [Henn B80r]

Singer, Samuel L. *Musical Courier* 139 (February 15, 1949): 24.   [Henn B80x]

95.   *Third Essay for Orchestra,* **Op. 47**

for orchestra
Commissioned by and dedicated to Audrey Sheldon (Poon).
Score 50481210

Holograph

NYPL: Toscanini Memorial Archive
         JNG 96-145: score, reproduced from holograph.

First performance: September 14, 1978

New York, Avery Fischer Hall; New York Philharmonic Orchestra, Zubin Mehta,
conductor.

Review

Smith, Patrick J. *High Fidelity/Musical America* 29 (January 1979): MA, 32–33.
[Henn B81d]

96.   *Toccata Festiva,* **Op. 36**

for organ and orchestra
Commissioned by Mary Curtis Zimbalist and written for the dedication of the
new Aeolian-Skinner organ at the Philadelphia Academy of Music.
Score 50339470 and reduction for organ and piano 50288920

Holograph

LOC: Music 1907
         item 40: short score

First performance: September 30, 1960

Philadelphia, Academy of Music; Paul Callaway, organ; Philadelphia Orchestra, Eugene Ormandy, conductor.

Reviews

"Barber's 'Toccata Festiva . . ." *PanPipes* 54, no. 2 (1962): 2, 5.

Briggs, John. *New York Times,* September 4, 1960, sect. 2, p. 9.

Day, Wesley A. *Diapason* 51 (November 1, 1960): 3.   [Henn B82c]

Schauensee, Max de. *Musical America* 80 (November 1960): 23.   [Henn B82j]

Singer, Samuel L. *Musical Courier* 162 (November 1960): 20.   [Henn B82k]

BAND MUSIC

97.   *Commando March*

Score 50348280 and set 50348270

Holograph

Eastman: Box 26, M2A 1, 4-2,3 (oversized)
       Folder 26/1: pencil score

First performance: May 23, 1943

Atlantic City, N. J., Convention Hall; Army Air Force Technical Training Command Band, Samuel Barber, conductor.

CHORAL MUSIC

98.   *Complete Choral Music*

Score 50313910

Review

Dickinson, Peter. *Musical Times* 122 (December 1981): 834.   [Henn B14a]

99.   *Ad Bibinem cum me rogaret ad cenam*

for chorus SATB
Text adapted by Barber from Venatus Fortunatus's "Ad Gogenem cum rogaret ad cenum."
First line: "Nectar vina cibus vestis"
Published in *A Birthday Offering to Carl Engel,* comp. and ed. Gustave Reese, New York: G. Schirmer, 1943. ML 55 .E5 B4

Holograph

LOC: Music 1907
        item 1: score plus notes
Unlikely to ever have been performed

100.   *Easter Chorale (Chorale for Ascension Day)*

for chorus, brass sextet, timpani, and optional organ
Text by Pack Browning.
First line: "The morning light renews the sky"
Score Choral octavo 50312080 and as a part of *Complete Choral Music*
Also: As part of *The Gloria in Excelsis Tower dedication book: the order of services and events for Ascension Day, May 7, 1964,* Washington, D.C.: Washington Cathedral publishers, 1964. (with 2 sound discs, 33 1/3 rpm)

Holograph

LOC: Music 1907
        item 52: as Chorale for Brass Choir,
        brass only, no choral parts

First performance: May 7, 1964 (Ascension Day)

Washington D.C., National Cathedral
For the dedication of The Gloria in Excelsis Bell Tower

101.   *God's Grandeur*

for double chorus a capella
Text by Gerard Manley Hopkins.
First line: "The world is charged with the grandeur of God"
Score 50482114 (not included in *The Complete Choral Music)*

Holograph

Copland's estate (according to Heyman, p. 179.)

First performance: January 31, 1938

Shippensburg Pa., State Teachers' College; Westminster Choir, John Finley Williamson, director.

New York Premiere: March 2, 1938

Carnegie Hall [Heyman, p. 179]

The Talbott and Contemporary American Music Festivals: May 23, 1938

Princeton, New Jersey, Princeton High School Auditorium
With members of various church choirs under the direction of John Finley Williamson.

102. *Let down the bars, O death,* **Op. 8, No. 2**

for mixed chorus a cappella
Text by Emily Dickinson
Score 50301430 and as a part of *Complete Choral Music*

Holograph

LOC: Music 1907
             item 11: score
Eastman: Box 1, M2A 1, 4-2, 3
             Folder 1/14: ink copy

First (documented) performance: October 17, 1950

West Chester, Pa.; West Chester State Teachers' College Choir, Samuel Barber, conductor.

103. *The Lovers,* **Op. 43**

for Baritone, mixed chorus and orchestra
Texts from poems by Pablo Neruda, from *Veinte Poemas de amor y una Canción,*
Translations by Christopher Logue and W. S. Merwin (with some changes by Barber)
Commissioned by the Girard Bank of Philadelphia
Score 50339740 and piano reduction 50332590

I.   "Body of a woman, white hills, white thighs," = "Cuerpo de mujer, blancas colinas." (Neruda, poem #1) [Merwin]

II.   "Lithe girl, brown girl," = "Niña morena y ágil." (Neruda, poem #19)
       [Logue]

III.   "In the hot depth of this summer" = "Es la mañana llena de tempestad."
       (Neruda, poem #4, first six lines) [Logue]

IV.   "Close your eyes, wherein the slow night stirs," = "Cierra tus ojos pro-
       fundos. Allí aletea la noche." (from Neruda, #8 "Abeja blanca zumbas;"
       starting at line eight.) [Logue]

V.   "The Fortunate Isles." (First line: "Drunk as drunk on trementine" =
       "Ebrio de trementina y largos besos," (Neruda, poem #9) [Logue]

VI.   "Sometimes it's like You are dead" = "Me gustas cuando callas porque
       estás como ausente." (Neruda, poem #15, first four lines) [Logue]

VII.   "We have lost even this twilight" = "Hemos perdido aun este crepúsculo."
       (Neruda, poem #10) [Merwin/Barber*]

VIII. "Tonight I can write the saddest lines," = "Puedo escribir los versos más
       tristes esta noche." (Neruda, poem #20) [Merwin/Barber]

IX.   "Cemetery of kisses, there is still fire in your tombs," = "Cemeterios de
       besos, aún hay fuego en tus tumbas," (last 26 lines of Neruda, "La Can-
       ción desperada") [Merwin/Barber]

Review of score

Music Review 39 (August–November, 1978): 299.

First performance: September 22, 1971

Philadelphia, Orchestra Hall; Tom Krause, baritone; Philadelphia Orchestra,
Eugene Ormandy, conductor; Temple University Choirs, Robert Page, director.

Reviews

"Philadelphians Hail Return . . ." *New York Times,* Sept 24, 1971, p. 36.   [Henn
B19g]

Webster, Daniel. *Philadelphia Inquirer,* September 23, 1971, p. 1, 8.

First New York Performance: October 5, 1971

Philharmonic Hall, same performers as above

Reviews

Derhen, Andrew. *High Fidelity. Musical America* 22 (January 1972): 23. [Henn B19b]

Kolodin, Irving. *Saturday Review* 54 (October 23, 1971): 14–15. [Henn B19e]

Schonberg, Harold C. *New York Times,* October 7, 1971. [Henn B19h]

Turok, Paul. *Music Journal* 30 (January 1972): 75. [Henn B19i]

104. *Prayers of Kierkegaard,* **Op. 30**

for soprano, mixed chorus, and orchestra
Texts by Søren Kierkegaard from *Unchangeableness of God* and *Christian Discourses.*
Commissioned by the Koussevitzky Music Foundation of the Library of Congress.
Dedicated to the memory of Serge and Natalie Koussevitzky.
Score 50339600, vocal score 50324640

1. "O thou who art unchangeable"

2. "Lord Jesus Christ"

3. "Father in Heaven"

Holograph

LOC: Music 1907
    item: 18 sketches
LOC: Music 1811
    item 3: orchestral score
    item 4: short score

Review of score

"Reviews of New Music." *Musical Opinion* 79 (December 1955): 157. [Henn B20r]

First performance: December 3, 1954

Boston, Symphony Hall; Boston Symphony Orchestra, Charles Munch, conductor. Soloists: Leontyne Price, soprano; Jean Kraft, contralto; Edward Munro, tenor; the Cecilia Society Chorus, Hugh Ross, director.

Review

B[roder], N[athan.] *Musical Quarterly* 41 (April, 1955): 227–228.   [Henn B20a]

Durgin, Cyrus W. *Musical America* 75 (January 1, 1955): 14.   [Henn B20d]

New York Premiere: December 8, 1954

New York, Carnegie Hall; Boston Symphony Orchestra, Charles Munch, conductor. Soloists: Leontyne Price, soprano; Mary McMurray, contralto; Earl Ringland, tenor; with Schola Cantorum, Hugh Ross, director.

Reviews

Bagar, Robert. *New York World Telegram and Sun,* December 9, 1954.

Downes, Olin. *New York Times,* December 9, 1954, p. 40.   [Henn B20c]

Eyer, Ronald. *Musical America* 75 (January 1, 1955): 17.   [Henn B20e]

H., W. C. *Musical Courier* 151 (January 1, 1955): 13.   [Henn B20g]

Johnson, Harriet. *New York Post,* December 9, 1954.

Kastendieck, Miles. *New York Journal American,* December 9, 1954.

Kolodin, Irving. *Saturday Review* 37 (December 25, 1954): 23.   [Henn B20l]

Lang, Paul Henry. *New York Herald Tribune,* December 9, 1954, p. 24.

"Next to Godliness." *Time* 64 (December 20, 1954): 57.   [Henn B20n]

"Performance Reviews." *Choral and Organ Guide* 7 (January 1955): 29.   [Henn B20p]

105.   ***Reincarnations,* Op. 16**

for mixed chorus a cappella
Texts by James Stephens, from *Honeycomb.*
Score 50301440, 50301450, and 50301460, sold separately; also as part of *Complete Choral Music*
"Mary Hynes"

First line: "She is the sky of the sun!"
"The Coolin"
First line: "Come with me under my coat"
"Anthony O'Daly"
First line: "Since your limbs were laid out"

Holograph

LOC: Music 1907
              item 21: sketches and later versions
              item 43: sketch for "The Coolin"
Curtis: score
Eastman: Box 1, M2A 1, 4-2, 3
              Folder 1/19: ink copy

Review of score

Orr, C. W. *Music Review* 4, no. 2 (1942): 120.   [Henn B21j]

First performance: April 23, 1940

Philadelphia, Curtis Institute of Music; Curtis Institute Madrigal Chorus, Samuel Barber, conductor. First performance of the last two choruses, "Anthony O'Daly" and "The Coolin," along with *A Stopwatch and an Ordnance Map,* Op. 15 (see Item 106 below).

106.   *A Stopwatch and an Ordnance Map,* Op. 15

for men's voices, brass ensemble, and timpani
Text by Stephen Spender, from *Poems About the Spanish Civil War.*
No score currently listed

Review of score

"Reviews of New Music." *Musical Opinion* 78 (February 1955): 285.   [Henn B22k]

First performance: April 23, 1940

Original Version (chorus and timpani); Philadelphia, Casimir Hall; Curtis Institute Madrigal Chorus, David Stephens, timpani; Samuel Barber, conductor.

107.   **Second version (with added brass)**

Full Score 50362250, chorus/timpani part 50301170; also 50334620 as part of *Complete Choral Music*

Holographs

LOC: Music 1907
              item 30: original score with brass parts added
Eastman: Box 1, M2A 1, 4-2, 3
              Folder 1/22: ink copy

Reviews of score

Keller, Hans. *Music Review* 16 (November 1955): 285.

"Reviews of New Music." *Musical Opinion* 78 (February 1955): 285.   [Henn B22k]

First performance: December 16, 1945

New York, Carnegie Hall; Collegiate Chorale, brass and timpani players of New York Philharmonic; David Machtel, tenor; Saul Goodman, timpani; Robert Shaw, conductor.

Reviews

Harrison, Lou. *Modern Music* 23 (Winter 1946): 52.   [Henn B22f]

Strauss, Noel. *New York Times,* December 17, 1945, p. 19.   [Henn B22l]

108.   *To Be sung on the Water,* **Op. 42, no. 2**

for mixed or women's voices a cappella
Text by Louise Bogan
First Line: "Beautiful, my delight"
Score for mixed chorus 50315310; for women's voices 50317050; also as part of *Complete Choral Music*

Holographs

LOC: Music 1907
              item 68: first draft
              item 69: score

109. *Twelfth Night,* Op. 42, No. 1

for mixed voices a cappella
Text by Laurie Lee, from *My Many-coated Man*
First line: "No night could be darker than this night"
Score 50315300; also 50334620 as part of *Complete Choral Music*

Holographs

LOC: Music 1907
     item 66: sketches and first draft
     item 67: score

110. *The Virgin Martyrs,* Op. 8, no. 1

for women's voices a cappella
Text by Siegbert of Gembloux, translated by Helen Waddell.
First line: "Therefore come they, the crowding maidens"
Score 50299760 also as part of *Complete Choral Music*

Holographs

LOC: Music 1907
     item 37: sketches and score
Eastman: Box 1, M2A 1, 4-2, 3
     Folder 1/25: ink copy

First performance: May 1, 1939

Philadelphia, Pa.; students of the Curtis Institute of Music, Samuel Barber, conductor; CBS Radio Broadcast.

VOCAL MUSIC

111. *Collected Songs*

Scores 50328790 (high voice) and 50328780 (low voice)

Review

Redlich, H. F. "Music from the American Continent." *Music Review* 19 (August 1958): 246–253.   [Henn B20q]

"Reviews of New Music." *Musical Opinion* 79 (December 1955): 157.   [Henn B36ff]

112. ***Andromache's Farewell,* Op. 39**

for soprano and orchestra
Text by Euripides, from *The Trojan Women,* trans. by J. P. Creagh.
Commissioned for the opening season of Lincoln Center.
First line: "So you must die, my son"
Score (piano/vocal) 50289570

Holograph

LOC: Music 1907
              item 3: full score, sketches, and short score
Eastman: Box 1, M2A 1, 4-2, 3
              Folder 1/7: piano vocal score and new introduction

Reviews of score

Dickinson, Peter. *Musical Times* 105 (May 1964): 371–372.   [Henn B26c]

Kullesreid, Eleanor. *Notes* 21, no. 3 (Summer 1964): 317.

Sigmon, Carl. *Musical America* 84 (January 1964): 70.   [Henn B26k]

First performance: April 4, 1963

New York, Philharmonic Hall; Martina Arroyo, soprano; New York Philharmonic,
Thomas Schippers, conductor.

Reviews

Biancolli, Louis. *New York World-Telegram and Sun,* April 5, 1963.

Davis, Peter G. *Music Journal* 21 (May 1963): 68.

Johnson, Harriet. *New York Post,* April 5, 1963.

Kastendieck, Miles. *New York Journal-American,* April 5, 1963.

Kolodin, Irving. *Saturday Review* 46 (April 20, 1963): 28.   [Henn B26f]

Lang, Paul Henry. *New York Herald Tribune,* April 5, 1963, p. 16.

Levinger, Henry W. *Musical America* 83 (June 1963): 22.   [Henn B26g]

Sargeant, Winthrop. *New Yorker* 39 (April 13, 1963): 153–154.   [Henn B26h]

Schonberg, Harold C. *New York Times,* April 5, 1963, p. 30.   [Henn B26i]

113.   *Despite and Still,* **Op. 41**

for voice and piano
Dedicated to "my friend" Leontyne Price.
Only as part of *Collected Songs;* not available separately.

1.   "A Last Song," text by Robert Graves, retitled from "A Last Poem"
   First line: "A last song, and a very last"

2.   "My Lizard," text by Theodore Roethke;
   retitled from "Wish for a Young Wife" from *The Far Field.*
   First line: "My lizard, my lively writher"

3.   "In the Wilderness," text by Robert Graves
   First line: "He of his gentleness"

4.   "Solitary Hotel," text by James Joyce, from *Ulysses,* the "Ithaca episode."
   First line: "Solitary hotel in mountain pass"

5.   "Despite and Still," text by Robert Graves
   First line: "Have you not read the words in my head"

Holographs

LOC: Music 1907
     item 62: first draft
     item 63: second draft
     item 64: pencil manuscript (without "Solitary Hotel")
     item 65: publishers' proofs

Review of score

Oberlin, Russell. *Notes* 26, no. 4 (June 1970): 849–50.   [Henn B31c]

First performance: April 27, 1969

New York, Avery Fisher Hall; Leontyne Price, soprano; David Garvey, piano.

Reviews

Henahan, Donal. *New York Times,* April, 28, 1969, p. 36.   [Henn B31a]

Moushon, George. *High Fidelity/Musical America* 19 (July 1969), MA section, p. 22.   [Henn B31b]

114.   *Dover Beach,* Op. 3

for medium voice and string quartet
Text by Matthew Arnold
First line: "The sea is calm tonight"
Score 50338840, set 50341380 and vocal score 50279610

Holographs

LOC: Music 1907
           item 39: score
Curtis: photocopy of manuscript
           photocopy of voice part
Eastman: Box 1, M2A 1, 4-2, 3
           Folder 1/9: Piano reduction
           Folder 1/10: full score in ink

Reviews of score

Copland, Aaron. *Modern Music* 14 (January–February 1937), 100.

Eyer, Ronald F. *Musical America* 16, no. 15 (October 10, 1936): 24.

First performance: May 12, 1932

Philadelphia, Curtis Institute of Music, Casimir Hall; Rose Bampton, mezzo-soprano; James Bloom and Francis Weiner, violins; Arthur Granick, viola, Samuel Geschichter, cello. 25th student concert

New York Premiere: March 5, 1933

New York, League of Composers' Concert, French Institute; Rose Bampton, mezzo-soprano; New York Art Quartet. [also Cello Sonata]

Review

H [ubbard] H [utchinson]. *New York Times,* March 6, 1933, p. 16.

115.   Four Songs, Op. 13

for voice and piano
Score 50328790 (high voice) and 50328780 (for low voice) as part of *Collected Songs*

1. "A nun takes the veil," text by Gerard Manley Hopkins ("Heaven-haven").
   First line: "I have desired to go where springs not fail"
   Dedicated to Rohini Coomara

2. "The Secrets of the Old," text by William Butler Yeats, from *The Tower.*
   First line: "I have old women's secrets now"

3. "Sure on this shining night," text by James Agee, from *Permit Me Voyage.*
   Dedicated to Sara

4. "Nocturne," text by Frederic Prokosch, from *The Carnival.*
   First line: "Close my darling both your eyes"

Holographs

LOC: Music 1907
      item 26: sketches and score
Eastman: Box 1, M2A 1, 4-2, 3
      Folder 1/16: ink copy of "A nun takes the veil"
      Folder 1/20: ink copy of "The Secrets of the Old"
University of Pa.: Marian Anderson Collection of Music Manuscripts
      MSS Coll 199, folders 52, 53, 54, 55:
      ozalid reproduction of holograph scores

Reviews of score

H., A. *Musical Times* 82 (September 1941): 336. [Henn B53f]

Orr, W. O. *Music Review* 2 (November 1941): 335–336. [Henn B53h]

First performance: April 4, 1941

Philadelphia, Curtis Institute of Music; Barbara Troxell, soprano; Eugene Bossart, piano.

New York Premiere: April 7, 1941 (No. 1 only)

New York, Town Hall; Povla Frijsh, soprano; Celius Dougherty, piano.

Review

Downes, Olin. *New York Times,* April 8, 1941, p. 33. [Henn B53b]

116. *Hermit Songs*, **Op. 29**

Commissioned by Elizabeth Sprague Coolidge Foundation of the Library of Congress for Founders Day Concert and dedicated to Mrs. Coolidge.
Score 50328820 (high voice) and 50328830 (low voice); also as part of *Collected Songs*.

1. "At St. Patrick's Purgatory" (anon., 13th century), tr. Sean O'Faoláin,
    First line: "What shall I do with a heart that seeks only its own ease"

2. "Church Bell at Night," tr. Mumford Jones,
    First line: "Sweet little bell"

3. "Saint Ita's Vision" (attributed to St. Ita), unpublished translation by
    Chester Kallman
    First line: "I will take nothing from my Lord"

4. "The Heavenly Banquet" (attributed to St. Brigid), tr. Sean O'Faoláin,
    First line: "I would like a great lake of beer"

5. "The Crucifixion," tr. Mumford Jones,
    First line: "At the cry of the first bird"

6. "Sea-snatch," tr. Kenneth H. Jackson,
    First line: "It has broken us, it has crushed us"

7. "Promiscuity," tr. Kenneth H. Jackson,
    First line: "I do not know with whom Edan will sleep"

8. "The Monk and His Cat," unpublished translation by W. H. Auden,
    First line: "Pangur, white Pangur"

9. "The Praises of God," unpublished translation by W. H. Auden,
    First line: "How foolish the man Who does not raise His voice and praise"
    To the memory of Mary Evans Scott

10. "The Desire for Hermitage," tr. Sean O'Faoláin,
    First line: "Ah! To be all alone in a little cell"

Holographs

LOC: Music 1907
        item 7: sketches
        item 8: copyist's manuscript
        item 18: sketches
LOC: Music 1571 score

Review of score

Kohs, Ellis. *Notes* 12, no. 2 (March 1955): 333–334.   [Henn B33n]

Sabin, Robert. *Musical America* 74 (December 15, 1954): 30.   [Henn B33u]

First performance: October 30, 1953

Washington, D.C., Coolidge Auditorium; Leontyne Price, soprano; Samuel Barber, piano.

Review

Hume, Ruth. *Washington Post,* October 31, 1953, p. 15.

New York Premiere: November 14, 1954

New York, Town Hall, same performers.

Reviews

Harrison, Jay. *New York Herald Tribune,* November 15, 1954, p. 15.

Parmenter, Ross. *New York Times,* November 15, 1954, p. 30.   [Henn B33r]

117.   *Hermit Songs* **[Dance Version]**

First performed: December 10, 1961

New York, Clark Center; Alvin Ailey American Dance Theater.
Solo dance by Alvin Ailey
Revived April 20, 1969, and 1971.

Review of revival:

Kisselgoff, Anna. *New York Times,* April 24, 1969, p. 42.   [Henn B33m]

118.   *Knoxville: Summer of 1915* **Op. 24**

for voice and orchestra
Text by James Agee, originally published in *Partisan Review,* later added (by the editors) as a preface to *A Death in the Family.*
First line: "It has become that time of evening"
commissioned by Eleanor Steber
Score 50339220; piano/vocal score 50285320

Holograph

LOC: Music 1907
              item 9: short score
              item 10: full score
Eastman: Box 1, M2A 1, 4-2, 3
              Folder 1/12: piano reduction

Review of score (piano-vocal)

Diamond, David. *Notes* 7, no. 2 (March 1950): 309.   [Henn B36d]

Glanville-Hicks, Peggy. *Musical America* 70 (January 15, 1950): 89.   [Henn B36n]

"New Publications in Review." *Musical Courier* 141 (February 15, 1950): 54. [Henn B36y]

First performance: April 9, 1948

Boston, Symphony Hall; Eleanor Steber, soprano; Boston Symphony Orchestra, Serge Koussevitzky, conductor.

Reviews

Durgin, Cyrus W. *Musical America* 68 (June 1948): 11.   [Henn B36f]

Riley, John W. *Boston Globe,* April 10, 1948.

"Summer, 1915." *Newsweek* 31 (April 19, 1948): 84–85.   [Henn B36ll]

June 19, 1949

radio performance by Eileen Farrell, soprano, Bernard Herrmann, conductor. Haggin, H. B. *New York Herald Tribune,* June 26, 1949, sect. 5, p. 5.

April 1, 1950; Revised version with chamber orchestra
Washington, D.C., Dumbarton Oaks; Eileen Farrell, soprano; William Strickland, conductor.

119.   *Knoxville: Summer of 1915* **[Dance Version]**

First performance: November 27, 1960

Alvin Ailey American Dance Theater
Revived April 22, 1969.

Review (from revival production)

McDonagh, Don. *New York Times*, April 23, 1969, p. 41.   [Henn B36w]

120. *Mélodies passagères,* **Op. 27**

for voice and piano
Texts by Rainer Maria Rilke, from *Vergers, Tendres Impôt à la France, Les Qua-trains Valaisans,* and *Poémes français.*
commissioned by William Strickland for Dumbarton Oaks
Dedicated to Pierre Bernac and Francis Poulenc
Score 50328950 (high voice) and 50328940 (low voice); also as part of *Collected Songs.*

1. "Puisque tout passe"
    First two lines: "Puisque tout passe faisons/ le mélodie passagère;"
    ("Since all things are passing, let us make a passing melody;")

2. "Un cygne"
    First line: "Un cygne avance sur l'eau"
    ("A swan moves across the water")

3. "Tombeau dans un parc"
    First line: "Dors au fond de l'allée"
    ("At the end of the avenue")

4. "Le clocher chante"
    First line: "Mieux qu'une tour profane"
    ("Better than a secular tower")

5. "Départ"
    First line: "Mon amie, il faut que je parte"
    ("My love, I must leave you")

Holographs

LOC: Music 1907
        item 14: sketches and score
Eastman: Box 1, M2A 1, 4-2, 3
        Folder 1/14: ink copy

Reviews of score

George, Earl. *Notes* 10, no. 3 (June 1953): 497.   [Henn B41b]

Goldman, Richard F. *Musical Quarterly* 38 (July 1952): 435–437.   [Henn B41c]

Levinger, Henry W. *Musical Courier* 146 (November 1, 1952): 29.

"Reviews of New Music." *Musical Opinion* 76 (October 1953): 33.   [Henn B41g]

Sabin, Robert. *Musical America* 72 (December 15, 1952): 26.   [Henn B41h]

First performance (of No. 1, 4, and 5): April 1, 1950

Washington, D.C., Dumbarton Oaks; Eileen Farrell soprano; Samuel Barber, piano.

First performance (complete set): February 10, 1952

New York, Town Hall; Pierre Bernac, baritone; Francis Poulenc, piano.

Reviews

Goldman, Richard F. *Musical Quarterly* 38 (July 1952): 436–437.   [Henn B41c]

H[arman], C[arter]. *New York Times,* Feb 11, 1952, p. 21.   [Henn B41d]

121.   *Nuvoletta,* **Op. 25**

for voice and piano
Text by James Joyce, from *Finnegan's Wake*
First line: "Nuvoletta in her lightdress"
Only as part of *Collected Songs,* not available separately.

Holographs

LOC: Music 1907
            item 17: score
Eastman: Box 1, M2A 1, 4-2, 3
            Folder 1/17: copyists manuscript in ink

Reviews of score

Carson, Leon. *Musical Courier* 147 (February 15, 1953): 39.   [Henn B46a]

F[lanagan], W[illiam.] *Musical America* 74 (February 15, 1954): 224.   [Henn B46c]

First performance: Date unknown

Eleanor Steber, soprano

New York Premiere: November 20, 1953

New York, Juilliard Concert Hall; Gayle Pierce, soprano; pianist unknown.

122.   **Ten Early Songs (1925–1937)**

for voice and piano
Score 50482014

1.   "Slumber Song of the Madonna" (1925), text by Alfred Noyes, from *Forty Singing Seamen and Other Poems.*
First line: "Sleep little baby, I love thee"

2.   "There's nae lark" (1927), text by Algernon Swinburne
First line: "There's nae lark loves the lift, my dear"

3.   "Love at the Door" (1934), text by Meleager of Gadara
First line: "Cold blows the winter wind"

4.   "Serenader" (1934), text by George Dillon, from *Boy in the Wind.*
First line: "I have nothing that is mine sure"

5.   "Love's Caution" (1935), text by William Henry Davies
First line: "Tell them, when you are home again"

6.   "Night Wanderers" (1935), text by William Henry Davies
First line: "They hear the bells of midnight toll"

7.   "Of that so sweet imprisonment" (1935), text by James Joyce, from *Chamber Music.*

8.   "Strings in the earth and air" (1935), text by James Joyce, from *Chamber Music.*

9.   "Beggar's Song" (1936), text by William Henry Davies
First line: "Good people keep their holy day"

10.   "In the dark pinewood" (1937), text by James Joyce, from *Chamber Music.*

Holograph

LOC: Music 1907
      item 43 sketches for no. 3, 8, 9
      "Early Songs" 1917–1927: no. 1

First performance (Songs 1–9): January 5, 1936

Rome, Villa Aurelia, American Academy; Samuel Barber, voice and piano.

123.   **Three Songs, Op. 2**

for voice and piano
Only as part of *Collected Songs,* not available separately.

1. "The Daisies," text by James Stephens, from *Songs from the Clay.*
    First line: "In the scented bud of the morning-O"
    Dedicated to Daisy (Barber's mother)

2. "With rue my heart is laden," text by A. E. Houseman
    Dedicated to Gama Gilbert

3. "Bessie Bobtail," text by James Stephens
    First line: "As down the road she wambled slow"
    Dedicated to Edith and John Braun

Holographs

LOC: Music 1907
            item 24: score of "With rue my heart is laden"
            item 38: score of "The Daisies"
            item 43: sketch for "Bessie Bobtail"
Curtis:
            "presentation copy" manuscript of "With rue my heart is laden"
Eastman: Box 1, M2A 1, 4-2, 3
            Folder 1/23: ink copy of all three songs

First performance: October 23, 1934

West Chester, Pa., New Century Club; Samuel Barber, voice; Yvonne Biser, piano. (Nos. 1 and 3)

124. **Three Songs, Op. 10**

for voice and piano
Texts by James Joyce from *Chamber Music.*
Only as part of *Collected Songs,* not available separately.

1. "Rain has fallen"
   Dedicated to Dario Cecchi
   First line: "Rain has fallen all the day"

2. "Sleep now"
   Dedicated to Susanna Cecchi

3. "I hear an army"

Holographs

LOC: Music 1907
     item 25: score, different versions

Review of score

H., A. *Musical Times* 81 (February 1940): 66.   [Henn B52c]

First performances (1 and 2 only): April 22, 1936

Rome, Villa Aurelia, American Academy; Samuel Barber, voice and piano.
(3 only): March 7, 1937
Philadelphia, Curtis Institute of Music; Benjamin de Loache, voice; Edith Evans
Braun, piano.

125. **Three Songs, Op. 45**

for voice and piano
Commissioned by the Lincoln Center Chamber Music Society for Dietrich
Fischer-Dieskau
Score 50333020 (high voice) 50333030 (low voice) and Score 50328790 (high
voice) and 50328780 (for low voice) as part of Collected Songs

1. "Now have I fed and eaten up the rose," text by Gottfried Keller, from
   Gedanken eines Lebendig-Begraben (Thoughts of a Living Burial), trans. by
   James Joyce.

2. "A Green Lowland of Pianos," text by Jerzy Harasymowicz (original:
   "Zielona nizina fortepianów"), trans. by Czeslaw Milosz.
   First line: "In the evening as far as the eye can see"

3. "O boundless, boundless evening," text by Georg Heym (original: "O weiter, weiter Abend"), trans. by Christopher Middleton.

First performance: April 30, 1974

New York, Alice Tully Hall; Dietrich Fischer-Dieskau, baritone; Charles Wadsworth, piano.

Reviews

Brewer, Robert. *Melos* 41 (July–Aug 1974): 238.   [Henn B57a]

Schonberg, Harold C. *New York Times,* May 2, 1974, p. 64.   [Henn B57c]

126. Two Songs, Op. 18

for voice and piano
Score 50328790 (high voice) and 50328780 (low voice) as part of *Collected Songs*

1. "The queen's face on a summery coin," text by Robert Horan, from *A Beginning.*

2. "Monks and Raisins," text by José Garcia Villa, from *Have Come, Am Here.* First line: "I have observed pink monks eating blue raisins"

Holographs

LOC: Music 1907
             item 30: score of "The Queen's Face"
Eastman: Box 1, M2A 1, 4-2, 3
             Folder 1/15: ink copy of "Monks and Raisins"
             Folder 1/18: ink copy of "The Queen's Face"

First performance: New York, February 22, 1944

CHAMBER MUSIC

127. *Mutations from Bach* (no opus no.)

based on chorale melody, "Christe du Lamm Gottes" as set by J. S. Bach in Cantata No. 23, "Du wahrer Gott und Davids Sohn."
Score and parts 50345250

Holograph

LOC: Music 1907
    item 54: score

Reviews of score

Bryan, Paul R. *Notes* 26, no. 2 (December 1969): 365.   [Henn B87a]

O'Loughlin, Niall. *Musical Times* 109 (November 1968): 1050.   [Henn B87d]

First performance: October 7 (or 8th), 1968

New York, American Symphony Orchestra, Leopold Stokowski, conductor.

128.   *Serenade,* **Op. 1**

for string quartet
Score 50341561 and parts 50341560

Holograph

LOC: Music 1907
    item 36: score

First performance: May 5, 1930

Philadelphia, Curtis Institute of Music, Casimir Hall; Swastika String Quartet (later the Curtis String Quartet): Jascha Brodsky, and Charles Jaffe, violins; Max Aronoff, viola; Orlando Cole, cello.

129.   **Sonata for Violoncello and Piano, Op. 6**

Dedicated to Rosario Scalero, but also inscribed "to Orlando [Cole]"
Score and part 50327230

Holograph

LOC: Music 1907
    item 35: score

Reviews of score

Copland, Aaron. *Modern Music* 14 (January–February 1937): 100.

Eyer, Ronald. *Musical America* 16, no. 15 (October 10, 1936): 24.

First performance: March 5, 1933

New York, League of Composers' concert; Orlando Cole, cello; Samuel Barber, piano.

Reviews

"Recitals of the Week." *Times* (London), June 25, 1937, p. 14.   [Henn B90t]

S., M. M. *Musical Times* 78 (July 1937): 645.   [Henn B90w]

130.   **String Quartet, Op. 11**

Score 50338950

Holograph

LOC: Music 1907
              item 19: Adagio movement
Curtis: string parts

First performance: December 14, 1936

Rome, Villa Aurelia; American Academy; the Pro-Arte Quartet.

American Premiere: 1938

Philadelphia; Curtis String Quartet (formerly the Swastika String Quartet): Jascha Brodsky, and Charles Jaffe, violins; Max Aronoff, viola; Orlando Cole, cello.

Review

Cohn, Arthur. *Modern Music* 15 (May–June 1938): 237.   [Henn B91c]

New York Premiere: March 15, 1938

New York, Town Hall; Curtis String Quartet.

Review

Taubman, Howard. *New York Times,* March 16, 1938, p. 20.   [Henn B91u]

131. *Summer Music,* Op. 31

for wind quintet
Commissioned by the Chamber Music Society of Detroit
Score and parts 5035030

Holograph

LOC: Music 1907
    item 32: score

Reviews of score

Bassett, Leslie. *Notes* 15, no. 1 (December 1957): 148–149.   [Henn B92a]

"Reviews of New Music." *Musical Opinion* 80 (July 1957): 599.   [Henn B92n]

First performance: March 20, 1956

Detroit Institute of Arts, Detroit, MI; Chamber Music Society of Detroit (First desk men, Detroit Symphony Orchestra: James Pellerite, flute; Arno Mariotti, oboe; Albert Luconi, clarinet; Charles Sirard, bassoon; Ray Alonge, French horn.)

Review

Mossman, Josef. *Detroit News,* March 21, 1956.

New York Premiere: November 16, 1956

New York, Carnegie Hall; New York Woodwind Quintet: Samuel Baron, flute; David Glazer, clarinet; Jerome Roth, oboe; Bernard Garfield, bassoon; John Barrows, French horn.

Review

Schonberg, Harold C. *New York Times,* November 17, 1956, p. 17.   [Henn B92q]

KEYBOARD MUSIC: PIANO

132. *Complete Piano Music*

score 50336700

Review of score

Svard, Lois. *Notes* 42, no. 3 (March 1985): 645–646.

133. *Ballade,* Op. 46

for piano
Commissioned by the Van Cliburn Foundation, funding by Mrs. J. Lee Johnson
Score 50335660 and 503336700 as a part of *Complete Piano Music*

First performances: September 11–15, 1977

Fort Worth, Texas; Fifth Van Cliburn International Quadrennial Piano Competition. Performed by various pianists, including Stephen De Groote, the winner of
the competition, who also received a gold watch from Neiman Marcus for "best
performance of a commissioned work."

Reviews

Ohendalski, Latryl. *Fort Worth Star Telegram,* September 19, 1977.

Silverman, Robert. *Piano Quarterly* 100 (Winter 1977–78): 15–18.

134. *Excursions,* Op. 20

four pieces for piano
Score 50328730 and 503336700 as a part of *Complete Piano Music*

1. Un poco allegro

2. In slow blues tempo

3. Allegretto

4. Allegro molto

Holograph

LOC: Music 1907
             item 6: score; sketches of 1, 2, and 4
Eastman: Box 1, M2A 1, 4-2, 3
             Folder 1/11: ink score

Review of score

Berger, Arthur. *Modern Music* 22 (May–June 1945): 267.   [Henn B94d]

First performance (1, 2, and 4 only): January 4, 1945

Philadelphia, Academy of Music; Vladimir Horowitz, piano.

Review

Schauensee, Max de. *Philadelphia Evening Bulletin,* January 5, 1945.

New York Premiere (1, 2, and 4 only): January 18, 1946

New York; Rudolf Firkusny, piano.

Review

Straus, Noel. *New York Times,* January 19, 1946, p. 19.   [Henn B94q]

First performance of complete set: December 22, 1948

New York, New York Times Hall; Jeanne Behrend, piano.
This program, featuring six pianists, was a benefit performance for the New York
Public Library to purchase several manuscripts of Louis Moreau Gottschalk.

Review

Downes, Olin. *New York Times,* December 23, 1948, p. 23.   [Henn B94g]

135.   *Excursions* **[Dance Version]**

First performance: October 19, 1975

Eliot Feld Ballet Company, with Christine Sarry

Review

Kisselgoff, Anna. *New York Times,* October 20, 1975, p. 45.   [Henn B94k]

136.   *Interlude I* **(Adagio for Jeanne)**

for piano
Score 50336700 and 503336700 as a part of *Complete Piano Music*

Holograph

LOC: Barber's Orchestration Book

First performance: May 12, 1932

Philadelphia, Pa., Curtis Institute of Music; Samuel Barber, piano.

137. *Nocturne* **(Homage to John Field) Op. 33**

for piano
Score 50288310 and 503336700 as a part of *Complete Piano Music*

Holograph

LOC: Music 1907
    item 71: score

First performance: Uncertain, possibly October 1959

Probably San Diego, CA (according to Heyman); John Browning, piano.

138. **Sonata, Op. 26**

for piano
Commissioned by Irving Berlin and Richard Rodgers in honor of the twenty-fifth
anniversary of the League of Composers.
Score 50328330 and 503336700 as a part of *Complete Piano Music*

Holograph

LOC: Music 1907
        item 22: two copies of score
Eastman: Box 1, M2A 1, 4-2, 3
        Folder 1/21: ink copy
Pierpont Morgan Library, Mary Flagler Cary Music Collection:
    sketches of the third movement

Reviews of score

A., R. "Piano." *Musical Times* 91 (September 1950): 357–358.   [Henn B98a]

Broder, Nathan. *Musical Quarterly* 36 (April 1950): 276–279.   [Henn B98k]

Kerr, Russell M. *Musical Courier* 141 (February 1, 1950): 29.   [Henn B98ww]

Kirkpatrick, John. *Notes* 7, no. 3 (June 1950): 448.   [Henn B98xx]

Krokover, Rosalyn. *Musical Courier* 141 (February 1, 1950): 29.   [Henn B98bbb]

Redlich, H. F. *Music Review* 11 (November 1950): 329.   [Henn B98nnn]

Sabin, Robert. *Musical America* 70 (February 1950): 332.   [Henn B98ppp]

First performance: December 9, 1949

Havana, Cuba; Vladimir Horowitz, piano.

New York Premiere: January 4, 1950

New York, Trustees Room of G. Schirmer, Co.; Vladimir Horowitz, piano.

Review

"New Piano Sonata," *New York Herald Tribune,* January 5, 1950.

First Public Performance in the United States: January 23, 1950

New York, Carnegie Hall; Vladimir Horowitz, piano.

Reviews

Downes, Olin. *New York Times,* January 24, 1950, p. 27.   [Henn B98t]

Gunn, Glenn Dillard. *Washington Times-Herald,* January 11, 1950.

"House in Mt. Kisco." *Time* 55 (February 6, 1950): 34–35.   [Henn B98mm]

Keith, Richard. *Washington Post,* January 11, 1950, p. 2B.

Levinger, Henry W. *Musical Courier* 141 (February 15, 1950): 42.   [Henn B98eee]

Washington, D.C., Premiere: April 1, 1950

Washington, D.C., Dumbarton Oaks; Rudolf Firkusny, piano.

Review

Hume, Paul. *Washington Post,* April 2, 1950.

November 24, 1951

New York, Hunter College Auditorium.

Review

Schonberg, Harold C. *New York Times,* November 26, 1951, p. 21.   [Henn B98ttt]

139. *Souvenirs,* **Op. 28**

for piano four hands
Dedicated to Charles Turner
Score 50286370

Holograph

LOC: Music 1907
  item 28 (a) sketch and (b) score

140. ***Three Sketches for Pianoforte*** (private edition, 1924)
  1. "Love Song" (dedicated "To Mother")
  2. "To My Steinway" (dedicated "To Number 220601")
  3. "Minuet" (dedicated "To Sara,")

Holograph

Chester County Historical Society Museum

KEYBOARD MUSIC: ORGAN

141. ***Wondrous Love (Variations on a Shape-Note Hymn),*** **Op. 34**

for solo organ
Commissioned by Christ Episcopal Church, Grosse Point, Michigan.
Dedicated to Richard Roeckelein.
Score 50288260

Holograph

LOC: Music 1907
  item 70: score

Review of score

Noss, Luther. *Notes* 17, no. 3 (June 1960): 479.

First performance: October 19, 1958

Grosse Pointe, Michigan, Christ Episcopal Church; Richard Roeckelein, organ.

ARRANGEMENTS OF BARBER'S WORKS, BY BARBER AND OTHERS

For Orchestra

142. *Commando March* (arranged for orchestra)

no Schirmer score listed

First performance: October 29, 1943

Boston, Symphony Hall; The Boston Symphony Orchestra, Serge Koussevitzky, conductor.

Review

Smith, Moses. *Modern Music* 21 (January–February 1944): 103–104. [Henn B86g]

For Voice and Orchestra

143. "I hear an army" from Op. 10, No. 3, arranged by Barber

Score: 50281230 (high voice), 50281480 (medium, low voice) 50328780
"Monks and Raisins" from Op. 18, No. 2, arranged by Barber
"Nocturne" from Op. 13, No. 4, arranged by Barber
"Sure on this shining night" from Op. 13, No. 3, arranged by Barber

Holographs

LOC: Music 1907
      item 23: pencil manuscript, without words

First performance: May 5, 1945

All four performed by Jennie Tourel, mezzo-soprano; CBS Symphony Orchestra, Samuel Barber, conductor.

144. *Music for Soprano and Orchestra* (Operatic and Concert Scenes)

In addition to the already published *Knoxville: Summer of 1915* and *Andromache's Farewell* are:

Three Scenes from *Vanessa*
    "Do not utter a word"
    "Must the winter come so soon"
    "Under the willow tree"
Two Scenes from *Antony and Cleopatra*
    "Give me some music"
    "Death of Cleopatra"
Score: 50331490

Holograph

LOC: Music 1907
    item 60: "Give me some music"

For Band or Wind Ensemble

145.   **Adagio for Strings,** from Op. 11,

arranged for clarinet choir by Lucien Caillet, 1963.
No score given

146.   **Adagio for Young Concert Band,** from Op. 11,

arranged for woodwind ensemble by Paul Jennings, 1991.
Score 50481483 and parts 50481482

147.   **Adagio,** from Op. 11,

arranged for woodwind ensemble by Calvin Cluster, 1992.
Score 50481485 and set 50481484

148.   **Adagio for Strings,** from Op. 11,

arranged for woodwind choir by John O'Reilly, 1967.
Score 50481483 and parts 50481482

149.   **First Essay,** from Op. 12,

arranged for band by Joseph Levy, 1994.
Score 50483400

150.   ***Intermezzo,*** from *Vanessa,*

arranged for band by Walter Beeler, 1962.
Score 50353800

151.   **"Medea's Dance of Vengeance"** from *Medea,* Op. 23a,

arranged for band by Frank M. Hudson, 1994.
Score 50482401

152.   **Overture to *The School for Scandal*** from Op. 5 arranged for band by
Frank M. Hudson, 1972.

Score 50363990 and set 50363980

Holograph

Eastman: Box 26, M2A 1, 4-2,3 (oversized)
        Folder 26/2: ink copy

153.   **Symphony No. 1 in One Movement,** from Op. 9

arranged for band by Guy M. Duker, 1970.
Score 50481641 and set 50481636

Choral Arrangements

154.   ***Agnus Dei,*** setting of *Adagio for Strings,* Op. 11,

for mixed chorus and optional piano or organ, text from Latin Mass, arranged by
Barber, 1967. Also in English as "Lamb of God."
Score 50313910 and 50334620 as a part of *Complete Choral Music.*

155.   **"The Monk and his Cat,"** from *Hermit Songs,* Op. 29, no. 8,

for mixed chorus and piano, arranged by Barber, 1953?
Score 50313900 and 50334620 as a part of *Complete Choral Music*

156.   ***Heaven-Haven*** ("A nun takes the veil,") from Op. 13, No. 1,

for voices a cappella, arranged by Barber, 1937.
Score 50308880; Also arranged for women's chorus
Score 50308900

157.   **"Sure on this shining night,"** from Op. 13, No. 3, for SATB voices and piano, arranged by Barber.

Score 50308930 and 50334620 as a part of *Complete Choral Music.*

Holograph

LOC: Music 1907
        item 23: score
Also for SAB voices and piano, arranged by Dick Averre, 1989.
Score 50480265

158.   **"Under the willow tree,"** from *Vanessa*, for mixed voices and piano, arranged by Barber.

Score 50308910 and 50334620 as a part of *Complete Choral Music.*
Also for mixed voices and orchestra

Holograph

LOC: Music 1907
          item 55 orchestral score (without words)
Curtis: pencil manuscript

159.   **"On the Death of Antony,"** from *Antony and Cleopatra*, for women's chorus or mixed voices and piano

First line: "Noblest of men, woo't die?"
Score 50334620 as a part of *Complete Choral Music;* not available separately.

160.   **"On the Death of Cleopatra,"** from *Antony and Cleopatra*, for women's chorus or mixed voices and piano

First line: "She looks like sleep"
Score 50334620 as a part of *Complete Choral Music,* not available separately.

Voice and Piano

161.   **"Lord Jesus Christ,"** from *Prayers of Kierkegaard*

Score 50287170

Chamber Music

162.   *Adagio for Strings,* from Op. 11,

for flute quartet, arranged by Rië Schmidt, 1991.
Score and parts 50481502

163.   *Adagio for Strings,* arranged for marimba ensemble.

no Score number from Schirmer

164.   *Adagio for Strings,* from Op. 11,

for violin and piano, arranged by Jerry Laning, 1996.
Score 50482603

165.   *Canzone* for flute or violin and piano, Op. 38a, 1959,

later to become the second movement of the Concerto for Piano.
Score and part 50289400 (flute) and 50289460 (violin)

Holograph

LOC: Music 1907
    item 53: pencil score

Review of score

Friedheim, Phillip. *Notes* 22, no. 1 (Fall 1965): 813.

Keyboard: Piano

166.   *Adagio for Strings,* from Op. 11,

for piano, arranged by Lawrence Rosen, 1987.
Score 50480216

167.   **"Under the Willow Tree,"** from *Vanessa,*

for piano, arranged by Henri Noel, contained in the education piano anthology,
American Classical Composers.
Score 50482216

168.   *Souvenirs* Op. 28, for piano, two hands, arranged by Barber, 1952

Score 50336680

169.   *Souvenirs,* Op. 28, for two pianos, arranged by Gold and Fizdale, 1953.

Score 50289800

First performance: July 1952

NBC Television; Arthur Gold and Robert Fizdale, pianos.

New York Premiere: March 11, 1953

New York, Museum of Modern Art; Arthur Gold and Robert Fizdale, pianos.

Review

"Gold, Fizdale . . ." *New York Times,* March 12, 1953, p. 23.   [Henn B78g]

Keyboard: Organ

170.   *Adagio for Strings,* for organ, arranged by William Strickland

Score 50284770

Review of score

Lester, William. *Diapason* 40 (November 1, 1949): 28.   [Henn B61dd]

171.   **Chorale Prelude on "Silent Night,"** from *Die Natali,* Op. 37,

for organ, arranged by Barber, 1961.
Score 50288900

Holograph

LOC: Music 1907
        item 16: score and sketches

Other Arrangements

172.   *Suite for Carillon*

1. "Prelude"
2. "Scherzetto"
3. "Andante, un poco meso"
4. "Toccata: allegro molto"

Score in preparation

UNPUBLISHED WORKS

The following pieces have never been published and are not easily available for study. This list should be considered a "works in progress" report, providing the names of many, if not all, of these pieces. Most are in manuscripts and are not yet catalogued. Heyman's forthcoming thematic catalogue will probably add other sources, give more detailed information, and clarify the relationships among the various manuscripts.

Opera

173. **"The Rose Tree,"** 1920

libretto by Annie Sullivan Brosius Noble (Barber family cook); first act complete, the rest incomplete

Holograph

LOC
also: excerpts from "The Rose Tree"
"Gypsy Dance," facsimile of first page, Heyman, p. 22
"Gypsy Song,"
"Dialogue for Act 1, scene 1,"
"Serenade for Act 1, scene 2" facsimile in Heyman, p. 27
complete libretto

Holograph

Chester County Historical Society

Orchestral Music

174. **"Adventure"** 1954

Holograph

LOC: Music 1907
  item 2: score
Facsimile of first 14 measures in Heyman, p. 346; a later passage is in Heyman dissertation, p. 535.

First performance: November 28, 1954

CBS television, "Adventure," hosted by Charles Collingwood, episode entitled, "The Language of Music." Music explained by Dr. Willard Rhodes; CBS Symphony Orchestra, Samuel Barber, conductor.
Dancers: John Butler, Glenn Tetley, and Mary Hinkson

175.   "Concerto for Piano and Orchestra," 1930

Holograph

LOC
Barber's orchestration notebook: sketch only; score is lost
Facsimile of one page in Heyman dissertation, p. 114.

176.   **"Horizon"** 1945

Written for the NBC radio program "The Standard Oil Hour."

Holograph

LOC
Facsimile of first page in Heyman, p. 362

First performance: NBC radio, June 17, 1945.

Choral Music

177.   **"Ave Maria"** (after Josquin) 1940

for chorus; an arrangement from Josquin des Prez's motet for the Curtis "Madrigal Chorus" for a performance of various works in 1940

178.   **"Christmas Eve"**

described as a "trio with solos;" one is a "Shepherd's Solo"
First line: "O Lord, what are we that thou should send a redeemer?"

Holograph

Chester County Historical Society
Melody of "Shepherd's Solo," hand copied (not facsimile), in Kreiling, p. 38.

179. **"Long Live Louise and Sidney Homer"** 1944

180. **"Mary Ruane"** 1936

four-voice mixed chorus
Text by James Stephens.
First line: "The sky-like girl that we knew"

Holograph

LOC: Music 1907
        item 11: sketch on verso side of "Let down the bars, O Death"

181. **"Motetto on words from the book of Job"** 1930

in three movements (I, II, and IV, with a third presumably missing), the first two
for SATB, the third for double choir;

Holograph

LOC

182. **"O the mind, the mind has mountains,"** c. 1939 (incomplete)

Text by Gerard Manley Hopkins, the sestet portion of Hopkin's sonnet, "No
worse, there is none."

Holograph

LOC
Brief sketch only, setting of a few lines

183. **"Peggy Mitchell,"** 1936

for four voices
Text by James Stephens, from *Honeycomb.*
First line: "As lily grows up easily"

Holograph

LOC
Partial sketch

Vocal Music

184.   **"Ask Me To Rest"** early 1920s

Text by E. H. S. Terry.

185.   **"Au clair de la lune,"** early 1920s

Described by Barber as a " modern setting" for voice and piano; to be played "mournfully, con moto."

Holograph

LOC
in Early Compositions 1917–1927
Dedication: "For Deems Taylor's class"

First performance: April 25, 1926

West Chester, Pa., home of the Barbers; Lilian Mc D. Brinton, mezzo-soprano, Samuel Barber, piano.

186.   **"Between Dark and Dark,"** 1942

for voice and piano
Text by Katherine Garrison Chapin (Biddle) from *Plain Chant for America.*

187.   **"The Dance"** 1927

for voice and piano
Text by James Stephens.
Score is lost; first line is likely to have been: "Left and right and swing around"; part of "In Green Ways"

First performance: March 7, 1938

Philadelphia Curtis Institute of Music, Casimir Hall; Rose Bampton, soprano, Edith Evans Braun, piano.

188. **"Dee Two Fella Joe"** early 1920s

for voice and piano
Text by an anonymous White Mountain Guide.
Written at camp Wyanoke (New Hampshire) in French-Canadian dialect (Heyman, p. 31).

Holograph

LOC
in "Early Compositions 1917–1927"

First performance: April 25, 1926

West Chester, Pa., home of the Barbers; Gertrude K. Schmidt, soprano, Samuel Barber, piano.

189. **"An Earnest Suit to His Unkind Mistress Not to Forsake Him"**

for voice and piano
Text by Sir Thomas Wyatt.

190. **"Fantasy in Purple,"** 1925

for voice and piano
Text by Langston Hughes, first printed in *Vanity Fair.*
First line: "Beat the drums of tragedy for me"

Holograph

LOC
in "Early Compositions 1917–1927"

First performance: April 25, 1926

West Chester, Pa., home of the Barbers; Lilian Mc D. Brinton, mezzo-soprano, Samuel Barber, piano.

191. **"Hunting Song,"** c. 1921

for voice and piano
Text by John Bennett.

Holograph

Chester County Historical Society

192.   **"I never thought that youth would go,"** 1925

for voice and piano
Text by J. B. Rittenhouse.

Holograph

Chester County Historical Society

193.   **"I seize the sphering harp"**

for voice and piano
Text by William Blake, from *Four Zoas*.

Holograph

LOC: Music 1907
        item 43: "An Old Sketchbook" short sketch

194.   **"In the Firelight,"** 1918

for voice and piano
Text by Eugene Field.
First line: "The fire upon the hearth is low"

195.   **"Invocation to Youth"**

for voice and piano
Text by Laurence Binyon.
First line: "Come then, as ever, like the wind at morning."

Holograph

Chester County Historical Society

First performance: April 25, 1926

West Chester, Pa., home of the Barbers; Lilian Mc D. Brinton, mezzo-soprano,
Samuel Barber, piano.

196.   **"Isabel,"** 1919

for voice and piano
Text by John Greenleaf Whittier.
Set as a waltz, showing Barber's "gift for parlor tunes," (Heyman, p. 12).

Holograph

LOC
in "Early Compositions 1917–1927"
facsimile in Heyman dissertation, p. 14

197. **"King David was a sorrowful man"**

for voice and piano
Text by Walter de la Mare, from *Peacock Pie: A Book of Rhymes*

Holograph

LOC: Music 1907
        item 43 in "An Old Sketchbook"
        10-measure sketch, words and melody only

198. **"Lady, when I behold the roses,"** early 1920s

for voice and piano
Anonymous text

Holograph

LOC
in "Early Compositions 1917–1927"

First performance: April 25, 1926

West Chester, Pa., home of the Barbers; Lilian Mc D. Brinton, mezzo-soprano, Samuel Barber, piano.

199. **"Little Children of the Wind,"** early 1920s

for voice and piano
Text by Fiona Macleod (pseudonym of William Sharp), from *Two Poems of the Wind*
First line: "I hear the little children of the wind"

Holograph

LOC
in "Early Compositions 1917–1927"

First performance: April 25, 1926

West Chester, Pa., home of the Barbers; Lilian Mc D. Brinton, mezzo-soprano,
Samuel Barber, piano.

200.   **"Longing,"** early 1920s

for voice and piano
Text by Fiona Macleod, from *Two Poems of the Wind,* 1924.
First line: "O would I were the cool wind that's blowing from the sea"

Holograph

in Louise Homer collection

First performance: April 25, 1926

West Chester, Pa., home of the Barbers; Lilian Mc D. Brinton, mezzo-soprano,
Samuel Barber, piano.

201.   **"Man,"** 1926

for voice and piano
Text by Humbert Wolfe.

Holograph

LOC
in "Early Compositions 1917–1927"

First performance: April 25, 1926

West Chester, Pa., home of the Barbers; Gertrude K. Schmidt, soprano, Samuel
Barber, piano.

202. **"Minuet,"** c. 1924

song for two voices

Holograph

in Louise Homer collection

203. **"Mother Goose Rhymes Set to Music,"** 1922

for voice and piano
"Dedicated to Sara" (also called "Nursery Songs" Op. VII)

      [1] "The Old Man from Jamaica"

      [2] "The Rockabye Lady"

      [3] "I Love Little Pussy"

Holograph

LOC
in "Early Compositions 1917–1927"
facsimile of no. 3 in Heyman, pp. 20–21

First performance: March 24, 1923

West Chester: First Presbyterian Church, Sara Barber, voice, Samuel Barber, piano.

204. **"Mother, I cannot mind my wheel,"** 1927

for voice and piano
Text by Walter Savage Landor
The poem is based on a fragment from Sappho, "Sweet mother, truly I cannot weave my web."

205. **"Music, When Soft Voices Die,"** c. 1926

for voice and piano
Text by Percy Bysshe Shelley.

Holograph

Chester County Historical Society

First performance: April 25, 1926

West Chester, Pa., home of the Barbers; Lilian Mc D. Brinton, mezzo-soprano, Samuel Barber, piano.

206.   **"My Fairyland,"** c. 1924

for voice and piano
Text by Robert T. Kerlin

Holograph

LOC
in "Early Compositions 1917–1927"

First performance: April 25, 1926

West Chester, Pa., home of the Barbers; Gertrude K. Schmidt, soprano, Samuel Barber, piano

207.   **"La Nuit,"** 1925

for voice and piano
Text by Alfred Meurath.

Holograph

LOC
in "Early Compositions 1917–1927"

First performance: April 25, 1926

West Chester, Pa., home of the Barbers; Lilian Mc D. Brinton, mezzo-soprano, Samuel Barber, piano.

208.   **"October Mountain Weather"** (October-Weather) c. 1923

for voice and piano
Text by Samuel Barber.
First line: "October mountain weather, With joy sing, ah!"

Holograph

LOC for version entitled "October Weather"
Chester County Historical Society, for version entitled "October Mountain Weather."

First performance: April 25, 1926

West Chester, Pa., home of the Barbers; Gertrude K. Schmidt, soprano, Samuel Barber, piano

209. **"An Old Song,"** 1921

for voice and piano
Text by Charles Kingsley.
First line: "When all the world is young, lad"

Holograph

Chester County Historical Society
Hand copy (not facsimile) of entire song, Kreiling, pp. 39–41.

210. **"Only of Thee and Me,"** c. 1927

for voice and piano
Text by Louis Untermeyer; poem is simply entitled "Song,"
First line: "Only of thee and me the night wind sings"

211. **"Peace,"** 1935

for voice and piano
Text from poetry of Bhartrhari, translated from the original Sanskrit by Paul Elmer More.

212. **"Prayer,"** 1921

for voice and piano
Anonymous text
Dedicated to Barber's mother.

213.   **"Rounds for Three Voices,"** 1927

A Lament	Shelley
To Electra	Robert Herrick
Dirge: Weep for the World's Wrong	Anon
Farewell	Robert Louis Stevenson from *Songs of Travel*
Not I	Robert Louis Stevenson
Of a Rose is Al Myn Song	Anon
Sunset	Stevenson
The Moon	Shelley
Sun of the Sleepless	Byron from *Hebrew Melodies*
The Throstle	Tennyson
When Day is Gone	Robert Burns
Late, Late, so Late	Tennyson from "Guinivere" portion of *Idylls of theKing*

Holograph

LOC
in "School Compositions, 1927–1928."

214.   **"The Shepherd to his Love,"** 1928

for voice and piano
Text by Christopher Marlowe ("The Passionate Shepherd to his Love").
First line: "Come live with me and be my love"

215.   **"The Nymph's Reply,"** 1928

for voice and piano
Text by Sir Walter Raleigh.

216.   **"Sometime,"** 1917

for voice and piano
Text by Eugene Field.

Holograph

LOC
in "Early Compositions 1917–1927"

217. **"Song of Enitharmon over Los,"** c. 1934 (inc.)

for voice and piano
Text by William Blake, from *Four Zoas.*

218. **"Stopping by Woods on a Snowy Evening,"** 1935

for voice and piano
Text by Robert Frost, from *New Hampshire.*

219. **"Summer is coming,"** 1924

for three voices
Text by Lord Alfred Tennyson.
(another name for "The Thostle"; see Item 213.)

220. **"Thy Love,"** 1926

for voice and piano
Text by Elizabeth Barrett Browning.

Holograph

LOC
in "Early Compositions 1917–1927"

First performance: April 25, 1926

West Chester, Pa., home of the Barbers; Lilian Mc D. Brinton, mezzo-soprano, Samuel Barber, piano.

221. **"Thy will Be Done,"** Op. V, c. 1922

A revised version of the song, "The Wanderer."

222. **"Two Poems of the Wind"** (songs), 1924; texts by Fiona Macleod

"Little Children of the Wind"
"Longing"
(See individual references, Items 199 and 200.)

223.   **"Two Songs of Youth,"** 1925

"I never thought that youth would go," J. B. Rittenhouse
"Invocation to Youth," Laurence Binyon
(See individual references, Items 192 and 195.)

224.   **"The Watchers,"** 1926

for voice and piano
Text by Dean Cornwell.

Holograph

LOC
Facsimile of last page, Heyman, p. 44.

First performance: April 25, 1926

West Chester, Pa., home of the Barbers; Lilian Mc D. Brinton, mezzo-soprano,
Samuel Barber, piano.

225.   **"Who carries corn and crown,"** 1935

for voice and piano
Anonymous text

226.   **"Why not?,"** 1917

for voice and piano
Text by Kitty Parsons.

CHAMBER MUSIC

227.   **"Commemorative March,"** 1941

for violin, cello and piano

Holograph

LOC
Score "composed for Susie's (my sister's) wedding in my New York apartment."

228. **Sonata for Violin and Piano,** 1928

Holograph

Manuscript, winner of the Joseph H. Bearns Music Prize; lost, possibly destroyed

229. **"Song for a new house,"** 1940

for voice, flute, and piano
Text by William Shakespeare; from *A Midsummer Night's Dream,* Act 5, scene 2; written for and dedicated to Mary Curtis Bok Zimbalist for her move to her new home.

Holograph

Curtis Institute of Music

230. **String Quartet** (second movement: Allegro molto) 1949

Holograph

LOC
seven pages
Facsimile of first page in Heyman, p. 160

KEYBOARD WORKS: PIANO

231. **"After the Concert,"** c. 1973

232. **"At Twilight,"** 1919

Holograph

LOC
in "Early Compositions 1917–1927"

233. **"Fantasie for Two Pianos Written in the Style of Joseph Haydn,"** 1924

Holograph

LOC
Facsimiles in Heyman dissertation, pp. 43–46; a later version of "Sonata in Modern Form" (see Item 241).

234. **"Fresh from West Chester (some Jazzings)":**
    1. "Poison Ivy, A Country Dance," 1925
       "A country dance that isn't/accredited to, and blamed on
       T. T. Garborinsky"
    2. "Let's Sit it Out, I'd Rather Watch," 1926

235. **"Largo,"** 1918

236. **"Lullaby,"** 1919

Holograph

LOC
in "Early Compositions 1917–1927"

237. **"Main Street,"** c. 1926

Kreiling p. 333: "looks like a piano/vocal score, but has no text."

Holograph

Chester County Historical Society

238. **"Melody in F,"** 1917

Holograph

LOC
in "Early Compositions 1917–1927"

239. **"Menuetto"**

Holograph

Chester County Historical Society
"Co-ed Music Book"

240. **"Petite Berceuse,"** c. 1924

Holograph

Chester County Historical Society
Facsimile in Heyman, dissertation, p. 36.

241. **"Sadness," 1917,** Op. 1, No. 1

Holograph

LOC
in "Early Compositions 1917–1927"

242. **"Sonata in Modern Form,"** Op. XVI (for two pianos)

Holograph

Chester County Historical Society
Piano II; includes part of Piano I

243. **"Themes,"** Op. X, No. 2; April, 1923

1. Theme in G Major
2. Theme in G Major "Andante Religioso"; later expanded as the last of "Three Sketches," published in 1924
3. Allegretto in C

Holograph

Chester County Historical Society

244. **"Three Essays for Piano,"** 1927

Holograph

LOC
A 1984 bequest of the Estate of Samuel Barber, in Box 3, manuscripts of Samuel Barber, "Early Compositions 1917–1927."

245. **"To Aunt Mamie, on her birthday,"** 1926

246. **"Two- and Three-voice fugues,"** 1927

Holograph

LOC
"School Compositions 1927–1928"

247. **"Two Interludes,"** 1931–32

Holograph

LOC
"Orchestration book," c. 1930
Facsimiles of both in Heyman dissertation, pp. 117–118.

248.   **"War Song,"** Op. I, No. 5; 1918

Holograph

LOC
in "Early Compositions 1917–1927"
Facsimile in Heyman, p. 14.

KEYBOARD WORKS: ORGAN

249.   **"Chorale for a New Organ,"** 1926

250.   **"Prelude and Fugue in B minor,"** 1927

Holograph

LOC
Manuscript of prelude, dated October 28, 1927

First performance: December 10, 1928

Curtis Institute of Music; performed by Carl Weinrich.

251.   **"Three Chorale Preludes and Partitas,"** for organ, 1927

252.   **"To Longwood Gardens,"** 1925

Hologram

LOC

KEYBOARD WORKS: CARILLON

253.   **"Pieces for Carillon"**
   1. Round
   2. Allegro

3. Legend
4. Dirge, 1930–31

Dirge has recently been published.

Holographs

Bok Tower Gardens, Anton Brees Carillon Library. Facsimiles in Heyman dissertation, pp. 125–126.

Chapter 3. Bibliography: Books, Theses, Dissertations, and Articles

This section is devoted to various sources about Barber and his music, primarily scholarly articles, excluding articles and newspaper reviews relating to first performances. The items vary in length from short reviews of the scores as they were received by various periodicals to full-length dissertations. Some of these documents are Masters' or D.M.A. theses, in which case the approach to any given piece of music will probably be rather general and descriptive. In the Ph.D. dissertations it will probably be more technically analytical. In general, the longer the work, the longer the annotation in this book is likely to be. Some of these works are listed on the RILM database, WorldCat, and a few on MLA. They can be found either by author or title, but also as part of the collection under "Barber, Samuel." Clicking the icon LIB will also tell you what libraries have copies of the sources, including the theses and dissertations, some of which will send a copy by interlibrary loan.

GENERAL BIBLIOGRAPHY: BOOKS AND DISSERTATIONS

The state of Samuel Barber research is not very extensive. There are only two biographies, one of which is out-of-date. The previous bibliographic study is also out-of-date and cumbersome to use.

254.   Broder, Nathan. *Samuel Barber.* New York: G. Schirmer, 1954. Reprinted Westport, Conn.: Greenwood, 1985. 111 p. ISBN 0-313-24984-9   Ml 410 B23 B7 [Henn W96]

This is the first book about the composer and his music and the only one until the appearance of Heyman's book nearly forty years later. Because it was published in 1954, it obviously does not contain references to Barber's mature music such as *Vanessa, Antony and Cleopatra,* and the Piano Concerto. The book is divided into two parts, the first devoted to "The Man" and the second to "The Music." The first part is itself divided into eight, short untitled sections, spanning the composer's life until the mid-1950s. The second part, a somewhat extended version of Broder's *Musical Quarterly* article of 1948 (see Item 261), begins with a section called "The Style." By means of 17 musical examples, Broder generalizes about several aspects of Barber's musical language, particularly his melodic structure as governed by tonality, and his varied and active rhythms. In the remainder of the second part, the author separates his discussion into genres: starting with "The Music for One Voice With Accompaniment," and continuing with "The Choral Music," "The Piano Music," "The Chamber Music," "The Concertos," "The Symphonies," and ending with "The Miscellaneous Orchestral Works." Each of these sections is quite short (from two to 10 pages) and contains very few examples, at least in the first sections. Broder does give several examples, however, from the violin and cello concertos, and from the two symphonies. The appendix is also very brief, with only a list of works, a list of available recordings at the time, and an extremely short list of eight articles. The book was not updated for its 1985 reprint.

Reviews of Broder

Frankenstein, Alfred. "Review of Books: *Samuel Barber* by Nathan Broder." *Musical Quarterly* 41 (January 1955): 105–106.   [Henn BG52]

Raynor, Henry. "*Samuel Barber* by Nathan Broder." *Music Review* 17 (May 1956): 164.   [Henn BG111]

Schonberg, Harold. "Book Reviews." *Musical Courier* 150 (November 1, 1954): 43.   [Henn BG128]

Talley, V. Howard. "*Samuel Barber* by Nathan Broder." *Journal of Research in Music Education* 3 (Spring 1955): 65–66.   [Henn BG138]

255.   Friedwald, Russell Edward. "A Formal and Stylistic Analysis of the Published Music of Samuel Barber." Ph.D. diss., Iowa State University, 1957. 357 p. [Henn: BG53, B33j, B36l, B41a, B51b, B52b. B53e. B56a. B67n, B71g, B76j, B77g, B79m, B80g, B85g, B86d, B88d, B90l, B98w]

The author begins with a preface that includes a brief sketch of Barber's career. In the body of the work he divides Barber's works into separate chapters on music for solo voice, choral music, piano music, chamber music, concertos, symphonies, and miscellaneous orchestral works. Because the dissertation was written in 1957, it naturally excludes the later works, such as the Piano Concerto and all three operas. No work is presented in very great depth. Musical examples and diagrams are included. A brief summary appears at the end along with a chronology of the works discussed and a short discography.

256. Hennessee, Don. *Samuel Barber: A Bio-Bibliography.* Vol. 3 in series, Bio-Bibliographies in Music. Westport, Conn.: Greenwood, 1985. 404 p. ISBN 0-313-24026-4   ML 134 .B175 H4

This is the first real bibliography of the composer. It is organized into several chapters, beginning with a brief biography, a list of works and a discography, as current as its publication date of 1985, which precludes the current technology of compact discs. The main body of the work is a bibliography of the material available by the mid-1980s. Much of the content consists of magazine and newspaper reviews of various performances of Barber works. Brief references to these reviews in the current volume can be supplemented with actual quotes as printed in Hennessee's work.

Reviews of Hennessee

Bassett, Leslie. "Review of *Samuel Barber: A Bio-Bibliography.*" *Sonneck Society for American Music: Bulletin* 13 (1987): 74.

O[ilver], M[ichael] E. "Hennessee: Samuel Barber." *Gramophone* 63 (March 1986): 1139–40.

"Review of *Samuel Barber: A Bio-Bibliography.*" *Central Opera Service Bulletin* 26 (1985–1986): 71.

S[immons], W[alter]. "Review of *Samuel Barber a Bio-Bibliography.*" *Fanfare* 9 (1986): 324–325.

257. Heyman, Barbara B. "Samuel Barber: A Documentary Study of His Works." Ph.D. diss., City University of New York, 1989.

This thesis is the basis of Heyman's later published book (see Item 258). This title is somewhat more appropriate than the book title, indicating her basic approach and the sources she used. Had this title also been used for the book, there might have been less criticism about her approach. Most of the same material is present here as in the book, but without the later chapter titles. Many chapters from the thesis were later reorganized and subdivided. For instance, the twelve chapters of the thesis later became eighteen in the book. Footnotes, while always given at the bottom of the page, are presented in a more readable form than in the book. However, she renumbers them, often within several parts of the same chapter. The bibliography is far more extensive than the one in the book.

258. Heyman, Barbara. *Samuel Barber: The Composer and His Music.* New York: Oxford University Press, 1992. 586 p. ISBN 0-195-06650-2   ML 410 .B23 H5

This is the most recent, most detailed, and the best published work on Barber to date. Heyman deals with Barber's life in strict chronological sequence. Instead of discussing his works in a separate section, she deals with them within the biographical chapters. Of the seventy-six musical examples, a third illustrate passages from holograph manuscripts, a feature that is especially important for the study of Barber's early unpublished works. Other examples allow valuable comparisons and contrasts between early manuscripts and later published versions. One example shows a passage from the holograph of *Knoxville: Summer of 1915* that Barber later cut from the published score. While there are extensive notes and references, the bibliography contains only "selected books and articles."

Reviews of Heyman

Anderson, Martin. "Samuel Barber: The Composer and His Music." (review), *Tempo,* no. 185 (June 1993): 37–40.

Hollander, Jeffrey. "Samuel Barber: The Composer and His Music." (review), *Choral Journal* 36, no. 7 (February 1996): 50–51.

Hurd, Michael. "Samuel Barber: The Composer and His Music." (review), *Music and Letters,* vol. 74, no. 3 (August 1993): 469–470.

Jackson, Richard. "Samuel Barber: The Composer and His Music." (review), *American Music,* vol 12, no. 2 (Summer 1994): 218–220.

Keller, James M. "Books." *Opera News* 57, no. 1 (June 1993): 52.

Mellers, Wilfrid. "Samuel Barber: The Composer and His Music." (review), *The Times Literary Supplement* 4693 (March 12, 1993): 16–17.

Olmstead, Andrea. "Samuel Barber: The Composer and His Music." (review), *MLA Notes* 49, no. 4 (June 1993): 1490–1492.

Pryce-Jones, Alan. "A Certain Courage." *The Yale Review* 80 (October 1992): 85–89.

Schwartz, Robert K. "Composers' Closet Open for All to See." *New York Times,* June 19, 1994, section 2, p. 2.

Warburton, Thomas. "Samuel Barber: The Composer and His Music." *College Music Symposium* 32 (1992): 166-169.

Valdes, Lesley. "Review of Barbara Heyman, Samuel Barber." *Philadelphia Inquirer,* November 29, 1992, Section H, p. 1.

Zondergeld, Rein A. "Samuel Barber: The Composer and His Music." (review), *Neue Zeitschrift fur Musik,* vol. 155, no. 1 (January 1994): 77–78.

GENERAL: PAMPHLETS AND ARTICLES

During the 1930s several articles mention Barber and his music, but it is not until the 1940s that whole articles are devoted specifically to him. The most important ones are by Horan (Item 273) in 1943, Henri-Louis La Grange (277) in 1946,

Nathan Broder (261) in 1948, and Harry Dexter (262) in 1949. By that time Barber's reputation is well established, and other general articles begin to appear.

259.   Ardoin, John. "Samuel Barber at Capricorn." *Musical America* (March 1960): 4–5; 46. [Henn BG5]

This is a very general article that describes the interior of Barber's and Menotti's home: drawings by Picasso and Cocteau; photographs of Toscanini, Walter, and Stravinsky; and scores by Copland, Berg, Schoenberg and (of all people) Boulez! Various visitors are mentioned, particularly Maria Callas, who sang through parts of *Vanessa* and didn't like it ("No melody!"). Barber mentions recordings of his works he liked (e.g. Toscanini's *Adagio for Strings),* and what works he would like to be recorded (e.g. the *Second Essay).* He also showed Ardoin two early works: "Sadness," his first composition at age 7; and "The Rose Tree," his incomplete opera, written at age 10.

260.   Briggs, John. "Samuel Barber." *International Musician* (December 1961): 23. [Henn BG14]

This is a very general article with a slight emphasis on the Violin Concerto. Near the end there is a reference to Barber's latest work, a piano concerto that is "making progress."

261.   Broder, Nathan. "The Music of Samuel Barber." *Musical Quarterly* 34 (July 1948): 325–335. [Henn BG15]

This is a preliminary study for Broder's later book, becoming, in revised form, its second half. In several examples Broder shows Barber's melodic structure, propensity for counterpoint, his "varied and active" rhythmic organization, and his strong feeling for form. The article concludes with a list of works (up to the forthcoming Piano Sonata) and first performances.

262.   Dexter, Harry. "Samuel Barber and His Music." *Musical Opinion* 72 (March 1949): 285–286; and 72 (April 1949): 343–344. [Henn BG30]

The first part of the two-part article contains a general discussion of Barber's works, primarily orchestral up to the then-current *Medea*. It is more of an annotated listing than a thorough discussion of the music. The second part retraces the chronology for a brief discussion of Barber's vocal and choral works.

263.   Emley, Joseph Frederick. "Melodic Characteristics of the Songs and Compositions for Violoncello of Samuel Barber." M. M. thesis, Eastman School of Music, University of Rochester, 1957. 93 p.

In Part I, the author discusses songs as divided into early and late periods, the former with diatonic tonalities and simple rhythms, and the latter with some modal melodies and complex and often quartal harmonies. He has many statistical charts. One shows many of the early and late characteristics of Barber's style. Part II concerns the Cello Sonata and Cello Concerto. With many charts, the author compares the two works. There are no footnotes or bibliography.

264.   Evett, Robert. "How Right is Right?" *The Score* 12 (1955): 33–37. [Henn BG40]

This very general article is about several prominent American composers, including Barber, and their reaction against German classicism. The author considers Barber a right-wing composer, but his gradual adoption of a more "astringent harmonic idiom" brought with it an intensity lacking in his earlier music.

265.   Ewen, David. "Modern American Composers." *Musical Times* 80 (June 1939): 415–416. [Henn BG43]

Barber gets only a brief mention in this two-page article. Yet Ewen sees great potential in the young composer, saying that he has already "written so fluently and professionally" that he may ultimately develop into a great composer.

266.   Flagler, Eleanor. "Toscanini Visit Started Him Off." *News and Courier* (Charleston, S.C.), May 28, 1978. [Henn BG51]

This article summarizes Barber's accomplishments as an introduction to the upcoming production of *Vanessa* at the Spoleto USA festival in Charleston, South Carolina.

267.   Gräter, Manfred. "Der Sänger von Capricorn." *Melos* 21 (September 1954): 247–250. [Henn BG56]

This very general article considers Barber's works up through *Mélodies Passagères*. The author thinks of Barber as a "Konservative Gemüter" (conservative spirit), and feels that his music represents a positive and constructive moment at a time when there has been much alienation between composers and their audience. There is a listing of Barber's works by opus numbers at the end.

268.   Hartshorn, William C. "Music In Our Public Schools: American Composers—Samuel Barber." *Musical Courier* 159 (February 1959): 41. [Henn BG62]

The article, obviously intended for young students, consists of a one-page biography urging students to listen to other works in addition to *Adagio for Strings*. He also recommends Broder's book for further reading.

269.   Heinsheimer, Hans W. "The Composing Composer: Samuel Barber." *ASCAP Today,* 2, no. 3 (December 1968): 4–7. [Henn BG65, B80j]

Written by the former director of publications at Schirmer (Barber's only publisher), this article includes a brief biography, including the author's personal recollections of the composer. The title means that Barber is among very few composers who make their living at composing, without relying on performing, conducting, or teaching. Included is an anecdote about Barber's Second Symphony, which Barber considered "not a good work." The two of them went to the office of Schirmer and literally tore up the copies! Much of this article is similar to the one that Heinsheimer wrote for *Saturday Review* two years earlier (see Item 292). There are several photographs, including Barber with the Kennedys at the White House.

270.   Heinsheimer, Hans W. "Samuel Barber, Maverick Composer." *Keynote* (February 1980): 7-11.

A short article about Barber by the director of publications at G. Schirmer. Not examined.

271.   Henahan, Donal. "I've Been Composing All My Life, Off and On: A Talk With Samuel Barber." *New York Times,* January 28, 1979, Sec. 2, pp. 19, 24. [Henn BG68]

This significant interview takes place after Barber's six-year "silence" from musical composition. When asked about this silence, Barber replied that "sometimes I just lose interest." He talks about his on-and-off friendship with Leonard Bernstein; after having several dinners together, they decided that they "just couldn't stand each other." He also describes Janet Baker's reaction to his songs and why she doesn't sing them; "They meant nothing to me," she said, according to Barber.

272.   Heyman, Barbara. "Gay Composers: Barber: No Need of Any Label," *New York Times*, July 10, 1994, section 2, p. 2.

Heyman answers the charge made by K. Robert Schwartz (see Item 282) that she fails to address Barber's homosexuality in her book. She says that she treats the composer's sexual orientation as a given and that the "lumping together of creative artists by sex or sexual orientation" tends to "obscure rather than reveal the individuality of the composer's voice."

273.   Horan, Robert. "American Composers, XIX: Samuel Barber." *Modern Music* 20, no. 3 (March–April 1943): 161–169. [Henn BG70, B22h, B56b, B61y, B66x, B68g, B79o]

Horan's study of the composer and his music was the first thorough discussion to appear in print. The author deplores much current music as having "fraudulent energy" and a kind of "middle age." On the other hand, Barber's music concentrates on the beauty and possibility of design; it is alive and has a moving personality and musical integrity. Barber is designated as a conservative due to larger aspects of his compositional architecture. His orchestration is simple and "aristocratic." His music is "non-urban" and often romantic. It is neither sinewy nor athletic, robust nor nervous because it is not overtly nationalistic. Horan then discusses several works: the Symphony in One Movement, the *Essay for Orchestra,* the *Second Essay,* the Violin Concerto, various songs, and his [then] recent choral work, *A Stopwatch and an Ordnance Map.* The article ends with a list of 31 pieces (by genre) that Barber had composed as of 1943.

274.   Kolodin, Irving. "A Farewell to Capricorn." *Saturday Review/World* (June 1, 1974): 44–45. [Henn BG80]

The author wrote this brief article shortly after Barber and Menotti sold their home, Capricorn, after living there for several decades. He mentions several important works, by both composers, that had their beginnings there. Yet he thinks the emotional ties between the two composers had "outrun its lifespan." The "rich promise" of their youth had "petered out" in later years.

275.   Kozinn, Allan. "Samuel Barber: the Last Interview and the Legacy: Part 1." *High Fidelity* 31 (June 1981): 44–46; 65–68. [Henn BG82, B80n]

In an interview conducted late in 1979, Barber answers diverse questions about his composing career, why he gave up conducting, and about the prospects of young composers in the 1980s. He thinks that the recording situation is "miserable and getting worse," and that foundations should fund recordings of rising composers. The last pages of the article are actually a discography of Barber recordings, evaluated and annotated by Kozinn.

276.   Kozinn, Allan. "Samuel Barber: the Last Interview and the Legacy: Part 2." *High Fidelity* 31 (July 1981): 45–47; 89–90. [Henn BG82, B80n]

This is a continuation of the previous month's article primarily extending the Barber discography with new listings and annotations. (See Discography, Item 516.)

277.   La Grange, Henri-Louis de. "D'Amérique: Un compositeur américain Indépendent." *Contrepoints* 4 (May–June 1946): 63–67. [Henn BG84]

This is one of the earliest European articles that singles out Barber as a significant American composer. His works do not have "an excess of folklorism" (perhaps a dig at Copland), a neglect of musical form, and a lack of metrical inventiveness. Barber's music has a deep inspiration. La Grange then mentions the merits of several Barber works: "Symphony in One Movement," the *Essay for Orchestra*, the *Second Essay*, and the *Excursions* for piano. The author also points out the importance of Barber's Second Symphony and the *Capricorn Concerto*. He thinks the slow movement of the Cello Concerto is particularly moving. He concludes by saying that Barber's works convince us that modern music can be beautiful without constant, "frictional" sonorities.

278.   Lipman, Samuel. "American Music: The Years of Hope." *Commentary* 71 (March 1981): 56–61. [Henn BG86]

Only one paragraph of this article is devoted to Barber's music, and in a very general way. Lipman points out the unforgettable quality of the *Adagio for Strings,* and hopes that *Antony and Cleopatra* may someday be considered among Barber's "finest achievements."

279.   Rands, Bernard. "Samuel Barber—a Belief in Tradition." *Musical Opinion* 84 (March 1961): 353. [Henn BG109]

This fairly short article deals with Barber's works in general, but with prominent mention of the String Quartet, Op. 11, which has movements of "inspired beauty," along with passages of "mechanical, academic writing." One constant problem in Barber's works is his reliance on traditional forms that are "already tired and overworked." Yet he avoids many theories and "novelties" of the last thirty years.

280.   Rorem, Ned. *Knowing When to Stop.* New York: Simon and Schuster, 1994. Chapter 20: "Paul, Sam, Marc," (pp. 306–311). ISBN 0-671-72872-5 ML 410 .R693 A3

Barber is the middle man in this chapter of Rorem's personal viewpoint of three composers. Most of his comments are not very favorable, e. g. the First

Symphony is "frantic and ill bred" and the piano *Excursions* are "trivial and vulgar." Much of his music is "too rarefied" and "elegant" for Rorem's taste; yet he was impressed by the "Piano Sonata."

281.   Salzman, Eric. "Great American Composers: Samuel Barber." *HiFi/Stereo Review* 17 (October 1966): 77–89. [Henn BG115, B5g, B61tt, B99a]

Barber is included as part six of the author's "Great American Composers" series. He takes a few biographical items from Broder's book, but says that Barber himself supplied "a number of anecdotes." While not strictly a review of *Antony and Cleopatra,* the article, was written during the preparation of the premiere performance of this opera and includes sketches of the costumes and sets.

282.   Schwartz, Robert K. "Composers' Closet Open for All to See." *New York Times,* June 19, 1994, section 2, p. 2.

The author criticizes Heyman's book for failing to address the issue of Barber's homosexuality. (See her reply, Item 272.)

283.   Teachout, Terry. "The Cream Will Rise." *Alberta Report/Newsmagazine* 23, no. 19 (April 22, 1996): 22.

After Barber's death his reputation is being "rehabilitated." Even though critics have often dismissed his works as being "traditional" or "unimaginative," his music has always been popular with audiences and conductors. Therefore the author feels that the current Barber revival is a "cheering sign."

284.   Teachout, Terry. "Samuel Barber's Revenge." *Commentary* 101 (April 1996): 55–58.

The "revenge" in the title refers to the fact that, despite critics' evaluations of Barber as being a conservative composer, his music has become more popular than ever after his death. It has undergone a "rehabilitation" due partly to his gift for composing "memorable melodies" and composing musical structures that are "conventional in form." Notice the similarity to the same author's article in the Alberta report (see Item 283).

285.   Turner, Charles. "The Music of Samuel Barber." *Opera News* 22 (January 27, 1958): 7. [Henn BG141, B61yy]

This short article mainly concerns *Vanessa,* but also extols the "great variety" in Barber's music from one work to another. It has none of the typically

"American" characteristics, such as "hard-drive rhythms, jazz or otherwise," or particularly dissonant harmonies. Yet it is highly personal. "There is nothing quite like it in American music."

286.   Wittke, Paul. *Samuel Barber: An Improvisatory Portrait.* New York: Schirmer, 1994. 58 p. ML 410 .B17 W5

This is essentially the first section of a sales catalogue of the works of Barber prepared by his publisher, G. Schirmer. This section is divided into six brief parts: an introduction; a short biography; a series of very short paragraphs on several Barber works; a discussion of the operas; a description of "Capricorn," Barber's and Menotti's home for many years; and finally a discussion of Barber's later years and his relationship with Menotti. This is followed by the actual Schirmer catalogue of Barber's music (pp. 32–53), compiled by Norman D. Ryan. Throughout the pamphlet are several photographs of Barber, some alone, some with others. Ryan's catalogue, with slight modifications and one new listing (an arrangement of *Adagio for Strings* for violin and piano) is now available online on the Schirmer website: www.schirmer.com/composers/barber_works.html

ADDITIONAL BIOGRAPHICAL MATERIAL

287.   Samuel Barber clippings file, New York Public Library

The file contains several folders of program notes, newspaper clippings, recordings, news releases, pictures, etc. Many of the newspaper items lack either the name of the newspaper, the date, or the page. The file is also available in microfilm format at Michigan State University.

INDIVIDUAL GENRES AND INDIVIDUAL WORKS

Opera And Ballet

288.   Jones, Stephanie. "The Political Tension Surrounding the Operas of Samuel Barber." M. A. thesis, Smith College, 1992. 96 p.

In her introduction, the author states that both *Vanessa* and *Antony and Cleopatra* were "suffocated by . . . the 'The American opera crisis.' " Critics never seemed to be able to define "American opera." Her biography chapter concentrates mainly on those events and attitudes in Barber's life that are related to opera. Because Gian Carlo Menotti had something to do with all three Barber operas, he is given a chapter of his own. Barber admits that he felt some jealousy of Menotti's success in opera and that may have delayed his own entry into the field for quite some time. In the fourth chapter the author delves into the question of "the great American opera" and how it differs from the "Broadway opera," the type that Menotti is known for. The author then discusses *Vanessa* (as a political victim) and *Antony and Cleopatra* (as an operatic disaster) and cites critical reviews about how each work fits the image of an "American opera." She also includes European reaction to both works. The passage of time and newer, more suitable productions may allow both operas to succeed, once they are "removed from the political hotbed" that formerly engulfed them.

289.   Mordden, Ethan C. *Opera in the Twentieth Century: Sacred, Profane, Godot.* New York: Oxford University Press, 1978. 357 p. ISBN 0-195-02288-2   ML 1705 .M67

    In his typical flippant attitude, Mordden (pp. 310–311) considers the first version of *Antony and Cleopatra* "at least an opera" while the second is just "scenes from an opera." He also points out the "clean, cascading lines," of *Vanessa,* but considers the work a "perfect throwback to the days of Sardou."

Antony and Cleopatra Op. 40

290.   Freeman, John W. "In the Grand Tradition: Barber's Music for Shakespeare also Holds True to Opera." *Opera News* 31, no. 2 (September 17, 1966): 41–42. [Henn B1n]

    Freeman mentions various adaptations necessary for shaping the libretto out of Shakespeare's original play, by "preserving the poet's lines" and replacing what is omitted with "musical amplification of mood and character." As to the music, he mentions the fugal section for Antony and Caesar's duet and Octavia's "passacaglia-like" bass theme. The score as a whole is sustained throughout by "musical imagination and energy."

291.   Gruen, John. "And Where Has Samuel Barber Been . . . ? *New York Times,* October 3, 1971, sec. 2, pp. 15, 21, 30. [Henn BG58, B1r, B19c]

    In an interview with Gruen, Barber discusses his operas, saying that *Vanessa* was received with "general praise" and *Antony and Cleopatra* with "general dismay." Since that operatic disappointment, Barber has lived in Italy in relative isolation (hence the title of the article) and has only now re-emerged at age 61 with his newest works, *The Lovers* and *Fadograph of a Yestern Scene.* Much of the rest of the article includes Barber's comments on his experience with the Metropolitan Opera production of *Antony and Cleopatra.* The Met "overproduced it," he himself had "little control over it," and the Met management supported the director, Franco Zeffirelli, in all things.

292. Heinsheimer, Hans W. "Birth of an Opera." *Saturday Review* (September 17, 1966): 49–50; 56–57. [Henn B1w]

The author, from G. Schirmer publications, talks about Barber as strictly a composer, one who does not rely on teaching, conducting, or performing. He discusses how *Antony and Cleopatra* went from pencil score to finished product, often with various scenes arriving at different times at the publishing house. He also includes an anecdote of how he and Barber went to the offices of Schirmer to destroy the scores of the Second Symphony. (See also the author's similar article, Item 269.)

293. Jolly, James Lester, Jr. "American Operas Based on the Plays of William Shakespeare, 1948–1976." (Volumes I and II) Ph.D. diss., Louisiana State University, 1985. 482 p.

The author begins with a history of Shakespearean operas from their origins to the present (1985), and then gives a brief biographical sketch of each of the composers whose operas he will discuss. He devotes the rest of the first volume to several operas based on Shakespeare comedies, which he divides into the categories "festive," "dark," and "late romance." The section on tragedies includes operatic versions of *Antony and Cleopatra* in settings by both Barber and Louis Gruenberg as well as Sam Raphling's setting of *Hamlet.* Jolly does not discuss each opera separately but intersperses them to discuss operatic tragedy in general. In this process, he emphasizes the voice classification of various characters and the instrumentation and size of the orchestra. He shows how the libretto is derived from the play, and how it may depart from certain aspects of the story line. Several musical examples illustrate points on musical characterizations (including a chart of leitmotifs in Barber's *Antony and Cleopatra).* The author then shows relationships among all the opera that he discusses.

294. Klein, Howard. "The Birth of an Opera." *New York Times Magazine* (August 28, 1966): 32–33; 107–110; 115. [Henn B1cc]

Barber speaks of his reluctant collaboration with Franco Zeffirelli on *Antony and Cleopatra,* and how the two of them worked together completing nearly the entire libretto in 15 days. Barber mentions the problems of Shakespeare's iambic pentameter, which had to be broken up "or else it would have trampled right over the music." Otherwise it would be difficult to avoid a "Purcellian sound." He also mentions some of the difficulties of the score, such as the fugal section for Antony and Caesar. The remainder of the article includes the invaluable role of Arnold Arnstein, who not only copied the orchestral parts, but also proofread and contributed various performance indications. After a few comments by Leontyne Price and Justino Diaz about their roles, Klein ends with a very short biography of Barber entitled, "Prodigy."

295.   Kupferberg, Herbert. "Barber, the Bard, and the Barge." *Atlantic* 218 (September 1966): 126–129. [Henn B1ff]

The author refers to the upcoming production of *Antony and Cleopatra* at the Metropolitan. He states that both Barber and Zeffirelli worked on the libretto, whereas only Zeffirelli is credited with it. Also included are portions of his interview with Barber commenting on his own working methods. Barber also reveals that he wanted Zeffirelli to direct the production, but that its "spectacular side is being more emphasized than it has to be." Smaller productions are also possible. He mentions the difficulty of setting Shakespeare's iambic pentameter lines to music (as he did in his interview with Klein; see Item 294).

296.   Littlejohn, David. " The Twentieth Century Takes On Shakespeare." In *The Ultimate Art: Essays Around and About Opera,* edited by David Littlejohn. p. 255–264. Berkeley: University of California Press, 1992. ISBN 0-520-07608-7   ML 1700 .L59

Littlejohn discusses Barber's *Antony and Cleopatra* along with Benjamin Britten's *A Midsummer Night's Dream,* and Aribert Reimann's *Lear* as three ways of adapting Shakespeare's plays for the operatic stage. He considers *Lear* to be the most successful and Barber's the least successful of the adaptations. One reason for Barber's lack of success is Zeffirelli's production and adaptation, "a terrible opera that bears no resemblance whatever, artistic or imaginative, to Shakespeare's original." While he points out "a few lyrical things," he laments Barber's "thick, plodding, old-fashioned and obvious" orchestral scoring. The "swooning strings" makes the music sound at times like the soundtrack from *Quo Vadis.* Yet Shakespeare's words may have presented an insurmountable problem: they are "too grand to be taken over by mere music." This article originally appeared in *San Francisco Opera Magazine* (program book of the San Francisco Opera), 1985.

297.   "Make Mingle With Our Tambourines That Heaven and Earth May Strike Their Sounds Together." *Opera News* 31 (September 17, 1966): 32–35. [Henn B1hh]

This article contains three separate interviews with Samuel Barber, Franco Zeffirelli, and Thomas Schippers about their collaborative production. Barber says that because the story line of *Antony and Cleopatra* is more difficult than *Vanessa*, the music is more difficult as well. Certain themes (leitmotifs are not mentioned) recur and are developed. Zeffirelli says that his concept started with the "central idea of the pyramid." Schippers calls the production "an enormous opera in every sense."

298.	Price, Leontyne. "What Opera Would I Like Revived?" *New York Times,* February 11, 1973, sect. 2, p. 17. [Henn B1 qq]

Price thinks that *Antony and Cleopatra* should be revived because the music is "glorious." If it were "quieted down," the opera could be given a "fair chance." She mentions programming the two scenes that Barber extracted from the opera for orchestral performance.

299.	Schmidgall, Gary. *Shakespeare and Opera.* New York: Oxford University Press, 1990. 394 p. ISBN 0-195-06450-X ML 3858 .S373

Chapter 30, "Barber's 'Pair So Famous,' " (pp. 298–305), is about Barber's *Antony and Cleopatra,* but the author devotes surprisingly few pages to this work. He talks about Barber's revisions from the first to the second version. While he considers the addition of "Take, oh, take those lips away" beautiful, he doubts that it contributes much to Shakespeare's conception of the couple's "torrid, violent, and self-destructive" love affair. He spends much of the time lamenting the passages from Shakespeare that Zeffirelli did not include in the libretto.

300.	Solomon, Jon. "The Spectacle of Samuel Barber's *Antony and Cleopatra.*" In *Opera and the Golden West: The past, present, and future of opera in the U.S.,* ed. by John Louis di Gaetani. Rutherford, N.J.: Fairleigh Dickinson University Press, 1993. ISBN 0-838-63519-9 ML 1711 .064

The author discusses the "memorable artistic disappointments" of two prominent presentations of the Cleopatra legend in the 1960s: Joseph L. Mankiewicz's film *Cleopatra* and Barber's opera *Antony and Cleopatra.* Both productions may have failed because the audience was tiring of grand epics, especially in movies, which had been so popular during the late 1940s through the early 1960s. Audiences no longer craved size, grandeur, and lavish spectacle. In addition, both productions suffered from a great deal of media "hype." The producers (especially Zeffirelli in the operatic version) "created expectations so excessive that they overwhelmed not only the audience and critics but the subject matter itself."

A Hand of Bridge, Op. 35

301.   Summers, Franklin W. *Operas in One Act.* Lanham, Md., and London: Scarecrow, 1997, pp. 34–35. ISBN 0-810-83222-4   MT 955 .S86

Barber's nine-minute opera clearly belongs in this survey of one-act operas. A brief list is given of cast requirements, instrumentation, synopsis of plot, and performance notes.

Medea Op. 23

302.   Graham, Martha. *The Notebooks of Martha Graham,* with introduction by Nancy Wilson Ross. New York: Harcourt, Brace, Jovanovich, 1973. 464 p. ISBN 0-151-67265-2   GV 1785 .G7 A35

This book contains the notes Graham made for several of her dance works, including *Cave of the Heart* (pp. 162–164).

303.   Stewart, Louis C. "Music Composed for Martha Graham: A Discussion of Musical and Choreographic Collaborators." D. M. A. thesis in conducting, Peabody Conservatory, 1991.

In general, this thesis reveals aspects of Graham's choices of music for her dances and how they are used to support the dramatic context. *Cave of the Heart* appears in the chapter, "Works on Greek Sources," one of five dances based on Greek drama. While this thesis deals only briefly with Barber's music, it shows how the musical themes reflect the nature of the characters, e.g., an angular theme for Jason, a more diatonic "playful" theme for the princess, and chromatic themes that parallel Medea's suffering and jealousy. There are eleven examples to illustrate the author's conclusions. He also includes a chronological list of works from the Graham repertory with details of the first performances.

Vanessa Op. 32

304.   Barber, Samuel. "Birth Pangs of a First Opera: Composer Learns Patience Awaiting *Vanessa* Libretto." *New York Times,* January 12, 1958, sect. 2, p. 9. [Henn B7e]

Barber relates his frustration with Menotti's constant delays in the completion of the *Vanessa* libretto. The end result, however, is perhaps Menotti's "finest and most chiseled" libretto, with Barber needing to change only a few words. He appreciates the "economy" and "utter simplicity" of Menotti's words, and his "unique sense of theatrical timing." Also mentioned is Sena Jurinac's illness, which prevented her from accepting the title role, and Elenaor Steber's "gallantry" in accepting it on such a short notice.

305.   Barber, Samuel. "On Waiting for a Libretto." *Opera News* 22 (January 27, 1958): 4–6. [Henn B7f]

Barber mentions that his first real opera was "The Rose Tree," written when he was very young. Regarding possible librettos, his early talks with Thornton Wilder "led to nothing" and his collaboration with Dylan Thomas was curtailed because of the war; but he was delighted when Menotti offered to write a libretto. When Menotti interrupted work on the libretto to write his own opera, *The Saint of Bleecker Street,* Barber stopped composing until the *Vanessa* libretto was completed (hence the title). Barber refers to Menotti's libretto as having "utter simplicity" and a "unique sense of theatrical timing." (These are the same words he used in a *New York Times* interview; see Item 304.) The title, "Vanessa," comes from a book entitled, *How To Name Your Child.* He also says, contrary to the opinion of critics, that the libretto is not a reflection of the sophisticated works of Isak Dinesen. This contradicts what he says in the *Theatre Arts* interview with Coleman (see Item 306).

This article is reprinted as a part of *Contemporary Composers on Contemporary Music,* edited by Elliott Schwartz and Barney Childs, with Jim Fox, expanded edition, New York: Da Capo Press, 1998, pp. 165–169.

306.   Coleman, Emily. "Samuel Barber and *Vanessa.* " *Theatre Arts* 42 (January 1958): 68–69; 86–88. [Henn B7q]

Printed in interview format, much of the conversation resembles the "On Waiting for a Libretto" from *Opera News,* including the story about "The Rose Tree." (Barber may have recycled much of this material for his own article. They both appeared in the same month.) Barber relates *Vanessa* to Isak Dinesen's "Seven Gothic Tales" (see Item 305). Why is the opera set in Europe? Menotti wanted to write "quasi poetry," which he thought did not lend itself well to American dialogue. Yet Barber still considers the work an "American" opera. It is an intimate, singer's opera with "set piece" arias, duets, and ensembles.

The author also asks him if he did his own orchestrations. Barber's abrupt reply shows his resentment of the question; Barber says huffily that every composer "worth his salt" from Mozart through Stravinsky did his own orchestration. How can someone hire someone else to make choices of tone, color, etc.?

307.   Ericson, Raymond. "Barber's *Vanessa*: a Guest Review." *American Record Guide* (November 1958): 178-179.

While the title suggests only a review of the opera, Ericson presents a full-fledged article, giving the work's inception, a plot summary, and a discussion of the music and libretto. He then goes on to a critique of the Met performance.

308. Larsen, Robert L. "A Study and Comparison of Samuel Barber's *Vanessa,* Robert Ward's The *Crucible,* and Gunther Schuller's *The Visitation.*" M. M. thesis, Indiana University, 1971. 179 p.

Larsen begins with a chapter entitled, "Background and Introduction," consisting of a historical overview of operas in the United States and a brief introduction to the three operas indicated in the title. The second chapter is devoted to *Vanessa*, and deals with its libretto, melodic characterization and "other linear concerns," harmony and tonality, rhythm, form, and orchestration. Twenty-seven examples help illustrate his points. Of particular interest is a thematic catalogue of various motives found throughout the opera. The author gives each a leitmotif-like name, and provides a chart of how these motives recur. Most of the names are indeed appropriate (e.g. "Vanessa's impatience"), but others are too dependent on their first appearance, when the contexts of their later appearances could provide better names. The later chapters on the Ward and Schuller operas are self-contained. Even the final chapter, "Reflections and Conclusions," does not contain much of a comparison of the three operas.

309. M. F. "Miracle on 39th Street." *Opera News* 22 (January 27, 1958): 15. [Henn B7hhh]

The author discussed *Vanessa* with the conductor of the opera, Dimitri Mitropoulos, who thinks that the work is a miracle in today's era. He thinks it took courage for Barber to write music in the "style of *Vanessa.*" It is singable with beautiful arias and duets, but Mitropoulos's favorite moments are the orchestral interludes. He thinks that the opera is "highly theatrical and dramatic."

310. Kolodin, Irving. "Barber, Menotti, and *Vanessa.*" *Saturday Review* (January 25, 1958): 41. [Henn B7xx]

The reviewer thinks that *Vanessa*'s highpoint is the quintet in the final act, a skillful canon that the composer should be proud of. The opera shows us a composer who can maintain our attention throughout a full-length work.

311. Resnik, Regina. "A New Role In a World Premiere." *Music and Musicians* 6 (March 1958): 18. [Henn B7yyy]

The mezzo-soprano who sang the role of the old Baroness in *Vanessa* discusses the "grand manner" of the opera. There are larger-than-life demands on the singers, both vocally and dramatically. Barber has written the music "with emotion" and in a "romantic vein."

312.   "Samuel Barber's First Opera." *Times* (London), January 15, 1958, p. 3. [Henn B7aaaa]

The article gives a brief summary of Barber's life and compositional career. It includes the cast of the upcoming Metropolitan Opera production of *Vanessa*.

313.   Turner, Charles. "The Music of Samuel Barber." *Opera News* 22 (January 27, 1958): 7; 32–33. [Henn BG141]

Turner extols the "great variety" from one Barber work to another, and that Barber always exhibits a "human touch" as in *Adagio for Strings*. Although Turner mentions other works, he focuses primarily on *Vanessa,* and points out that many features of Menotti's libretto reflect Barber's own personal tastes: for instance, fine food, reading aloud, skating, snowy landscapes, and church hymns and waltzes. (Menotti says much the same thing in Ardoin's *The Stages of Menotti;* see Item 495). Turner says that the vocal lines in *Vanessa* require considerable technique and sensitivity on the part of the singers. The article concludes with a section called, "What to read and listen to," a miniature bibliography and discography of Barber's works as of 1958.

314.   "Vanessa Makes Ready." *Opera News* 22 (January 27, 1958): 10–11.

This is not an article, but a picture survey of the staging of *Vanessa* for the Met production, including the "menu reading" scene at the beginning of Act I, and the love duet in Act III.

315.   "Violets in the Snow." *Opera News* 22 (January 27, 1958): 20–21.

This anonymous article describes much of the scenery and costumes of *Vanessa* as devised by Cecil Beaton. Relating to the works of Isak Dinesen, the set might be described as "Edwardian Gothic," with brocades and overstuffed furniture. Regarding the costumes: Anatole is often seen in grey tweed and brown velvet; Vanessa is always in some kind of velvet outfit, contrasting with Erika's silks and taffeta.

Instrumental: General

316.   Besedick, Stephen T. "Samuel Barber's Cantilena Slow Movements: a Study of Textural Relationships." M. M. thesis, Florida State University, 1986. 117 p.

This analytical study includes Barber's *Adagio for Strings,* and the "Adagio mesto" movement from the Piano Sonata. Not examined.

317. Coke, Austin Neil. "An Analysis of Some of the Purely Instrumental Works of Samuel Barber between the Years 1930–1950." M. A. thesis, California State College at Long Beach, 1968. 82 p. [Henn BG19]

This is a brief survey of orchestral works, chamber pieces, and piano pieces that Barber composed during the 1930s and 1940s. The author states his method of procedure, then discusses the innovations in the music of Stravinsky, Schoenberg, and Bartók. After a short biographical sketch, the author then presents his analyses, only about half the length of the entire thesis. The works discussed are Overture to *The School for Scandal;* The Cello Sonata; the First Symphony; the String Quartet; the *Second Essay* for Orchestra; the Second Symphony; the piano *Excursions;* the *Capricorn Concerto;* and the Piano Sonata. In most cases, Coke presents a chart of the work, giving measure numbers, "subjects" (i.e. themes), the key area of that subject, and a brief comment.

318. Wathen, Lawrence Samuel. "Dissonance Treatment in the Instrumental Music of Samuel Barber." Ph.D. diss., Northwestern University, 1960. 141 p. [Henn BG149]

After a brief preface and introduction, the dissertation is divided into two main sections: Chapter 1 deals with contrapuntal dissonance and chapter 2 with harmonic dissonance. Chapter 1 is further divided into separate sections on: the suspension, appogiaturas, anticipations, auxiliary tones, passing tones, cambiatas and echappées, and free tones. Chapter 2 is subdivided into sections on the seventh chord, the fourth chord (two superimposed fourths), and miscellaneous treatment of harmonic dissonances, including polychords and pedal points. In general, the author treats all the dissonances in the very traditional approach of basic tonal theory. The date of the dissertation (1960) precludes the inclusion of the later instrumental works, such as the Piano Concerto, the *Ballade, Fadograph of a Yestern Scene*, and the *Third Essay.* Yet because the approach is by dissonance type and not by individual pieces, many generalizations may well apply to these later works as well.

Orchestral Works: General

319. Downes, Edward. *Guide to Symphonic Music.* New York: Walker and Company, 1981. pp. 28–34. ISBN 0-802-77177-7   MT 125 .D68

In his survey of symphonic music, Downes includes a brief discussion of the Piano Concerto, the Violin Concerto, the *Essay for Orchestra* and *Second Essay,* and the Overture to *The School for Scandal.* He includes several musical examples.

Orchestral Works: Individual Titles

Adagio for Strings Op. 11

320. Rawlinson, Harold. "Famous Works for String Orchestra, no. 20: *Adagio for Strings.*" *Strad* 60 (April 1950): 372–374. [Henn BG110]

The author considers *Adagio for Strings* to be a "forceful" work that "holds our interest," perhaps because it is not "outrageously modern." Yet as a whole it "lacks vivid personality."

Adventure

321. "Composers Corner." *Musical America* 74 (December 1954): 31. [Henn B62a]

This short article concerns the composition that Barber was commissioned to compose for the CBS television program *Adventure,* for which he was asked to use various instruments from the American Museum of Natural History, including nose flute, Burmese cymbals, etc.

Capricorn Concerto, Op. 21

322. Anderson, W. R. "Round About Radio." *Musical Times* 87 (November 1946): 339. [Henn B85a]

This article is from the British viewpoint. The work is in concerto grosso form, but the author thinks that it sounds "desiccated and squeaky."

323. Anderson, W. R. "Round About Radio." *Musical Times* 88 (September 1947): 323. [Henn B85b]

Here is more of the same author's typical British viewpoint. Anderson now inexplicably compares *Capricorn Concerto* to Mussorgsky's *Pictures at an Exhibition,* and says that like so much American music, "it doesn't jell."

324. Berger, Arthur. "Scores and Records." *Modern Music* 23, no. 1 (Winter 1946): 66. [Henn B85c]

The "Brandenburgian" final movement has an "asymmetry" and "attention to interest that recalls the later Stravinsky." Berger looks forward to Barber's next works.

325. Mills, Charles. "Over the Air." *Modern Music* 23, no. 1 (Winter 1946): 74. [Henn B85j]

Mills reviews the CBS Radio broadcast of the *Capricorn Concerto* and explains that the title is not from the Zodiac, but from Barber's and Menotti's home at Mt. Kisco, New York, where it was written. He thinks it is a "delightfully clear and brilliant score" and hears a Copland influence in it.

326.   Smith, Cecil. "Big Names in Chicago." *Modern Music* 22, no. 2 (January–February 1945): 121. [B85o]

Even though Smith hears a Stravinsky influence, Barber has, in this work, his own themes and maintains them by his own kind of "rhythmic urging." He orchestrates with his own "pointed economy." The work as a whole is "friendly and communicative."

Concerto for Piano and Orchestra, Op. 38

327.   Bals, Karen Elizabeth. "The American Piano Concerto in the Mid-Twentieth Century." D. M. A. diss., University of Kansas, 1982. 124 pp.

The introductory chapter is an overview of the piano concerto in Europe during the Classical and Romantic eras and its developments in the first half of the twentieth century. The second chapter continues with the genre as it develops in America at that time with an emphasis on the concertos of Gershwin and Copland. In chapter 3 the author covers the concerto during the 1940s and 1950s, discussing, in particular, works by Schuman, Bloch, Sessions, and Cage. The section devoted to Barber's Concerto then appears in her fourth chapter on works in the 1960s and is necessarily quite brief. She discusses each movement and gives several examples.

328.   Deguchi, Tomoko. "Unity and Variety: Motivic Transformation in Three Selected Piano Concerti by American Composers." M. A. thesis, University of Wyoming, 1999. 63 pp.

The author discusses how "themes, motives, and figures" contribute to structural aspects in the piano concertos by Aaron Copland, Samuel Barber, and John Corigliano. Accomplishing this in 60 pages necessitates a fairly superficial treatment. He gives background information on the three composers, including very brief biographies. The main chapter is called "analysis," but the author seldom goes beyond a short description of each concerto. In the chapter entitled "Treatment of the Materials" some aspects of the discussion (e.g. additive motives, fragmentation, augmentation) apply very little or not at all to Barber. However, Barber is featured more prominently in the section on the relationship between motives. The "selected" bibliography at the end is very generic and does not contain Heyman's book (which devotes ten pages to the Barber Concerto).

329. Gamble, Linda DiGiustino. "Samuel Barber's Piano Concerto Op. 38." D. M. A. [thesis], West Virginia University, 1973. 60 p.

In this work, described as a "project for advanced study," the author discusses each of the three movements of the concerto, including the role of counterpoint, the use of motives, and other thematic relationships. For the outer movements, she presents charts of the forms, originally in color, but in the library photocopy they are in black and white, thereby losing some of their effectiveness.

330. Hanson, John Robert. "Macroform in Selected Twentieth-Century Piano Concertos." Ph.D. diss., Eastman School of Music, University of Rochester, 1969. 404 p. [Henn B65r]

Barber's Piano Concerto is alphabetically first among the 33 works that the author discusses regarding form in relation to classical formal prototypes. He does much of this by means of diagrams. He mentions aspects of thematic relationships in each of the three movements of Barber's concerto and illustrates the unity and contrasts of thematic sections. In the summary and again by means of diagrams, he gives general characteristics and lists of movements sharing common formal plans.

331. Hayden, Paul Murray. "The Use of Tonality in Four Concertos by American Composers." D. M. A. diss., University of Illinois, Urbana-Champaign, 1982. 181 p.

Barber's Piano Concerto is included (chapter 1) along with three other concertos: Ned Rorem's *Concerto in Six Movements* (chapter 2); John Corigliano's Piano Concerto (chapter 3); and George Rochberg's Violin Concerto (chapter 4). Hayden discusses Barber's Concerto first, partly because it is the earliest of the four, but also because he finds in it basic and more traditional aspects of twentieth-century tonality that he can refer to in the chapters on the other three composers. In each concerto, Hayden looks for how and where tonal centers are established, the relationships among different tonal centers, and the place, if any, of traditional tertian harmonies. He notes, especially in the Barber Concerto, that tonality is most ambiguous when "contrapuntal considerations are paramount."

There are many musical examples, some of which are direct quotations from the score, while others are illustrative "Schenkerian" derivations that illuminate the inner direction and harmonic implications of the themes. Because the author sets forth essential definitions in the Barber chapter, he is then able to refer back to these in the chapters on the other composers. In his conclusion he says that while there is much tonal ambiguity in the other three concertos, Barber tends to reject ambiguity and that his progressions "tend to move toward a goal."

332.   Kolodin, Irving. "Music to My Ears: Barber Concerto—Campora, di Ste-
        fano." *Saturday Review* 46 (November 23, 1963): 33. [Henn B65z]

While starting out as a review of a performance by John Browning and Josef
Krips, it actually becomes a full critique of the music itself. Kolodin thinks the
first movement "carries less persuasion" than the other two and that few other
slow movements by Americans (including Gershwin) "succeed so eloquently in
establishing a mood and making a whole experience of it." The final movement is
"brilliantly conceived."

333.   Lu, Emily. "The Piano Concerto of Samuel Barber." D. M. A. thesis, Uni-
        versity of Wisconsin, Madison, 1986. 117 p.

In her first chapter, the author discusses the forms and principle motives of
each of the three movements. She then devotes a separate chapter to various
aspects of style and compositional elements that Barber uses throughout the concerto. Chapter 2 deals with counterpoint, particularly Barber's use of canon in the
first two movements. Chapter 3 deals with ostinatos, including a comparison with
the composer's use of this device in his Piano Sonata and *Excursions*. In chapter
4, she discusses rhythm, specifically "rhythmic displacement" and "written-out
accelerandos." She also deals with Barber's "frequent but fluid" meter changes.
Chapter 5, entitled "Lyricism and Drama," illustrates what she considers to be
Barber's two strong points. For her discussion of lyricism she compares the slow
movement of the Concerto to the slow movement of Ravel's Concerto in G major,
using musical examples to support her theory. She illustrates Barber's sense of
drama with examples showing his use of percussion, harmonic tonal clusters, and
rapid arpeggios figures. In the concluding chapter (6), she states that the Concerto
is a "fusion of traditional formal procedures with contemporary rhythmic and harmonic languages." The appendices include a brief biographical sketch, a survey
of Barber's solo piano works, an analysis of the fugue from the Piano Sonata, and
a discography of his piano music.

334.   Meyer, John A. "The Solo Piano Concerto in the Twentieth Century."
        Ph.D. diss., University of Western Australia, 1973. 435 p.

This dissertation is a huge undertaking, describing hundreds of twentieth-
century piano concertos (from Jean Absil to Mario Zafred), dividing them into various style categories and often making interesting comparisons. Barber's Concerto
receives about four pages in the chapter entitled, "The Post-Romantic Piano Concerto," along with works of Medtner, Khachaturian, and Vaughan Williams. The
author compares the "declamatory" piano introduction with the cadenza in Bliss's
Piano Concerto. He also thinks that such "deliberate virtuosic gestures" may be

intended as a parody of the nineteenth-century Romantic piano concerto. Yet he does not doubt the "sincerity" of Barber's romanticism in the slow movement. Other brief references to this concerto appear throughout the dissertation, and it is included in the alphabetical list of first performances in the final appendix.

335.   Smith, Steven H. "The Piano Concerto after Bartók." D. M. A. diss., Eastman School of Music, University of Rochester, 1978. 509 p.

The work begins with a general history of the piano concerto to 1900, followed by a discussion of works by Schoenberg and Bartók. In part 2 the author discusses the form after World War II, organized primarily by country. Part 3 is devoted to eight "recent" piano concertos, divided into these categories: radical concertos; those of the new "mainstream"; and concertos of the "standard literature," which logically includes Barber's concerto but also one by Ginastera. The author discusses the two concertos, not in separate sections, but by going back and forth from one to the other and making comparisons throughout the chapter.

Concerto for Violin and Orchestra, Op. 14

336.   Baer, Verna Lucile. "The Concerto for Violin and Orchestra by Samuel Barber." M. M. thesis, Eastman School of Music, University of Rochester, 1945. 70 p.

In her preface, the author states that her viewpoint is that of a performer and she will approach the concerto primarily through violinistic style. Note too that, because the concerto was only recently composed at the time of her writing, hers is an early study, perhaps the earliest to be devoted to the work. Because not much had been written about Barber as of 1945, her biography is often based on "first hand" information, e.g. student reports at Curtis, and interviews, for example, with Barber's parents. In other words, it is not just a summary of other people's efforts. Chapter 2 is the historical background to Barber's Concerto; the author notes various performances, including American and European newspaper reviews. For chapter 3, the main analysis of the work, she divides her study into the following sections: A. formal structure; B. rhythmic structure; C. relationship of the solo instrument to the orchestra; and D. violinistic style. As part of her conclusion, she states that the concerto is a "musical entity with virtuosity; an accompanying result rather than a generating factor."

337.   "Barber Concerto." *New York Times,* June 29, 1980, sect. 2, p. 22. [Henn B66c]

This article relates the story of Samuel Fels's commission for the concerto and how he refused to pay the commission when he saw the difficulty of the third movement.

338.   "Concert and Opera: Violin Concerto by Samuel Barber to Have Premiere in February." *New York Times,* December 29, 1940, sect. 9, p. 7. [Henn B66g]

The article states that Barber's Violin Concerto, which he completed last summer, will have its "baptism" on February 7 when Eugene Ormandy and the Philadelphia Orchestra play the work with Albert Spalding as solo violinist. It will then be performed on February 11 in New York's Carnegie Hall.

339.   Gorer, R. "Review of Music." *Music Review* 11 (November 1950): 327. [Henn B66u]

Gorer prefers the middle movement of Barber's Violin Concerto ("powerful and moving") to the outer two, which seem to him "rather unsatisfactory" by comparison. Yet even those movements are "perfectly competent."

340.   Kim, Sunhee. "A Performer's Approach to Samuel Barber's Violin Concerto." D.Mus. thesis, Florida State University, 1987. 74 p.

After the usual introduction and biographical chapters, the author then discusses the concerto by means of "selected elements of style," dividing the chapter into areas on rhythm, melody, and orchestration. In the section on rhythm the author mentions Barber's frequent meter changes, irregular accents, cross rhythms, and the use of ostinato. In the section on melody, she points out Barber's lyricism and smooth melodic lines. In the orchestration section, she discusses Barber's instrumentation, his preferred instrumental combinations (particularly, clarinet, bassoons, horns, and strings), orchestration to achieve a variety of expression, and the use of instruments for coloristic effects. Chapter 3 contains a "codification of technical virtuosity," especially Barber's use of higher violin positions, finger shifting, and the use of harmonics and double stops.

341.   Mills, Charles. "Over the Air." *Modern Music* 22, no. 2 (January–February, 1945): 139. [Henn B66ii]

In the author's review of a radio concert, he considers the materials of the concerto "innocuous" and their treatment "naive and cute at best;" more like a neatly scored "three-part bagatelle." He likes the slow movement, however, which is comparatively fresh in quality.

342.   Walters, Willard Gibson. "Technical Problems in Modern Violin Music as Found in Selected Concertos, with Related Original Exercises and Etudes." Ph.D. diss., State University of Iowa, 1958. 252 p.

Barber's violin concerto is one of the "selected" works the author uses in discussing technical problems for the violinist. While the work "presents no extreme problems," it does demand the use of extension (i.e. stretching the fingers) and replacement fingerings to achieve greater facility. Yet the principle theme of the first movement requires careful use of the second and fourth positions, and the performer should not make use of shifting.

Concerto for Violoncello and Orchestra, Op. 22

343.   Dale, S. S. "Contemporary Cello Concerti. XV: Samuel Barber." *Strad* 84 (January 1974): 529–535. [Henn B67e]

Dale spends almost half of his article on a biography of Barber and a discussion of many of the works preceding the Cello Concerto. He thinks the work is unusually dissonant for Barber but it still concentrates on melody. It demands perfect technique, requiring many double stops and harmonics. He calls the slow movement a "lyrical cantilena," and mentions several features of the finale: "dry configurations," a "strange ostinato," and a "feverish passage." As a whole, the concerto is "Barber at his finest."

344.   Taubman, Howard. "Music: Cello Concerto." *New York Times,* January 31, 1959, p. 12. [Henn B67z]

The author thinks that the concerto shows both the composer's strongest and weakest facets. In the slow movement Barber "sings with romantic ardor."

345.   Tobias, Paul. "Much-maligned Masterpiece." *The Strad* 107, no. 1272 (April 1966): 388–392.

Tobias calls the Barber Cello Concerto "an exuberant, virtuosic *tour de force,* " and considers it a stronger work than either the Violin Concerto or Piano Concerto. He includes a discussion of its premiere in 1946 and many of its subsequent performances. The article is very similar to Item 346.

346.   Tobias, Paul. "The Rocky Road of an American Orchestral Masterpiece." *Journal of the Conductors' Guild* 16, no. 2 (Summer–Fall 1995): 91–95.

The author gives the performance history and reception of Barber's Cello Concerto. He considers it "possibly the most important cello piece written by an American" (a statement the author also makes in the *Strad* article; see Item 345), and compares it favorably with Elgar's Cello Concerto. While it is often performed in Europe, Barber's Concerto gets few professional performances in the

United States. American cellists seem to be daunted by its difficulties. Much of the fault lies with the Garbousova's overedited cello part in the published score. Tobias thinks that if more cellists could play from a transcription of Barber's original manuscript, they might have a different, freer approach. When the author himself played parts of the Concerto for Barber with faster "more propulsive" tempos, the composer approved.

Music for a Scene from Shelley, Op. 7

347.   Smith, George Henry Lovett. "Forecast and Review: Martinu's Second Symphony." *Modern Music* 21, no. 1 (November–December 1944): 44.

While the review is essentially about the Martinu work (as the title indicates), the reviewer does discuss the recent revival ("more than justified") of Barber's *Music for a Scene from Shelley*. It remains a "work of substance," which creates its mood "quickly and persuasively." Its musical texture is "lustrous."

Second Essay for Orchestra, Op. 17

348.   Mills, Charles. "Over the Air." *Modern Music* 22, no. 3 (March–April 1945): 209.

Mills says that the work has an ability to "exploit stale materials in an attractive layout of eloquent sounds." Barber is "least boring" when he writes simply and quietly, as opposed to the "inevitable bombast" of his fortissimo scoring.

Symphony No. 1 in One Movement, Op. 9

349.   Leuch, Ruth. "An Analysis of the *First Symphony in One Movement* by Samuel Barber." M. M. thesis, Eastman School of Music, University of Rochester, 1949. 115 p.

Leuch divides her thesis into six main chapters. The first chapter deals with form, citing the use of three principle themes and their transformations throughout the four large sections. In the second chapter, she notes meter changes and rhythmic developments, and in the third, describes melodic characteristics, such as Barber's balance of conjunct and disjunct motion and his outlining of triads and 7th chords. She also includes a multipage chart of intervallic usage. In the chapter on contrapuntal characteristics, she includes Barber's use of imitation, canon, ostinato, pedal point, stretto, and the combination of fragments from several themes. For harmonic characteristics, she concentrates on types of chords, use of common tones, cross relations, and polytonality. The fifth chapter is devoted to a discussion of Barber's traditional orchestration, including charts on ranges of instruments and on typical instrumentation for specific themes. In her conclusion she mentions the highly unified nature of the symphony, especially the themes that are contrasting but having common characteristics, and the strong harmonic background of the work.

350. McAlexander, John. "A Stylistic Analysis of the First Symphony (in One Movement), Op. 9 by Samuel Barber." M. M. thesis, Texas Tech University, 1976.

This thesis is somewhat more comprehensive than Leuch's (see Item 349), but both authors give a good view of Barber's methods of symphonic construction. McAlexander discusses the four sections of the symphony: the sonata-form aspects of the first, the scherzo-like sound of the second, the ternary form of the third, and the passacaglia form of the fourth. He presents a chart of these sections both by length in measures and by minutes (based on a recording). He also mentions cadences and tonal centers, along with providing a multipage chart (Appendix B). In "Elements of the Composition," the author discusses scale formations, vertical structures, melodic construction, and aspects of rhythm and meter. For these latter two he presents a chart (Appendix A) that illustrates many thematic metamorphoses. He then discusses counterpoint, showing Barber's contrapuntal devices from simple two-voice imitation to complex imitative textures (e.g. in the passacaglia section); and then to orchestration, comparing the Barber work to Sibelius's 5th Symphony. The author also gives a chart on how frequently Barber uses the various sections of the orchestra. In the concluding chapter, he summarizes much of his previous information.

351. Pleasants, Henry. "First Time Fever." *Modern Music* 16, no. 2 (January–February 1939): 84–85. [Henn B79w]

The Barber portion of this article is only one paragraph long, where the author comments on the various performances of the First Symphony.

Second Symphony, Op. 19
352. Pollack, Howard. "Samuel Barber: Second Symphony." *MLA Notes* 47, no. 3 (March 1991): 958–959.

This brief but informative article comments on the reissue of the Second Symphony in 1990, after the composer withdrew it in 1964. The author mentions that Barber transformed the second movement into *Night Flight* (a fairly well-known fact), but also mentions that he "recycled" some material from this work into his scores for *Antony and Cleopatra* and *Fadograph of a Yestern Scene* (lesser-known facts). He provides no musical examples, but see Heyman, p. 456 for the *Antony and Cleopatra* material. He then gives a brief description of each of the three movements. The work "stands up well as a distinctive contribution to the American symphonic repertory," and is generally "a better and more interesting work" than the First Symphony.

Third Essay for Orchestra, Op. 47

353.   Alps, Tim. "Concerto: Modern." *Music and Musicians* 28 (January 1980): 66. [Henn B81a]

Alps considers the definition of the word "essay" as a work "with a tendency to explore a single aspect of a subject." Barber's piece fits this definition. The music begins with basic melodic and rhythmic materials, which then build up in various orderings, eventually growing into long lyrical lines that are "sumptuous" and "compelling." While the harmonies "rarely extend beyond Scriabin," the work is "strongly constructed and richly imagined."

354.   Simmons, Walter. "Barber: Essay No. 3." *Fanfare* 4 (May–June 1981): 49–50.

While this article starts out as a review of a recording, it is mostly a discussion of the work itself. Barber's last major work "seems somehow to echo half-heartedly the gestures of his earlier days." It lacks the "cumulative, episodic drama" of his early works and merely "parades a couple of attractive themes through a lavish orchestral wardrobe." Barber's "paralyzed harmonic motion is ultimately frustrating."

Toccata Festiva, Op. 36

355.   "Stoplists." *American Organist* 43 (December 1960): 19. [Henn B82m]

The reviewer of the score considers the work to be far more than a virtuoso showpiece. The "carefully designed inter-play" between organ and orchestra is "exceptionally and imaginatively well conceived." The work has "drama, pulse, driving rhythm, winging line, beauty, shape, and purpose."

Choral and Vocal Music

356.   Fahey, John. "Samuel Barber, A Portrait in Poetic Voice." M. A. thesis, California State University, Fullerton, 1983. 99 p.

Because Fahey deals with textual interpretations in Barber's music, it is logical that he should choose his examples from both the composer's vocal and choral repertoires. In his introduction (chapter 1) he explains his choice of music and states his method of procedure. Chapter 2 is devoted to four songs from the early "Bessie Bobtail" through "Now have I fed and eaten up the rose," one of Barber's last. He uses a similar approach for three choruses in chapter 3. In the last chapter, entitled "A Portrait in Poetic Voice," the author makes some general statements based on his findings, concluding that Barber selected texts that express "aloneness" and give him the opportunity to compose "sadly pensive" music for them. He also suggests that such poetry is often abstract in meaning, allowing Barber to "express himself honestly," but at the same time allowing him to protect aspects of his privacy, particularly his spirituality and his sexuality.

In an appendix, Fahey reprints letters from various people he consulted during the writing of the thesis, including Ned Rorem, William Schuman, and Virgil Thomson. (For a summary of the Fahey-Thomson correspondence, see chapter 6, Thom [17], [18], and [19]. Some of the letters are informative [e.g. Rorem's and Schuman's] while others are not [e.g. John Browning].)

357.   Voorhees, Larry Donald. "A Study of Selected Vocal-Choral Works of Samuel Barber." M. A. thesis, Eastern Illinois University, 1965. 105 p.

In his introduction, Voorhees explains his reason for dividing Barber's choral and vocal repertoire into compositions before and after 1940. While this may make sense for Barber's music in general (it is basically Broder's idea), for the song and choral repertoire it splits various opus numbers, e.g. for *Reincarnations*, it puts "Mary Hines" in the former category and "The Coolin" in the latter. Voorhees next briefly discusses the choral works and the vocal works in these two categories. Most discussions begin with a chart of the vocal range, and some include diagrams of the tonal plan. The most informative chapter is his "Summary of Style," in which he generalizes about melody, method of construction, tonality vs. modality, counterpoint, and other musical relationships.

Choral Music: General

358.   Castleberry, David Henry. "The Choral Music of Samuel Barber: A Conductor's Guide." D. M. A. thesis, University of Texas at Austin, 1992. 295 p.

The author's aim is to present information about Barber's choral music that will "assist the conductor in understanding the composer's musical language and methods of textual expression." He emphasizes common themes in the texts that Barber chooses as well as the composer's use of text inflection and phrasing. Barber favors traditional forms that are enhanced by "varied resources, textures, and structural formats." Not examined. [Based on dissertation abstracts.]

359.   Dolph, Heather Marie. "Choral Arrangements of Samuel Barber." M. F. A. thesis, University of California, Los Angeles, 1991. 21 p.

Not examined, but must include discussions of the *Agnus Dei* (based on *Adagio for Strings)* and two choruses from *Antony and Cleopatra.*

360.   Horowitz, Linda. "Literature Forum: The Choral Music of Samuel Barber." *Choral Journal* 21 (December 1980): 26-29. [Henn BG 72, B7rr, B14b, B15a, B18b, B19d, B20j, B21e, B22i, B23a, B24a, B25a, B34a, B54a, B55a]

The author discusses Barber's choral works in reference to their texts, structure, rehearsal problems, and performance practicality (all in four pages). She briefly discusses all the choral works, the unaccompanied (e.g. "Let down the bars, O death,"), those with full orchestra (e.g. *Prayers of Kierkegaard),* and one arranged from other sources (e.g. *Agnus Dei,* arranged from *Adagio for Strings).* There is barely room for a brief appraisal of each.

361.   Johnson, Randall Daley. "The Choral Music of Samuel Barber." D. M. A. diss., University of Washington, 1992. 198 p.

A discussion of 16 Barber choral works, including those that the composer arranged from other pieces, e.g. "Sure on this shining night," and choral selections from *Antony and Cleopatra.* However, it excludes *God's Grandeur, Ad Bibinem cum me rogaret ad cenam,* and Barber's two major choral works with soloists and orchestra, *Prayers of Kierkegaard* and *The Lovers.* The approach is the same for all works. Each begins with "Commentary and Associated Information," giving the circumstances surrounding the composition including aspects of first performances. The text of each work is then presented, followed by a discussion of form, motivic function, harmonic idiom, and rhythmic activity. Most of this discussion is very rudimentary. There are numerous musical examples, sometimes reprinting nearly the entire movement (e.g. "Let down the bars, O death," and *Chorale for Ascension Day).* The dissertation ends with a brief chapter of conclusions and a bibliography.

362.   Manzo, Ralph Dan. "A Study of Selected Choral Works by American Contemporary Composers." Ph. D. diss., Colorado State College, 1961. 270 p.

This thesis is geared toward the prospective choral director, giving advice on technique, musicianship, knowledge of the voice, aspects of music theory, and interpretation. Barber is among the nine composers selected for the study, with discussions of "Let down the bars O death," and *Reincarnations.*

363. Nally, Donald John. " 'To Immerse Myself in Words': Text and Music in Selected Choral Works of Samuel Barber." D. M. A. diss., University of Illinois, Urbana-Champaign, 1995.

Nally discusses ten "smaller" choral works by Barber (thereby excluding the large-scale *Prayers of Kierkegaard* and *The Lovers),* analyzing texts in regard to poetic devices, meter, and rhythm, and Barber's musical setting of them. (The phrase, "to immerse myself in words" is Barber's own.) Each work is given a separate chapter, eight altogether because *Reincarnations* contains three movements. Each of these chapters begins with a substantial section on the author of the text, including a brief biography and a short discussion of that author's poetic output. This is, in fact, the most valuable portion of the dissertation, because some musicians may not be aware of the literary side of these choral works. The discussion of the music itself is somewhat superficial, more of a description than an analysis.

364. Pisciotta, Louis Vincent. "Texture in the Choral Works of Selected Contemporary American Composers." Ph.D. thesis, Indiana University, 1967. 416 p. [Henn BG108]

After an introductory chapter stating objectives, scope, and procedures of the study, the author then discusses his topic of texture in all Barber's choral works, including his arrangements of "Sure on this shining night," and "A Nun Takes the Veil." In the final summary the author concludes that in his early choral works, Barber is much more likely to employ either homophony or polyphony throughout the work, whereas in his later works, he is more likely to mix the two textures together. Barber figures, but not prominently, in the author's concluding chapter.

365. Skoog, William M. "The Late Choral Music of Howard Hanson and Samuel Barber." D. A. diss., University of Northern Colorado, 1992. 353 p.

Skoog's dissertation presents a comparison of choral music of two conservative American composers, distinguishing between their specific compositional techniques. Approximately half of the dissertation is devoted to the late (i.e., after 1953) choral music of Barber, including *Prayers of Kierkegaard* and *The Lovers.* After a chapter on general considerations, the author presents substantial biographies of the two composers, with Barber receiving fifteen pages, longer than most biographical studies in such dissertations. The remainder of the chapter includes ideas from previous dissertations such as those by Pisciotta, Dailey, Wathen, and Friedewald. (See Items 364, 373, 318, and 255, respectively.)

The organization of the main chapter on Barber's choral music (chapter 4) is not chronological by title, but by specific aspects of the composer's style, the same process used in chapter 3 for Howard Hanson's choral music. He first discusses structure and texture, then melody, themes, harmony, counterpoint, development, rhythm, meter, accompaniment, and finally the relationship of text and music. Then in chapter 5, "Summary and Conclusions," he ties together these aspects for the music of both composers.

366.　　Svaren, J. Cornell. "Choral Style of Samuel Barber: A Lecture-Recital." M. S. thesis, Moorhead State University, 1976. 41 p. (includes one sound cassette).

After a brief chapter of biographical material, the author discusses three choral pieces that Barber adapted from his previous music and then three of the composer's original choral works. The three adapted works are: "Lamb of God," from *Adagio for Strings*, "Heaven-Haven" from the solo song, "A Nun Takes the Veil," and "Under the willow tree" from *Vanessa*. In all three cases the author shows, sometimes through musical examples, what kind of adaptations were necessary to transform the solo vocal work into the later choral one. The original choral works are "Let down the bars, O death," *A Stopwatch and an Ordnance Map*, and *Easter Chorale,* with his description of them being fairly brief and straightforward. The work ends with a short summary.

Choral Music: Individual Titles

Agnus Dei (based on *Adagio for Strings*)
367.　　Mueller, John William. "A Conductor's Analysis of Selected Works: by William Byrd, Antonio Lotti, George Frideric Handel, Samuel Barber, Gustav Holst, and Daniel Pinkham." M. M. thesis, Southwestern Baptist Theological Seminary, 1992. 198 p.

Mueller discusses only one choral work by each of the composers named in his title. For the Samuel Barber segment (chapter 4), it is the *Agnus Dei,* derived from his *Adagio for Strings.* The author devotes over twenty pages to the work and uses the same approach as he does for all six: first some biographical information, then aspects of performance practices, analysis (the most substantial part of the chapter), and finally some performance considerations. There is no separate introduction or conclusion to the thesis.

Easter Chorale (Chorale for Ascension Day)
368.　　*The Gloria in Excelsis Tower dedication book: The order of services and events for Ascension Day, May 7, 1964.* Washington, D.C., Washington Cathedral (publishers), 1964. 176 p.

This publication contains the musical score, 2 sound discs (33 1/3 RPM), important dates in the history of Washington Cathedral, and biographical information on the composers of the ten works performed on the occasion of the dedication of the bell tower. [Not examined.]

The Lovers, Op. 43

369. Hicks, Anne Matlack. "Samuel Barber's *The Lovers.*" D. M. A. thesis, University of Cincinnati, 1991. 215 p.

The Lovers is placed in the context of Barber's other choral works, and approached primarily through the poems of Pablo Neruda. The thesis begins with a brief biography. The second chapter is devoted to a general discussion of Barber's choral works prior to *The Lovers.* In chapter 3, the author discusses the specific poems by Neruda that comprise the text of *The Lovers,* including a comparison of the two translations that Barber used (W. S. Merwin and Christopher Logue, although Barber occasionally substituted a few of his own lines). Hicks then writes about each of the nine poems and their musical settings (one chapter each). She then ends with a discussion of the reviews of various performances and gives some general conclusions.

370. Kolodin, Irving. "Music to My Ears." *Saturday Review* 54 (October 23, 1971), 14. [Henn B19e]

This is a three-paragraph description of *The Lovers,* which "breaks the long silence" after the adverse response to Barber's *Antony and Cleopatra.* It is essentially a critique of the first performance of the Philadelphia Orchestra at New York's Philharmonic Hall (yet to be designated as Avery Fisher Hall), but with additional comments. He believes that Barber has maintained "his craftsmanship and his artistic balance" in this work. The main motive (A-C-B) reminds him of one in Ravel's *Chansons madécasses.* Yet the work is "slightly synthetic."

371. "Philadelphia: Orchestra and Bank Combine to Make Music." *New York Times,* January 24, 1971, sect. 3, p. 15. [Henn B19f]

A fairly brief announcement that the Girard Bank of Philadelphia has commissioned Barber to compose a work (as yet untitled) for the Philadelphia Orchestra for the 1971–72 season.

372. Webster, Daniel. "Samuel Barber: Reading Love Poems in the Board Room." *Philadelphia Inquirer,* September 19, 1971, p. 8.

This article relates the incident when Barber became a bit frustrated with the board's straight-laced attitude and asked them "Don't you have love affairs in Philadelphia?" One board member then replies, "It's all we have left."

Prayers of Kierkegaard, **Op. 30**

373. Dailey, William Albert. "Techniques in Composition Used in Contemporary Works for Chorus and Orchestra on Religious Texts as Important Representative Works from the Period 1952–62." D. M. A. thesis, Catholic University, 1965. 334 p. [Henn 20b]

In addition to Barber's *Prayers of Kierkegaard,* Dailey also presents studies of Hovhaness's *Magnificat* and Stravinsky's *Canticum Sacrum.* Chapter 1 is not just a description of *Prayers,* but a systematic orderly analysis of it, movement by movement. One particularly useful feature is the inclusion of charts showing a Schenkerian analysis of individual sections of the work. This is one of the few chapters of any dissertation on Barber's music that shows a true understanding of the composer's tonal language.

In the remaining chapters the author takes us through various aspects of *Prayers* (always the first of the three choral works discussed). Chapter 4 deals with text setting, chapter 5 with structural design and the use of motives, and chapter 6 with tonal, modal, and harmonic organization. Barber's main contrapuntal practice of canon is the subject of chapter 7 as is rhythm and meter in chapter 8. Melodic line is discussed in chapter 9. The last main chapter is a rather catchall category, illustrating idiomatic choral practice, voice leading, choral grouping, choral fabric, and instrumental accompaniment. The dissertation ends with a "Summation and Conclusion." Because the three works are very diverse, the author does not make many comparisons, but the reader can at least see the compositional techniques of three different, leading twentieth-century composers.

374. Hicks, Anne Matlack. "Samuel Barber's *The Lovers.*" Item 369, pp. 39–49.

While most of this thesis is obviously concerned with *The Lovers,* the last section of chapter 2, "The Choral Music," is devoted to *The Prayers of Kierkegaard,* an unexpected bonus. The ten-page discussion includes five musical excerpts.

375. Redlich, H. F. "Music from the American Continent." *Music Review* 19 (August 1958): 246–253. [Henn B20q]

The passage in this very general article on *Prayers of Kierkegaard* is only on one page (p. 247). Redlich shows how the composer uses passages from

Kierkegaard's "religious, speculative, and self-analytical writings," to write a "serious hymnlike composition." He thinks that the work sounds like music written by a German "sometime between 1910 and 1935," but is also somewhat comparable to Delius's *Mass of Life* (on texts by Nietzsche) and Kaminski's *Introitus und Hymnus*. Redlich also reviews the Schirmer edition of Barber's songs (see Item 111).

Reincarnations, Op. 16

376. Birch, Courtney Ann. "An Analysis of Samuel Barber's *Reincarnations.*" M. A. thesis, University of Virginia, 1991. 17 p.

While this study is short, it is not as superficial as it may seem. The author's insight goes well beyond the brief descriptions typical of program notes. It is, in fact, more like a journal article. She discusses each of the movements primarily in terms of their motivic content and development and ends with a discussion of similar motives in all three pieces. There is no significant bibliography.

377. Castleberry, David Henry. "The Lyric Voice in Samuel Barber's *Reincarnations.*" *The Choral Journal* 33, no. 7 (February 1993): 17–23.

Castleberry discusses the rather complex legacy of the texts in *Reincarnations*, starting with Anthony Raftery, through Douglas Hyde, to James Stephens, the version Barber uses. In particular, he mentions how Stephens "translates" and/or "re-works" poetic passages of the previous authors, and even shows us some of the early forms of the texts. While he discusses and quotes musical examples from all three movements, he actually says very little about Barber's musical settings. This article should be read in connection with Heinz, "New Light" (see Item 378).

378. Heinz, William, Jr. "New Light on Samuel Barber's *Reincarnations.*" *Choral Journal* 25, no. 3 (November 1984): 25–7.

Heinz gives information on James Stephens's poetry, the text for Barber's music. While not as detailed as the Castleberry article (Item 377), it is still a good starting point for understanding the complex relationships of the texts. On the other hand, Heinz says even less about Barber's music than Castleberry.

Vocal Works: General

379. Coutts, Greg Alan. "A Formal, Melodic and Harmonic Analysis of the Published Solo-Song Compositions of Samuel Barber." Ph.D. diss., Northwestern University, 1991. 359 p.

In his introductory section, Coutts gives his method of analysis and a brief biography of the composer. He then proceeds methodically through all thirty-six songs in order of opus numbers. Each chapter deals first with the original texts and Barber's modification to them (if any). In the case of some of the *Hermit Songs,* he provides other translations as well as the ones Barber used. He illustrates his ideas with 140 musical examples, either linear Schenkerian melodic diagrams or full texture excerpts from the score, almost always with his own Roman numerals, showing his interpretation of the harmonies. His concluding chapter is not just a summary of the previous chapters, but a reorganization by various categories: text types and settings; formal types; melodic, harmonic, and tonal elements; and cadence types. Throughout the last chapter he gives various tables showing the frequency of poetic types, nationality of authors, plus the sources and chronology of the texts.

380.   Elson, James. "The Songs of Samuel Barber." *NATS Bulletin* 34, no. 1 (October 1977): 18–19. [Henn BG36]

Elson gives a brief biography before mentioning several Barber songs. In a two-page article, he can only give a short comment on the various songs that he lists. The article is meant for voice teachers, primarily to let them know what kind of song repertoire is available to them.

381.   Fredrickson, Sigurd G. "Arts Songs of Aaron Copland, Samuel Barber, Norman Dello Joio: An Analysis and Comparison." D. Mus. Research Project, Northwestern University, 1959. 64 p.

After a brief introduction, the author devotes a chapter each to the three composers in the order given in the title. The organization for all three chapters is very much the same: a biographical sketch; a list of songs; and some general comments about them. The two most revealing chapters, however, are Prosody (4) and Melody (5) which compares how these composers handle these aspects. Barber receives a great deal of attention in the prosody chapter. Here the author gives several examples from five songs illustrating how rhythmic accents of the music "blend into oneness with the text." Other examples show "pictorialization." While Barber does not figure as much in the chapter on melody, the author does mention the way he links the words with the music, mainly by means of their "expressive contents." The author concludes that Barber gives an "overall verbal picture of the texts."

382.   Gregg, Thomas Andrew. "Song Composers and Their Poetry Choices: An Analysis of the Literary Background and Textual Selections of Twelve Composers." D. M. A. document, Ohio State University, 1989. 277 p.

The author divides his twelve composers into three categories: The German lied; the French *mélodie;* and the American art song. Barber is among four composers that the author selects for study in the third category, exploring their particular textual choices. The discussion includes the composers' educational and literary background, their choice of sources, their preferences in "non-native languages," and their personal contact with the poets (if any). A comparative summary of all twelve composers is included at the end.

[Not examined. Derived from dissertation abstracts.]

383.   Haldeman, William K. "The Art Songs of Samuel Barber: An Analysis of Style." M. A. thesis, Claremont College, 1958. 42 p.

In this brief survey of Barber's songs, the author begins with a chapter stating the nature of "the problem" and his methodology. The second chapter presents short descriptions of each of the songs for solo voice up through the *Hermit Songs.* (It excludes the cycle, *Despite and Still,* and the Three Songs, Op. 45, which were not yet composed as of the date of this thesis.) The survey also includes *Dover Beach* and *Knoxville: Summer of 1915.* The work ends with a concluding chapter, a bibliography, and a list of Barber's published songs.

384.   Kimball, Carol. *Song: A Guide to Style and Literature.* Seattle: Pst...Inc., 1996. 514 p. ISBN 1877761680   MT 120 .K55 S6

Since Barber composed a great number of songs, it is not surprising that these songs should figure prominently in this general bibliography of song repertoire. Barber's name first appears in a section called "style sheets." Here various aspects of the composers' style are delineated according to melody, harmony, rhythm, accompaniment, poets, and musical form (pp. 28–29). In the chapter on "American Song" (pp. 254–259) Kimball describes each of the songs.

385.   King, James Stephen. "A Performer's Guide to the Selected Songs of Samuel Barber." D. M. A. thesis, Southern Baptist Theological Seminary, 1991. 125 p.

The purpose of King's study is to provide teachers and voice students with a guide to twenty selected songs by Barber. After an introductory chapter on the composer's life and musical style, the author discusses the songs of Op. 10, Op. 13, Op. 27, and Op. 41. King apparently chooses these songs because they span most of Barber's career. The approach to each song is consistent: he first prints the text, describes aspects of the poem, and provides information about the poet. He then lists the song's major characteristics, such as key, range, and tempo, but also includes the degree of difficulty for the performers, both singers and pianists.

After describing the musical elements of the song, he adds some performance suggestions. In the appendix, he gives a phonetic transcription of the texts.

386.   Kreiling, Jean Louise. "The Songs of Samuel Barber: A Study in Literary Taste and Text Setting." Ph.D. diss., University of North Carolina, Chapel Hill, 1986. 379 p.

Kreiling begins with a general discussion of the relationship of words and music, with occasional references to Barber songs. The main organization of the dissertation is unusual but logical. Chapter 3 is a lengthy chapter on works using texts by James Joyce, one of Barber's favorite poets, including the then unpublished song, "Strings in the earth and air." Chapter 4 deals with songs on texts of American authors, which includes a substantial section on James Agee's text that becomes the basis for Barber's *Knoxville: Summer of 1915.* Chapter 5 is devoted to songs on texts by British poets, such as Matthew Arnold's *Dover Beach* and the various authors and translators of the texts for the *Hermit Songs.* Through sketches, she shows how a short musical passage from "The Heavenly Banquet," from the *Hermit Songs,* undergoes many transformations before it reaches its final version.

The next chapter is a catchall category of songs on texts in other languages, including the *Mélodies passagères* on poems of Rainer Maria Rilke. Yet the most valuable chapter of the dissertation is, perhaps, chapter 2, which deals with some of Barber's early songs, especially those found in manuscripts at the Chester County Historical Society. Kreiling presents and discusses the texts and sometimes includes musical examples from these works. At the end she presents a list of these works, and includes various sketches, manuscripts, and correspondences at the Library of Congress. Her bibliography contains literary sources of the texts as well as secondary sources of both music and literature.

387.   McCann, June. "The Solo Songs of Charles Griffes and Samuel Barber." M. M. thesis, Kent State University, 1960. 280 p.

McCann, after discussing Griffes's songs in the first part of her thesis, discusses Barber's solo songs in the second part. She begins with the usual and expected biography. She divides Barber's song repertoire into the Early Period, from op. 2 through op. 13, and the Later Period, from op. 18 through the *Hermit Songs*, the latest he had composed at the time of her writing. She then discusses the poets and their poetry, and in a discussion of the music, includes much chord analysis and some form diagrams. She also indicates various characteristics of the 'later period' that contrast with those of the early one.

388.   Quillan, James W. "The Songs of Samuel Barber." *Repertoire* 1 (October 1951): 17–22. [Henn B36dd, B46d, B51e, B52d, B53j, B56c]

In a few short pages, the author gives a brief description of all of Barber's songs composed through 1951 (Opus numbers 2, 10, 13, and 18). For some reason he includes *Knoxville: Summer of 1915* but not *Dover Beach*.

389. Ramey, Philip. "Samuel Barber at Seventy: The Composer Talks About His Vocal Music." *Ovation* (March 1980): 15–20.

Ramey begins the article with a brief biography of the composer and then goes on to the interview itself, subtitled, "A Talk with Samuel Barber." He asks him about his early songs and prints a copy of his first program, held in his home, that included many of these songs. Barber says that he is not very impressed by twelve-tone songs or the songs of Charles Ives. He mentions aspects of the *Mélodies passagères* (he was living in France and was, he supposes, "in a French mood,") and his own recording of *Dover Beach*. He then discusses, at length, *Knoxville: Summer of 1915*. The article includes several pictures: one with Barber and the author; one with Barber and his aunt Louise Homer (whom he discusses); and three of the composer alone, including a beautifully photographed portrait of him at age sixteen.

390. Redlich, H. F. "Music from the American Continent." *Music Review* 19 (August 1958): 246–253. [Henn B20q, B33s]

While reviewing the Schirmer edition of Barber's songs, Redlich makes some critical observations. In the *Hermit Songs* Redlich hears, perhaps, an influence of Hindemith, Pfitzner, and Britten. *Nuvoletta* catches "something of Joyce's Irish whimsy," and the *Mélodies passagères*, while being "quite anachronistic," nevertheless recreate "charmingly the stylistic conditions of the young Ravel."

391. Rorem, Ned. *Setting the Tone: Essays and a Diary.* New York: Coward, McCann, and Georghean, 1983. 383 p. "Samuel Barber" is a part of the chapter entitled, "The American Art Song." ISBN 0-879-10024-9   ML 410 .R69 A33

In this chapter, Rorem presents a series of strictly personal opinions about Barber's music with no attempt at any orderly investigation. He asserts that Barber's early songs, particularly "Sure on this shining night," "lack profile" and that one "searches in vain for a personal signature." In a slightly more conciliatory mood, he states that many of Barber's compositions, especially the song cycles, "are from the pen of a musician who, so far as elegance is concerned, stands alone."

392. Satterfield, Jacqueline Creef. "Samuel Barber: A Study of His Style and Music for Solo Voice and Piano." M. M. thesis, University of Houston, 1970. 68 p.

This brief and rather superficial work begins with a short and irrelevant history of music in America, from the colonists, through Francis Hopkinson and John Knowles Paine. The next chapters deal with Barber's life, musical education, and career. Chapter 4 finally gets to a "study of his music for solo voice and piano," but includes only four songs: "The Daisies," "A Nun Takes the Veil," "Sure on this shining night," and "Monks and Raisins." She presents the text for each song, gives a brief biography of the author of the text, and then, usually in only a page or two, discusses the music.

Individual Songs or Cycles

The citations given below range from short, early reviews of songs, written when first published, to more substantial theses and dissertations about them.

Andromache's Farewell, Op. 39

393.   Follet, Diane Weber. "A Comprehensive Analysis of Samuel Barber's 'Andromache's Farewell': A Study in Musical Relationships." M. M. thesis, University of Arizona, 1997. 86 p.

The author discusses the "variety of musical materials" that Barber skillfully uses to create "dramatic impact" in *Andromache's Farewell,* and uses these materials to reveal the style and structure of the work. She includes aspects of the musical language, the text, orchestration, and performance problems. [Not examined. Based on dissertation abstracts.]

Despite and Still Op. 41

394.   Berry, Treda Sheryl. "Program Notes for a Voice Recital: A Thesis." M. A. Appalachian State University, 1976. 35 p.

Berry's thesis contains a few brief notes on various vocal works that she performed on her master's recital, including the song cycle, *Despite and Still.*

395.   Cobb, Nedra Patrice. "Rhyme and Reason: A Critical View of Poetry and Prose Used in Twentieth-Century American Art Song." D. M. A. thesis, University of Wisconsin, Madison, 1992. 73 p.

Among the songs by various composers that Cobb considers (e.g. those by Ned Rorem, Paul Bowles, and Aaron Copland), is the "Solitary Hotel" from Barber's *Despite and Still.* The author begins with some general considerations of poetry and its relationship to prose. Her main chapters show the scansion of the texts of the art songs she selects, how that compares to the melodic rhythm and contour of the music, and the composers' musical response to the poetic imagery. In the case of the Barber song, the text is prose and requires a slightly different approach. [Not examined. Based on dissertation abstracts.]

396.   Gibbons, Bruce Leslie. "The Role of the Piano in Samuel Barber's *Despite and Still.*" D. M. A. diss., Louisiana State University, 1987. 118 p.

The author systematically discusses each of the five songs of the cycle, using a precise series of criteria based on the role of the piano in the traditional nineteenth-century art song. He discusses each song, beginning with a commentary on the text and its author, and then investigates the role of the piano: [1] as partner, mentioning harmonic support, doubling of, and/or imitation of the voice line; [2] as commentator, using text illustration and creation of mood; and [3] as unifier, with emphasis on melodic and rhythmic material, harmonic and tonal relationships and pianistic figurations. Many musical examples illustrate these devices. In the final chapter, "The Cycle as Whole," he provides convincing evidence that the songs constitute a cycle in the traditional sense of the word. Finally, he recommends further study of the use of piano in Barber's songs, particularly the *Hermit Songs,* and suggests a comparison of pianistic devices in the songs with those in his solo piano works.

Dover Beach, Op. 3

397.   Coroniti, Joseph A., Jr. "Poetry As Text in Twentieth-Century Vocal Music: From Stravinsky to Reich." *Studies in the history and interpretation of music* no. 35. Lewiston, NY: Mellen Press, 1992. 101 p. ISBN 0-773-49774-9   ML 3849 .C7

Dover Beach is just one of six twentieth-century compositions that the author examines with regard to text and music. It is included in the chapter entitled, "What Anvil, What Dread Grasp?: Imitation or expression in the modern musical setting," pp. 49–71. The discussion of *Dover Beach,* however, is barely two pages long and deals primarily with text painting (which the author refers to as "imitation"). The single musical example illustrates Barber's declamatory style. Kreiling's dissertation (see Item 386), pp. 226–245, has an extensive analysis of this work.

Four Songs, Op. 13

398.   Friedberg, Ruth C. *American Art Song and American Poetry, Volume III: The Century Advances.* Metuchen, N. J.: Scarecrow, 1987. 343 p. ISBN 0-810-81460-9   ML 2811 .F75

The chapter, "The Second Decade" (pp. 7–22), contains a brief discussion of "Sure on this shining night," with brief biographies of Barber and James Agee and comments about their works.

Hermit Songs, Op. 29

399.   Albertson, John Emery. "A Study of the Stylistic Elements of Samuel Barber's 'Hermit Songs' and Franz Schubert's 'Die Winterreise.' " D. M. A. thesis, University of Missouri, Kansas City, 1969. 101 p. [Henn BG2, B33a]

This thesis was designed to accompany the author's recitals of these two song cycles, he therefore treats them separately but approaches them in a similar way. There is no concluding comparison of the two cycles. The Barber portion of the thesis (comprising 36 pages) begins with a "background of compositional characteristics" of the composer. In the second chapter, called "a stylistic analysis," but more of a general description, the author briefly discusses each song of the cycle and includes musical examples. As with the Davis thesis (Item 402), the author hardly ever mentions the texts. Then, in the third chapter, he generalizes about some of the musical characteristics mentioned in the previous chapter. He organizes the chapter into several subheadings: Meter-Rhythm, Harmony, Melody, and Form.

400.   Barr, Clara Anne Myers. "Samuel Barber and His Song Cycle Entitled, *Hermit Songs.*" M. M. thesis, Northwestern State University of Louisiana, 1971. 86 p.

Since Barr's thesis is referred to as a "recital thesis" on the title page, one might expect a set of program notes, but it is actually more than that. In her introduction she states the importance and limitations of her study, mentions her methodology of analysis, and defines a few terms. The second chapter provides a fairly lengthy biography of the composer and introduces songs from publications prior to the *Hermit Songs.* After a brief chapter on Barber's musical style, she discusses each of the *Hermit Songs,* concentrating on musical phrases, recurring rhythmic figures, and "pictorialization" of words within the texts. The length of discussion of each song is comparable to the length of the song itself, ranging from about three pages each for "Church Bell at Night" and "Promiscuity," to over nine pages for the longer "At Saint Patrick's Purgatory." Fifteen musical examples support the author's views.

401.   Brown, Jimmy Lee. "An Analysis of Performance Practices in Samuel Barber's *Hermit Songs,* Op. 29." M. M. performance document, Northwestern State University of Louisiana, 1990. 55 p.

In his introductory chapter, the author states the importance of his study, and defines some of the terms he will use in the later chapters. Chapter II, "Samuel Barber—The Man and His Songs," contains a brief biography, and a discussion of songs other than the *Hermit Songs*. He generalizes about Barber's style in the *Hermit Songs* and then discusses each of the individual songs in a short chapter. Brown's discussions of the text and music are not as comprehensive as those by Davis (see Item 402).

402.   Davis, Alycia Kathleann. "Samuel Barber's 'Hermit Songs,' Opus 29: An Analytical Study." M. M. thesis, Webster College, 1983. 94 p.

The author presents a brief biography of the composer, and then discusses the origins and translations of each of the ten texts used in the *Hermit Songs,* including references to translations that Barber did not use. Since each text receives only three or four short paragraphs, a detailed description is not possible.

She then presents an analysis of each song, discussing its structure, meter, melody, and rhythm, occasionally using Alan Forte's system of set theory analysis. A form diagram is given for each song and many musical examples illustrate motivic and intervallic relationships. However, because texts are seldom included in this section, the author hardly ever deals with Barber's concept of text setting. This thesis, however, is somewhat more substantial than the ones by Albertson (Item 399) and Brown (Item 401).

403.   Lansford, Julia Ann. "The Hermit Songs of Samuel Barber." M. M. thesis, North Texas State University, 1964. 73 p.

This early academic study of the *Hermit Songs* begins with the usual biography of the composer, which is fairly extensive but does not extend beyond the composition of the *Hermit Songs*. In the second chapter, Lansford discusses the forms of the songs in the cycle, but does not include diagrams. Later chapters are devoted to the accompaniments of the songs, including their rhythmic aspects and melodic construction. In the last part, she summarizes various features discussed throughout the thesis. Twenty-four musical examples illustrate some of the author's main points.

404.   McClusky, Nicki R. S. "A Study of Manuel de Falla's 'Seven Spanish Popular Songs' and Samuel Barber's 'Hermit Songs.' " M. A. thesis, California State College, Hayward, 1971. 71 p.

This thesis, meant as a companion document to the author's graduate recital, is necessarily short and limited in scope. After a general introduction, she first presents songs of Manuel de Falla and then, using a similar approach, those of

Barber. Instead of discussing the *Hermit Songs* in order one at a time, she incorporates all the songs in sections devoted to melody, rhythm, texture, harmony, and form. In a concluding chapter she mentions a few common features of both composers.

405.   Rickert, Lawrence Gould. "Selected American Song Cycles for Baritone Composed Since 1945—Part 2." *NATS Bulletin* 23 (December 1966): 8. [Henn B33t]

The author believes that Barber's cycle continues the great tradition of song cycles of the past. In it he hears an influence from Stravinsky. (It is curious that he considers it a baritone cycle when most performances and only recordings are sung by sopranos.)

406.   Scherler, David Kent. "Tonal Definition and Texture in the *Hermit Songs* by Samuel Barber." M. M. thesis, East Texas State University, 1983. 32 p.

After a brief preface, the author discusses each of the songs in the cycle by first dealing with "tonal definition," including aspects of form. He then goes on to "texture," usually meaning the use of ostinato, rolled chords, etc. The author's limited approach does not allow very much detail for the construction and style of the songs.

407.   Sperry, Linda Kay. "Analysis for Performance and Interpretation of Selected Songs of Debussy, Griffes, and Barber." M. A. thesis, Eastern Illinois University, 1966. 98 p.

Although it is not apparent from the title, the "selected" songs by Barber are all from the cycle, *Hermit Songs*. Sperry devotes a chapter to each of the three composers, with Barber's section coming in between the other two (unlike the order in the title). Because she is performing only five of the songs, and out of the usual order, she discusses just those and in her performance order: "The Desire for Hermitage" (X), "St. Ita's Vision" (III), "Sea-Snatch" (VI), "Crucifixion" (V), and "At Saint Patrick's Purgatory" (I). While this procedure might have resulted in mere program notes, her discussion is actually rather comprehensive, including many melodic, harmonic, and structural features of the songs.

Knoxville: Summer of 1915 **Op. 24**

408.   Alcorn, Carla Olivia. "Samuel Barber's 'Knoxville: Summer of 1915': An Analysis and Performance Suggestions." M. M. thesis, Bowling Green State University, 1980. 39 p.

The author begins with discussions of the lives of both Barber and James Agee. She then discusses Agee's text for *Knoxville* and Barber's setting of it. In the section devoted to the music, she provides charts on form and rhythm. Because she performed the work on a recital with piano accompaniment, that is the format she discusses throughout the thesis. Her performance suggestions for both the singer and pianist are fairly straightforward.

409.   Belt, Byron. "Four Voices of America." *Music Journal* 25 (December 1967): 89–90. [Henn B36a]

Belt thinks that the work evokes a special aura of nostalgia and the "questioning spirit of youth." He considers it a "superbly lyrical and meaningful setting of Agee's great prose poem."

410.   Dressler, Jane K. "The Prose-Poetry of James Agee: Samuel Barber's Response." D. M. A. thesis, University of North Carolina at Greensboro, 1989. 115 p.

First Dressler defines Agee's term, "word music," and how Barber's music is a logical response to the concept. She then applies this term more specifically to Agee's text for *Knoxville: Summer of 1915,* relating various poetic terms to examples from the text itself. She emphasizes Agee's use of word repetition, punctuation, and "distinctive one-syllable words." Then, by means of many musical examples, she discusses Barber's "response" to many of Agee's textual devices, such as agogic, dynamic, metric, and rhythmic accents. In her final chapter she presents various critics' reactions to Barber's handling of the Agee text. (See also Item 411.)

[Not examined. From dissertation abstracts.]

411.   Dressler, Jane K. "The 'Word Music' of James Agee: Samuel Barber's Melodic Response," *NATS Journal,* 47, no. 1 (September–October 1990): 4–8.

This article is obviously derived from the author's dissertation (see Item 410). In a more concise form, she defines Agee's term "word music" and how Barber's music is a logical response to the concept. As in her dissertation, she then applies this term to Agee's text, relating various poetic terms to examples from the text itself: e.g. assonance, alliteration, onomatopoeia, and word repetition. Relating such devices to Barber's music is somewhat less successful. She relies on only brief references to rhythmic emphasis (for alliteration), "low pitched locust sounds" for onomatopoeia, and rhythmic variation for word repetitions.

412.   Janssen, Nancy R. "Metaphor Set in Musical Symbols: A Study of the
       Relation between Music and Text." M. A. thesis, Sarah Lawrence College,
       1969. 233 p.

A discussion of Barber's *Knoxville: Summer of 1915* is included among
other diverse vocal works, such as J. S. Bach's *Jesu, meine Freude,* Monteverdi's
Orfeo, Josquin des Prez's *De profundis,* Schubert's *Winterreise,* and Britten's *The
Holy Sonnets of John Donne.* [Not examined. Based on thesis abstracts.]

413.   Lickey, Eugene Harold. "An Analysis of Samuel Barber's *Knoxville: Sum-
       mer of 1915."* M. M. thesis, Indiana University, 1969. 37 p.

This thesis is one of two by the author devoted to twentieth-century vocal
works (the other being Britten's *Serenade* Op. 31). They are separate documents,
bound together. The Barber thesis begins with an introduction, continuing with
discussions of form, melody (including motives), "modal resources," declamation
and rhythm, and harmony. In the final chapter the author discusses performance
considerations.

414.   McInnish, Lynda. "An Analysis of Samuel Barber's *Knoxville: Summer of
       1915."* M. M. thesis, Chicago Conservatory College, 1973. 19 p.

The author discusses the composition's form, motivic development (with
charts of musical motives), tonality, meter, tempo, dynamics, and the composer's
musical treatment of the text. Finally she compares the work to the song cycles of
Gustav Mahler. [Not examined. Based on RILM abstracts. The Chicago Conservatory College, for which the author wrote this thesis, has since closed and the
whereabouts of the library's holdings, including this work, are unknown.]

415.   O'Keefe, Marian Bodnar. "A Background Study and Analysis of Text-
       Setting Techniques Used in Samuel Barber's *Knoxville: Summer of
       1915."* M. M. thesis, California State University, Long Beach, 1991. 86 p.
       + 1 cassette.

After stating the problems of setting prose to music, O'Keefe gives brief
biographies of both Barber and Agee. She gives general comments about text setting: Should music reflect the sound of the words or the emotion and meaning of
them? The next chapter is basically an analysis of *Knoxville* discussing harmonic
changes and recurring melodic motifs, often quoting from previous dissertations
by Dressler (Item 410) and Kreiling (Item 386). The last chapter deals with performance considerations, often relating them to the principles of David Craig's
On Singing on Stage (New York: Schirmer Books, 1978), a work that deals with

Broadway musicals. Thus O'Keefe relates the singing of English texts in two very different dramatic genres.

416.   Rockwell, Janeanne. "*Knoxville: Summer of 1915*. Symphonic Poems of James Agee and Samuel Barber." M. A. E. thesis, Wayne State College, 1993. 31 p. + 1 cassette.

Much of this thesis deals with James Agee's concept behind his prose-poem. After a general introduction, the author gives a brief definition of the symphonic poem. The next section is called: "Agee's Vision of the Symphonic Poem." Here she presents various ideas found in the text: "comfort in routine;" "tension among people;" and the "question of identity." She compares some of Agee's "nature sounds" with the poetry of Walt Whitman. In "Barber's Re-vision of 'Knoxville,' " she shows how some of Barber's musical themes mirror those of Agee. While Agee's concept is of an "adult-as-child," who has control over his sorrow and emotions, Barber seems to emphasize the actual child, and his sense of wonder.

417.   Tebow, James Francis. Part I: "Lyricism, Narrative, and Drama in Samuel Barber's *Knoxville: Summer of 1915*." (Part II: is his own song cycle, "This, and My Hear Beside"). Ph.D. thesis, UCLA, 1991. 155 p.

The key words in the title, "lyricism, narrative, and drama" are derived from Edward T. Cone's book *The Composer's Voice* and are first applied to several of Barber's vocal compositions, including the opera, *Vanessa*. While lyricism is predominant in many of these works, the author finds all three aspects to be present in *Knoxville: Summer of 1915*. Somewhat off his main subject, the author also deals with the work in terms of intervallic sets. [Not examined. Based on dissertation abstracts.]

Mélodies passagères, Op. 27

418.   Shinaberry, Cathleen Stettner. "Samuel Barber's *Mélodies passagères* with Performance Implications." M. M. thesis, Bowling Green State University, 1978. 39 p.

The author begins with a brief biography, which concentrates on Barber's vocal works, divided into early and late periods. She then discusses the texts and their sources, provides English translations, and shows Barber's handling of elisions and accents in his text setting. The analyses of the songs are quite short. After a summary, she then considers aspects of performance problems, most of which are straightforward and fairly obvious. Despite it shortcomings, this is the only thesis that deals so directly with this cycle of songs.

Ten Early Songs (without opus numbers)
These are previously unpublished songs from 1925 to 1937, first published in 1994.

419.   Wittke, Paul. "Ten Early Songs (without opus numbers)" Preface to the Schirmer piano-vocal score. New York: G. Schirmer, 1994.

This is a brief description of the songs, often comparing style characteristics in them that appear in his later, more mature vocal pieces. For example the author sees in "Love at the Door" an "intensity of characterization" comparable to Erica in *Vanessa,* and in "Serenader" he finds "strong hints" of *Antony and Cleopatra.*

Three Songs, Op. 2
420.   Cary, Stephen. "A. E. Housman and the Renaissance of English song." *NATS Journal,* 49, no. 1 (September–October 1992): 17–18.

In such a short article the author can only briefly mention aspects of Barber's "With rue my heart is laden." It is included along with works of nine other composers who set Housman texts to music.

Three Songs, Op. 10
421.   Madsen, Jean. "A Discussion and Analysis of Some of the Songs of Schütz, Wolf, Duparc, Falla, and Barber." M. A. thesis, University of Iowa, 1971. 87 p.

Although you cannot tell it from the title, "some of the songs" by Barber are the three Joyce settings of Op. 10. In her introduction, the author discusses the meaning of style and the problem of interpretation in all the songs to be discussed. She then devotes individual chapters to the songs of each composer, ending with a ten-page discussion of Barber's Op. 10, which is necessarily brief. She discusses each of the three songs, giving information in the manner of program notes. On her title page she refers to the document not as a thesis, but as "a series of essays presented as a supplement to [her] graduate recital."

Three Songs, Op. 45
422.   Knowles, Sebastian D. G. "Opus Posthumous: James Joyce, Gottfried Keller, Othmar Schoeck, and Samuel Barber." *Bronze By Gold: The Music of Joyce.* New York: Garland, 1999, pp. 107–149. ISBN 0-8153-2863-X PR 6019 .09 Z52633

While this chapter has very little discussion of Barber's songs themselves, it does relate good information about the Joyce texts that the composer set to music, including Joyce's translation of Keller's poem. Knowles also prints several other poems from Keller's collection.

423. Kreiling, Jean Louise. "A Note on James Joyce, Gottfried Keller, and Music." *James Joyce Quarterly,* 25, no. 3 (Spring 1988): 349–356.

Kreiling's article concerns the genesis of the text for Barber's song, "Now have I fed and eaten up the rose." The original German poem, "Da hab' ich die Rose aufgegessen," was written by Gottfried Keller in 1846. James Joyce heard a song by Othmar Schoeck using a shorter version of the text in 1935. It is this version of the poem (probably altered by Schoeck) that Joyce translated, and consequently set to music by Barber in 1972. This article is derived but greatly expanded from chapter 6 of the author's dissertation (see Item 386). Because the article is aimed at a literary rather than a musical reader, she considerably reduces the coverage discussing Barber's musical setting of the text.

424. Lamont, Carolyn. "The Last Three Songs of Samuel Barber (Opus 45)." M. M. thesis, Boston University, 1989. 28 p.

The author's short introduction contains some biographical information, but mainly presents a generic discussion of Barber's songs and their musical style. She then discusses each of the three songs of Op. 45, first giving the translation that Barber used in his musical setting and then showing some of the composer's musical devices. These devices include manipulation of motives, melodic construction, "chromatic shifts," and rhythmic and metric activity. Incidentally, this study is even shorter than the number of pages would indicate due to the use of a large computer font and large format musical examples. Nevertheless, the author's analyses, while brief, are still informative.

Chamber Music: General

425. Laverty, Paul H. "Samuel Barber: A Formal Analysis of Three Chamber Works." M. M. thesis, Eastman School of Music, University of Rochester, 1955. 84 p.

The three chamber works of the title are *Dover Beach,* the String Quartet, and the *Capricorn Concerto,* which are noted in the introduction as spanning sixteen years of Barber's early career. The author then discusses each work in a separate chapter. For *Dover Beach,* Matthew Arnold's text has the main influence on the formal structure of the music, which is constructed in a large ABA form. For the String Quartet, he illustrates the sonata structure of the opening movement, the "monothematic" nature of the slow movement, and how the thematic material for the final coda is derived from the first movement. The *Capricorn Concerto* consists of an opening movement in Baroque concerto grosso form (including two fugato sections). The slow movement is basically a 3-part song form in ABA, and the third movement resembles the French rondeau form: ABACADA. In his conclusion, the author points out some common characteristics of all three works.

Serenade for Strings, **Op. 1**

426.   Mills, Charles. "Over the Air." *Modern Music* 20, no. 3 (March–April 1943): 213.

Mills believes the *Serenade* is "essentially lyric in character and not unattractive" but the sound is "woefully conventional and romantic" in a "lukewarm way."

Sonata for Violoncello and Piano, Op. 6

427.   Cowling, Elizabeth. *The Cello.* 2nd ed., London: B. T. Batsford, 1983. p. 161. ISBN 0-684-17870-2   ML 910 .C7

The author considers the work to be "affirmative, strong, passionate" and "eloquent." It keeps a good balance between the cello and piano parts.

428.   Edel, Oliver. "Sonatas for Cello and Piano." *Repertoire* 1 (October 1951): 50–51. [Henn B90h]

The Cello Sonata maintains a good balance of the two instruments, and while the work is modern, it helps create for the audience "a sympathy for contemporary composition."

429.   Scedrov, Igor. "A Study of the Reciprocal Relationship Between the Composer and the Performer in Selected Works for the Cello by Samuel Barber, Elliott Carter, and Charles Wuorinen." D. M. A. thesis, Temple University, 1994. 95 p.

As indicated by the title, the author discusses the relationship between composer and performer in three works for cello. The section on the Barber sonata (chapter 2) is the shortest of the three (only 13 out of the 95 pages). It begins with a two-page biography of the composer followed by a shorter one of the cellist, Orlando Cole, and a brief description of the sonata itself. The main part of the chapter consists of the 1992 interview the author had with Cole. Perhaps, because he is so far removed in time from his initial dealings with Barber and the sonata, Cole is not always very informative, especially regarding some of the changes that Barber made to the work. Yet he does recall that both he and Barber agreed on some changes during rehearsal periods. In appendix A the author gives 21 examples from the sonata, often illustrating the change from manuscript version to the printed score. (For these exact manuscript passages, see chapter 5 on Holographs.) In his fifth chapter, the author compares Cole's contribution with the other performers of their respective works. Anyone performing the work would benefit from at least some of Cole's comments.

430. Stevens, Denis. "Duet Sonatas Without Wind Instruments (From 1700)." In *Chamber Music,* edited by Alec Robertson. Baltimore, Md.: Penguin, 1957, p. 286.

Referring to Barber's Cello Sonata as an established work in the repertory since its publication in 1932, Stevens regards it as "one of the finest cello sonatas of the century."

431. Watson, Jeffrey. "The Contemporary Dilemma: A Performance Project." D. M. A. document, University of Maryland, College Park, 1995. 24 p.

This brief work documents the author's desire to create programs that "embody the spirit of our time and place," and to include works that are "rarely, if ever, performed." Barber's Cello Sonata was one of the works he selected as part of this project.

Summer Music, Op. 31

432. Wooden, Lori Lynn. "Excerpts of Woodwind Quintet Music for Bassoon: Selections, Pedagogy, and Practice." D. M. A. document, University of Wisconsin, Madison, 1996. 254 p.

Barber's *Summer Music* is among the five twentieth-century woodwind quintets the author studies with the intent of developing a pedagogical approach to help students learn difficult passages. She begins with a short biographical note of the composer, short program notes, and information on recordings. She then presents the excerpts with suggested fingerings, practice techniques, and related studies. She provides notes to facilitate the first rehearsal, as an aid to professional musicians, students, amateur bassoonists, and even "instructor/coaches" who may not play the bassoon.

Solo Piano Works: General

433.   Carter, Susan Blinderman. "The Piano Music of Samuel Barber." Ph.D.
       thesis, Texas Tech University, 1980. 188 p. [Henn BG17, B65f, B93a,
       B94e, B97b, B98m]

This very comprehensive study begins with a chapter called "The Man"
showing how early events shape Barber's life and work, followed by a discussion
of the elements of musical style. The main body of the work has a chapter devoted
to each of Barber's works for piano, both solo pieces and the concerto. Many
chapters begin with critical responses to the works when they first appeared, and
then deal with aspects of form, thematic treatment, etc. She includes comments
on interpretative and technical performance problems at the end of all the chapters. The "Concluding Summary" presents generalizations on Barber's piano
style, including form, tonal harmony, counterpoint, and motivic unity. In the
appendix she includes the script for a lecture recital that she gave on Barber piano
music, which is primarily a summation of the material in the thesis.

434.   Fairleigh, James P. "Serialism in Barber's Solo Piano Works." *Piano Quar-
       terly* 72 (Summer 1970): 13–17. [Henn BG45]

In this short article, Fairleigh continues in the tradition of Hans Tischler (see
Items 461 and 462), who presented the idea several years earlier that Barber
employed his own unique version of twelve-tone rows in his Piano Sonata. The
author furthers the idea by illustrating similar serial techniques in Barber's *Nocturne*. The composer combines his personal use of row manipulation with a more
traditional tonal method, creating a hybrid of twentieth-century compositional
techniques.

435.   Lerner, Bennett. "The Spirit of American Music: Three Musical Discover-
       ies." *Keyboard Classics* (July–August 1986): 4–5.

In this very brief article the author mentions how he discovered Barber's
piano piece, *Love Song,* in the Schaum collection, *American Composers of the
Twentieth Century* (Schaum Publications, 1969). He devotes one paragraph to an
"interpretation" of the piece and includes three measures of the score. He thinks it
has the "character of a slow waltz." The other two "discoveries" are Marc
Blitzstein's *Variation II* and Paul Bowles' *Orosí.* The Barber piece is listed in
Maurice Hinson's *Guide to the Pianist's Repertoire* (Indiana University Press,
1979); but does not appear in Schirmer's *Samuel Barber: Complete Piano Music.*

436.   Miller, Elaine. "A Study of Samuel Barber's Piano Music." M. M. thesis,
       Kent State University, 1960. 67 p.

The author provides a biographical sketch of the composer and a discussion of his piano works from the *Excursions* through the *Nocturne*. (The *Ballade* had not yet been composed at the time of her writing.) She describes each of the four *Excursions,* giving examples of bass patterns, motives, etc. She then discusses each of the four movements of the Sonata in much the same way and includes a chart of the fugal movement. Her discussion of the *Souvenirs,* however, is virtually nonexistent, presenting musical examples "without comment." She returns to a more descriptive style for the *Nocturne,* which she describes as a "character piece" of the Romantic period, but with 12-tone elements. In her summary, she comments that in these works Barber is "less conservative" than in works before 1939, has developed a skill at "working out" his subject matter, and "exploits brilliant and percussive qualities" of the piano.

437. Oswalt, Lynda Lee Freeman. "The Piano Music of Samuel Barber: A Brief Stylistic Analysis." M. M. thesis, University of Nebraska, 1971. 198 p.

Even though the title contains the word "brief," Oswalt's thesis is actually one of the more comprehensive studies of Barber's piano music up through and including the Piano Concerto. The *Ballade* had not been composed at the time of her thesis. The author's introduction includes a brief biography of Barber, and an introduction to both his piano pieces and a few of his other works as well. This section concludes with a section described as "forces influencing Barber's musical style," which may be applicable to the composer's output in general, but is less successful when applied to the piano works in particular.

The main body of the thesis contains individual chapters on the *Excursions,* the *Piano Sonata, Souvenirs,* and the Piano Concerto. Each chapter begins with introductory remarks (e.g. thematic relationship between movements in the Sonata and the different arrangements for *Souvenirs).* The author then discusses each movement, concentrating on thematic motives and tone rows, when relevant. She includes many musical examples for illustrations (especially good for comparisons), and gives a chart for each movement (some several pages long) that deal with melodic content, texture, and tonal centers.

438. Owens, Jeanette. "Aspects of Interpretation in the Solo Piano Music of Samuel Barber." M. M. thesis, Royal College of Music, London, 1993.

[Not examined.]

439. Sifferman, James Philip. "Samuel Barber's Works for Solo Piano." D. M. A. diss., University of Texas, Austin, 1982. 140 p.

The author investigates the writing style, formal structure, and compositional techniques in Barber's solo piano music, including: traditional forms,

Romantic expression, and typical American idioms, such as jazz and folk music. *Excursions* exhibits more "Americanisms" than most other Barber works, with only "small doses" in the Piano Sonata. The author considers Barber's *Nocturne* more influenced by Chopin than Field, despite the designation, "Homage to John Field." He thinks both it and the *Ballade* are parodies of typical romantic character pieces. In the final chapter he discusses Barber's few ventures into 12-tone rows, in the first and third movements of the Sonata and in the *Nocturne*. [Based on RILM and dissertation abstracts.]

440. Young, Lauri L. "The Solo Piano Music of Samuel Barber." D. M. A. thesis, University of Cincinnati, 1989. 209 p.

As the title implies, this thesis deals with only the solo piano works, not the Piano Concerto. After a brief biographical sketch, the main part of the thesis presents individual chapters on *Excursions,* the Sonata, *Nocturne,* and the *Ballade.* Each work receives a great deal of attention (100 pages on the Sonata, alone) with many charts and examples from the Barber works and from other composers' works to offer comparisons and contrasts. For example, she compares Barber's "Hoedown" from the *Excursions* to Copland's "Hoedown" from *Rodeo,* and Barber's *Nocturne* to various works by Chopin in the same genre. There is, however, no final chapter with conclusions.

Ballade, Op. 46
441. Bang, Keumju. "The Study of Representative Twentieth-Century Piano Compositions Appropriate for Use in Contemporary College Piano Literature Classes." Ed. D. diss., Columbia University, 1987. 136 p.

Bang studies four very diverse twentieth-century piano pieces for several important aspects of style: Bartok's Suite, Op. 14 for folk music; Gershwin's Preludes for jazz; Schoenberg's *Klavierstücke* Op. 33a for twelve-tone technique; and Barber's *Ballade*, Op. 46 to illustrate the concept of neo-romanticism. The first chapter introduces the author's methodology and the second chapter briefly covers general characteristics of twentieth-century piano music. The next chapters analyze the four compositions showing what kind of pianistic techniques can be learned by studying these pieces. The thesis concludes with "educational implications in music learning," including affective, psychomotor, and especially cognitive aspects.

Excursions, Op. 20
442. A., R. "Piano." *Musical Times* 91 (September 1950): 357–358. [Henn B94a, B98a]

The author states that rhythms in these pieces are "characterized by regional American idioms" and that a fine pianist is required.

443.   Schneider, Albrecht. "Musik sehen—Musik horen: Über Konkurrenz und Komplementaritat von Auge und Ohr." *Hamburger Jahrbuch fur Musikwissenschaft* 18 (1995): 123–50.

The author discusses the differences between visual and aural perception, first as a general discussion, and then in relation to Barber's *Excursions, * Op. 20. The work also includes an investigation into the semantic qualities and strategies of the *Excursions* and attitudes of listeners. Not examined. [Based on RILM abstract.]

Nocturne, Op. 33
444.   Browning, John. "Samuel Barber's *Nocturne.*" *Clavier,* 25, no. 1 (January 1986): 20–21.

Browning states that the Barber *Nocturne* is more of a tribute to Chopin than it is to John Field. He gives many tips on the performance of the work: for instance, use a "warm, expansive style," with as much pedal as necessary to get a "lush atmosphere." Always consider the "skeleton melody" when playing the embellishments. Use the same type of rubato as in the playing of Chopin or Schumann. Grace notes should be "easy and gentle, never jerky." Think of "the big Chopin-Scriabin sound when you play this work."

445.   Jones, Brent M. "The Nocturne in Piano Literature from John Field to Samuel Barber." M. M. thesis, Brigham Young University, 1971. 112 p.

[Not examined. However, a study of Barber's *Nocturne* in relation to earlier pieces in the genre sounds promising.]

Piano Sonata, Op. 26
446.   Arlton, Dean Luther. "American Pianos Sonatas of the Twentieth Century: Selective Analyses and Annotated Index." Ph.D. diss., Columbia University, 1968. 400 p.

Arlton devotes over fifty pages of his dissertation to Barber's Piano Sonata, proceeding clearly and methodically from movement to movement. In the first movement he mentions motives and row formations. He discusses the two main themes of the second movement and their various transformations. In the third movement he points out row formations and shows similarities in several passages. He compares this movement to a "dirge-like baroque lament." In the fugue, he illustrates the two main parts of the subject, the nature and transformation of the countersubject, and the climatic final stretto.

447.   Carr, William Bernard. "An Analysis of the Compositional Style of
        Samuel Barber with Detailed Analysis of the Piano Sonata, Opus 24 and
        Other Contemporary Piano Works, (lecture recital)." D. M. A. document,
        Catholic University of America, 1982. 43 p.

[Not examined.]

448.   Chittum, Donald R. "The Synthesis of Materials and Devices in Non-serial
        Counterpoint." *Music Review* 31, no. 2 (May 1970): 122–35. The section
        specifically on Barber, pp. 125–130. [Henn B98n]

    The final movement (fugue) of Barber's Piano Sonata is discussed in relation
to the fugal movements of Beethoven's String Quartet, Op. 59, no. 3 and Bartók's
Music for Strings, Percussion and Celeste. He includes nine examples from the
Barber fugue and discusses the subject on the basis of its subdivision into head,
tail, and codetta. He considers the head as an arpeggiated I9 chord in E-flat minor,
and then discusses various entries of the subject as they illustrate stretto, augmentation, and splitting the single line into two component parts.

449.   Everett, Donald Malin. "Samuel Barber's Piano Sonata Op. 26." M. M.
        thesis, Eastman School of Music, University of Rochester, 1951. 108 p.

    Within each chapter, the author discusses each of the four movements, start-
ing with form and tonality (e.g. sonata-allegro, rondo), harmonic study (e.g. vertical sonorities of two, three, or more tones, quartal harmonies), melodic study
(e.g. chromatic devices, row structure), and rhythm (e.g. use of triplets with 16th
notes, polymeter, displacement of rhythmic pattern). There is a brief summary at
the end.

450.   Foster, Thomas K. "A Formal and Stylistic Analysis of Barber's Piano
        Sonata Op. 26." M. M. thesis, Ball State University, 1987. 22 p.

    In this brief document, Foster discusses the Piano Sonata with an emphasis
on structural design and how it relates to various technical details, such as
melody, counterpoint, harmony, and rhythm.

451.   Haberkorn, Michael. "A Study and Performance of the Piano Sonatas of
        Samuel Barber, Elliott Carter, and Aaron Copland." Ed. D. diss., Columbia
        University, 1979. 120 p. [Henn B98cc]

    The author discusses three important piano sonatas composed in the 1940s,
and considers their harmonic explorations, new rhythmic schemes, and discovery

of new acoustical possibilities of the piano. [Not examined. Based on RILM abstracts.]

452.   Heist, Douglas R. "Harmonic Organization and Sonata Form: The First Movement of Samuel Barber's Sonata Op. 26." *Journal of the American Liszt Society* 27 (January–June 1990); 25–31.

The article focuses on Barber's harmonic procedures, his handling of form, and how he achieves contrast through texture, dynamics, and rhythmic devices. The movement's tonal ambiguity between C-flat major and E-flat minor contributes to its "intense restlessness."

453.   Lee, Gui Sook. "Aspects of Neoclassicism in the First Movements of Piano Sonatas by Barber, Sessions, Copland, and Stravinsky." D. M. A. document, Ohio State University, 1996. 151 p.

In the introductory chapter, the author establishes the principles of sonata structure by comparing two groups of works: the "classical model" with movements by Mozart, Haydn, and Beethoven; and the "romantic model" with music of Beethoven, Schubert, Brahms, and Schumann. The second chapter covers the twentieth-century composers listed in the title, and illustrates the proportion of exposition, development, and recapitulation sections in their works. Chapter 3 involves key relationships and harmonic structure. In the Barber portion of this chapter, the author discusses mainly the use of row structure, thereby digressing from the principle "neo-classical" focus of the document. The remaining chapters return more to this focus with a chapter on parallels between the exposition and recapitulation. Chapter 5 shows the developmental process, which in Barber's case includes canonic procedure and the use of ostinato and sequential patterns. Only the first 64 pages of this document deal with the topic in the title; the remaining pages (over half the work) contain the author's own String Quartet.

454.   Mathes, James Robert. "Texture and Musical Structure: An Analysis of First Movements of Select Twentieth-Century Piano Sonatas. Ph.D. diss., Florida State University, 1986. 271 p.

This dissertation consists of highly technical analyses of the first movement of Barber's Piano Sonata in relation to Prokofiev's Sonata no. 7, Roger Sessions's Second Sonata for Solo Piano, and Boulez's Second Sonata for Piano. These sonatas have a wide variety of musical styles, yet they are all constructed in twentieth-century variants of sonata form, as can easily be seen in the tables that accompany the discussion of each work. Mathes first presents a general introduction to analytical techniques, including definitions, and aspects of musical texture as related to density and linear relationships. He then discusses the four sonata movements using the same approach for each one. First, as an introduction, he presents the history and general style features of all four sonata movements. He then discusses structural design and how texture contributes to the articulation of divisions within the movement. His discussion of "hierarchic structure" shows many similarities and differences of textural processes. For Barber, each section of the movement often begins with "new textural configurations." In the concluding chapter Mathes shows how all four sonata movements have "a number of comparable textural processes" that "shape structural units and clarify structural functions."

455.   Mathias, Michele A. "Samuel Barber's Piano Sonata Op. 26." M. M. thesis, Bowling Green State University, 1977. 31 p.

After a biographical introduction, the author proceeds with a discussion of Barber's style characteristics, and briefly examines the composer's solo piano works (excluding the *Ballade*, which had not yet been written). In the main chapter (3), the author discusses each of the four movements of the Sonata, giving some musical examples but no charts. The fugal movement receives the most attention, including a comparison to Brahms's *Variations on a Theme by Handel*. Musical examples in this area would have enhanced the comparison. She then sums up many of her ideas in the concluding chapter.

456.   Parmenter, Ross. "The World of Music Commissions." *New York Times,* December 11, 1949, sect. 2, p. 9. [Henn B98jjj]

Ross mentions that Barber's Piano Sonata, taking a half hour, will be performed by Vladimir Horowitz. It was commissioned by the League of Composers with money donated by Richard Rodgers and Irving Berlin.

457.   Regueiro, Allen. "A Linear Analysis of Barber's Piano Sonata, Op. 26." M. M. thesis, Indiana University, 1976. 124 p.

Chapter 1 is an introduction and chapter 6 is a summary and conclusion; each chapter in between is devoted to one movement of the Sonata. The subdivisions of each chapter are always the same: (1) primary melodic material; (2) distinguishing characteristics of that material; and (3) development of that material. He illustrates his ideas with at least ten short examples from each movement. In Movement I (Ch. 2), the author gives his sonata diagram and lists motives "a" through "k." Movement II (Ch. 3) is diagrammed as a "scherzo-like" rondo. In Movement III (Ch. 4), he discusses the ternary design, with introduction and coda, and Movement IV (Ch. 5) as a fugue in three sections. In his conclusions,

Regueiro pulls a great deal of his information together by using examples from all four movements. Here he discusses types of melodic material, motivic connections between this material, types of melodic treatment, serialism, rhythm, meter, tonality, and form.

458. Roberts, Alice Parker. "A Comparative Analysis of the First Movements of Sonata in B-flat major Op. post. by Franz Schubert; Sonata in C major Op. 1 by Johannes Brahms; and Sonata in E-flat Minor Op. 26 by Samuel Barber." Archive Manuscript, Georgia Southern University, 1971. 30 p.

In the Introduction, the author states that all three sonatas may be compared because they all utilize a classical sonata-form structure and contain romantic harmonic relationships. In the analysis section, she describes the sonata structure of each movement separately, including themes, motives, and tonal aspects. She then compares the three movements and gives a chart (p. 24) showing the sections along with their tonal centers. She concludes that Brahms and Barber are more alike in their developmental techniques, thematic content, and style. All three composers like to use mediant and submediant relationships.

459. "Sonata to Honor League." *New York Times,* September 24, 1947, p. 20. [Henn B98bbbb]

An announcement that Irving Berlin and Richard Rodgers have commissioned Barber to write a piano sonata in honor of the League of Composers' twenty-fifth anniversary.

460. Thomasson, Elizabeth Erikson. "The Sonata for Piano Op. 26 by Samuel Barber." M. M. Scholarly Paper. Brigham Young University, 1976. 119 p.

After an introduction, the author devotes a chapter to the general structure of the Piano Sonata, including a presentation of recurring ideas (e.g. "expanding" and "diminishing" interval motives). She then thoroughly discusses each of the movements in a separate chapter, presenting a diagram of the form. She gives many musical examples, often showing thematic transformation, and then provides performance suggestions on articulation (especially when Barber is not always clear), and pedaling (including half-pedal and use of the sostenuto pedal). Although the paper presents many of the author's own original ideas, she often relies on Arlton's dissertation (Item 446).

461. Tischler, Hans. "Barber's Piano Sonata Op. 26." *Music and Letters* 33 (October 1952): 352-354. [Henn 98eeee]

In this article, similar to his JAMS piece (Item 462), Tischler discusses aspects of the Sonata which combine traditional forms (e.g. sonata-forms, fugue) with contemporary ideas, such as twelve-tone techniques. The work stands "head and shoulders" above any other American sonata and is "a classic of our times."

462. Tischler, Hans. "Some Remarks on the Use of Twelve-Tone and Fugue Technics [sic] in Samuel Barber's Piano Sonata." *Journal of the American Musicological Society,* 5, no. 2 (Summer 1952): 145–146. [Henn 98ffff]

This is a brief abstract of a paper Tischler presented at the midwestern chapter of AMS at a meeting on April 19, 1952. The abstract mentions Tischler's view that the third movement, while using a twelve-tone row, is not a true twelve-tone composition since it also contains many other non-serial procedures. He also points out that the three-measure fugue subject for the last movement is often split into two component parts.

463. Van Meter, Robert Dwayne. "Fugue Within the Sonata: A Study of Fugal Techniques in the Final Movements of the Sonata for Piano Op. 26 by Samuel Barber and the Third Piano Sonata, 1936 by Paul Hindemith." M. M. thesis, Indiana University, 1962. 65 p.

This is one-third of the author's thesis project, and is bound with two other short projects on the keyboard music of Sweelinck and Mussorgsky. The first chapter is an introduction entitled, "Fugue and Sonata Form," tracing the historical relationship between traditional fugues and those in contemporary sonatas. Chapter 2 is devoted entirely to the fugue in Barber's Sonata. The author deals with this movement in relation to the other three movements. He then examines the fugue subject and countersubject, gives an outline of the main contrapuntal structure of the movement, and a more specific analysis of the fugue, illustrating Barber's employment of conventional fugal techniques. The study of Hindemith's fugue is a totally separate section and does not refer back to Barber's fugue for any comparison.

464. Woods, Benjamin. "The North American Piano Sonata in Transition from Tonal to Atonal styles." D. M. A. diss., University of South Carolina, 1991. 115 p.

Barber's Sonata is one of ten selected from nearly two hundred North American piano sonatas (1870–1970) to be analyzed, particularly in relation to the traditional sonata-allegro form of eighteenth-century sonatas. The aim of the thesis is to show the "definite but inconsistent continuum" in the use of this form, from tonal to atonal styles.

[Based on dissertation abstracts.]

Piano Sonata and Piano Concerto

465.   Lee, Kichoung. "Stylistic Analysis and Performance Practice of the Piano Sonata and the Piano Concerto of Samuel Barber." D. Mus. thesis, Northwestern University, 1994, 124 p.

In the preface, the author gives a brief biography of the composer along with aspects of his musical style. He proceeds with a discussion of performance practice in the Sonata, including expression, phrasing, fingering, and pedaling, among other aspects. He discusses each movement and gives appropriate (but unnumbered) examples from the score with his own markings, circled notes, etc. He discusses each of the three movements of the Concerto in much the same manner. In the final section, the author gives form diagrams for the movements of the Sonata and Concerto, and summarizes his conclusions of performance practice.

Organ Works: General

466.   Hettinger, Sharon L. *American Organ Music of the Twentieth Century.* Warren, Mich.: Harmonie Park Press, 1997, pp. 20-22. ISBN 0-899-90076-3   ML 106 .U3 H47

Although Barber is not a major composer of organ music, he still receives a three-page listing of works along with a few articles and the obituaries printed in the standard organ periodicals.

Wondrous Love, Op. 34

467.   Adrian, Sabrina Lynn. "Twentieth-Century American Organ Compositions: Selected Composers and their Works." D. M. A. thesis, University of Texas, Austin, 1995. 106 p.

Chapter 1 deals with a historical background of American organ music. Chapter two explores twentieth-century organ works that are "conceived along traditional lines," including what she refers to as "neoclassical aesthetics." This is therefore the chapter in which she discusses Barber's use of hymn-tune variation in his *Wondrous Love.* In later chapters she focuses on more contemporary techniques such as twelve-tone methods, other serial procedures, interval cycles, and cellular construction. The last chapter contains a discussion of even more avant-garde techniques, including aleatoric procedures. [Based on dissertation abstracts.]

468.   McCandless, William Edgar. "Cantus Firmus Techniques in Selected Instrumental Compositions, 1910–1960." Ph.D. thesis, Indiana University, 1974. 309 p. [Henn BG88]

The author discusses textural, rhythmic, and tonal treatments of preexistent melodies in 10 twentieth-century compositions, including Barber's *Wondrous Love.* He first discusses the source of the hymn tune and presents it in its original shape-note form. Then, after a brief biography of Barber, he discusses how the composer uses the tune in each variation, including where the tune is presented (e.g. pedals in variation four) and the nature of the contrapuntal material surrounding it.

469.   Rhoades, Larry Lynn. "Theme and Variation in Twentieth-Century Organ Literature: Analyses of Variations by Alain, Barber, Distler, Dupré, Dureflé, and Sowerby." Ph.D. diss., Ohio State University, 1973. 297 p. [Henn B101f]

The author's method of analysis is based on Robert Nelson's *The Technique of Variation* (Berkeley: University of California Press, 1948) and on Jan LaRue's *Guidelines for Style Analysis* (New York: Norton, 1970), but with modifications. Emphasis is on patterns and changes of patterns. Rhoades begins with a historical background of variation sets: cantus firmus; melodico-harmonic; harmonic; and free. The first two of these are the most relevant for the twentieth-century compositions that he presents. The procedure used for Barber's *Wondrous Love,* basically the same for the other pieces as well, consists of background and general structure; the nature of the melody itself (in this case an American shape-note hymn from the nineteenth century); and the melodico-harmonic texture of the theme and its successive variations (modality, use of open fifths, etc). Rhoades then discusses aspects of registration (generally from simple to complex) and technical demands on the performer (not great). In the section on dynamics, the author mentions that most changes can be accomplished through changes of registration, but others (mainly in variation 4) need the use of choir and swell pedals. The section on rhythm shows how two variations use a "rhythmic-melodic module" in the lines surrounding the theme, while others use a diminution of the theme itself. At the end of the chapter, the author presents a chart of the whole variation set. After discussing the remaining compositions, he concludes with a comparison of all six compositions and provides a chart for easy reference. Rhoades's study is a bit more comprehensive than the one by McCandless (Item 468).

470.   Smith, Rollin. "American Organ Composers." *Music* (American Guild of Organists) 10 (August 1976): 18. [Henn B821]

This article contains only a brief mention of Barber's *Wondrous Love,* including a discussion of the origin of the hymn tune, plus a short description of the four "highly evocative and original variations" that Barber composes for it.

RELATED MATERIAL: PEOPLE, PLACES, AND PERFORMERS IN BARBER'S LIFE

The following books are about other people in Barber's life, such as his life-long companion Gian Carlo Menotti, the choreographers Alvin Ailey and Martha Graham, the conductors Koussevitzky and Toscanini, and performers such as Vladimir Horowitz and Leontyne Price. The list also includes performing groups such as the N.B.C. Symphony Orchestra and the New York Woodwind Quartet. While these works only occasionally mention Barber, they sometimes present additional insight into the composer.

Several Colleagues

471.   Chotzinoff, Samuel. *A Little Night Music.* New York: Harper and Row, 1964. 151 p. ML 385 .C48

This work contains interviews with several people associated with Barber including: Vladimir Horowitz, Gian Carlo Menotti, and Leontyne Price. Both Menotti and Price mention Barber briefly.

Alvin Ailey

472.   Ailey, Alvin. *Revelations: The Autobiography of Alvin Ailey.* (with A. Peter Bailey). Secaucus, N. J.: Carol Publishing Group, 1995. 183 p. ISBN 1-559-72255-X   GV 1785 .A83 A3

Ailey gives many insights into his life and career in this work, including his love for Barber's music. He also relates his own feelings of a boy growing up in Texas to that of James Agee's text that Barber used for *Knoxville: Summer of 1915* (pp. 57–58). Echoing Agee's final line, Ailey states that his family and friends "had no notion of who I was."

473.   Defrantz, Thomas Faburn. " 'Revelations': The Choreographies of Alvin Ailey." Ph.D. diss., New York University, 1997. 485 p.

Defrantz presents a study of Ailey's development as a choreographer and an assessment of his intentions and achievements. It includes a complete chronology of his choreographic output. [Not examined. Based on dissertation abstracts.]

474.   Dunning, Jennifer. *Alvin Ailey: A Life in Dance.* Reading Mass.: Addison-Wesley, 1996. 496 p. ISBN 0-201-62607-1   ML GV 1785 .A38 D85

Dunning says that Barber is one of Ailey's favorite composers, and mentions his choreographic versions of *Knoxville: Summer of 1915* and of the *Hermit*

Songs. She considers Ailey's choreography for *Antony and Cleopatra* to be "one of the few elements of the lavish, moribund opera that received any praise."

Jeanne Behrend

475. Hostetter, Elizabeth Ann. "Jeanne Behrend: Performer of American Music, Pianist, Teacher, Musicologist, and Composer." D. M. A. thesis, Arizona State University, 1990. 282 p.

This thesis concerns the life of Jeanne Behrend, whom Barber got to know when they were both students at the Curtis Institute of Music. She became one of his closest friends, and a performer of some of his piano works. She played his *Interludes* and encouraged the composition of his *Excursions.*

Leonard Bernstein

476. Peyser, Joan. *Bernstein: A Biography,* Rev. and updated. New York: Billboard Books, 1998. 510 p. ISBN 0-823-08259-8   ML 410 .B566 P5

Barber's name only appears occasionally in this work, devoted mostly to his composing and conducting colleague. They did not have a particularly close relationship.

Rudolf Bing

477. Bing, Sir Rudolf. *5000 Nights at the Opera.* Garden City, New York: Doubleday, 1972. 360 p. ISBN 0-385-09259-8   ML 429 .B52

There is a brief reference (pp. 210–211) to the Metropolitan Opera production of *Vanessa,* which Bing calls "first-rate," and that he "rather liked" the opera "despite its dull libretto." He also gives an account of the infamous opening night of *Antony and Cleopatra,* including the comment that he, the director Franco Zeffirelli, and others were "somewhat doubtful about the music."

Elizabeth Sprague Coolidge

478. Barr, Cyrilla. *Elizabeth Sprague Coolidge: American Patron of Music.* New York: Schirmer, 1998. 436 p. ISBN 0-02-864888-9   ML 429 .C64 37

Barr relates events of Mrs. Coolidge's life in chapters entitled "Coming of Age" and "Marriage and Motherhood," etc., and of her establishment of the Coolidge Auditorium. Barber's name is mentioned in connection with the Founder's Day concert of his *Hermit Songs.*

479. Coolidge, Elizabeth Sprague. *Da Capo.* Washington D. C.: Library of Congress, 1952. 14 p. ML 429 .C64 A32

This is a paper that Mrs. Coolidge read before the Mother's Club of Cambridge, Mass., on March 13, 1951. While she never mentions Barber in this presentation, it does give us an insight into her own personality and accomplishments.

Aaron Copland

480. Copland, Aaron. *Copland II: Since 1943.* (with Vivain Perlis). New York: St. Martin's Press, 1989. 463 p. ISBN 0-312-03313-3   ML 410 .C73 A3

There are many references to Barber throughout the book, including one mention of him as one of the ten leading composers "to represent American culture to European nations." Copland mentions Barber's teaching at Tanglewood in the late 1940s and the 1959 performance of Stravinsky's *Les Noces,* in which the two of them were featured as pianists (the other two being Lukas Foss and Roger Sessions). Three letters from Barber are quoted (see Cop [1], [8], and [12].)

481. Pollack, Howard. *Aaron Copland: The Life and Works of an Uncommon Man.* New York: Henry Holt, 1999. 690 p. ISBN 0-805-04909-6   ML 410 .C756 P6

This is the most recent and most comprehensive biography of Copland. Pollack mentions Barber occasionally and includes quotes from two letters (see Cop [8] and [13]).

Dumbarton Oaks

482. Thatcher, John, editor. *Music at Dumbarton Oaks: A Record, 1940 to 1970.* Washington, D.C.: Privately Printed, 1976. 92 p. ML 200.8 .W32 D8

In his preface, the author gives a very brief history of Dumbarton Oaks, the venue for several Barber performances. The main part of the book, however, is merely a list of the various programs and their contents, including the all-Barber concert featuring Eileen Farrell's performance of *Knoxville: Summer of 1915,* and Rudolf Firkusny's performance of the Piano Sonata.

Dietrich Fischer-Dieskau

483. Whitton, Kenneth S. *Dietrich Fischer-Dieskau: Mastersinger.* New York: Holmes and Meier, 1981. 342 p. ISBN 01-8419-0728-5   ML 420 .F51 W5

The author briefly mentions Fischer-Dieskau's recording of *Dover Beach* (p. 252), regarding it as one of the singer's "major contributions to the cause of twentieth-century music."

Martha Graham

484. Bliss, Paula Marlene. "Mutually Influential: The Collaboration of Modern Dance Choreographer Martha Graham and Sculptor Isamu Noguchi." M. A. Thesis, Texas Woman's University, 1988. 173 p.

This work not only tells us about Graham as a choreographer but of her working relationship with Noguchi. Each had an understanding and respect for the other's art. Among their 21 theatrical collaborations was *Cave of the Heart*, performed to the Barber score.

485. Chung, Ok Jo. "Martha Graham as a Theatre Artist: an Analysis of the Use of Stage Properties in Three Major Works: *Appalachian Spring, Cave of the Heart, Night Journey.*" M. F. A. Thesis, University of California, Irvine, 1984. 55 p.

Stage "props" sometimes play a significant role in Martha Graham's dances. Chung investigates their usage in three works, including *Cave of the Heart*. [Not examined.]

486. De Mille, Agnes. *Martha: The Life and Works of Martha Graham*. New York: Vintage Books, 1956 and 1992. 509 p. ISBN 0-679-74176-3   GV 1785 .G7 D4

Graham's contemporary choreographer Agnes de Mille gives a reverential but candid account of her life. There are several references to *Cave of the Heart*.

487. Graham, Martha. *Blood Memory*. New York: Doubleday, 1991. 277 p. ISBN 0-385-26503-4   GV 1785 .G7 A3

The book, which unfortunately has no index, is very conversational and "chatty," with endless supply of "name dropping" on nearly every page. (Graham did, after all, know many famous people.) She briefly mentions a performance of *Cave of the Heart* in Burma where one action of the choreography was referred to as an "elephant going amok."

488. Nimri, Keram. "A Study of the Selective Theatrical Environment Exploring the Internal Symbols Between Graham's Choreography and Noguchi's Set-Sculptures (1946–1947 Productions)." Ph.D. diss., Ohio University, 1995. 292 p.

Cave of the Heart figures prominently in this study of the relationship between Martha Graham's choreography and Noguchi's stage sets. The author uses Rudolf Laban's Effort-Shape theory to help analyze the choreography and L. R. Rogers' method of sculptural analysis to examine the set-sculpture. Both Graham and Noguchi sought self-recognition and searched for new sources of inspiration. [Based on dissertation abstracts.]

Sidney Homer

489.   Snider, Jeffrey Alan. "The Songs of Sidney Homer." D. M. A. document, University of North Texas, 1996. 89 p.

This document gives us insight into the "all but forgotten" songs of Sidney Homer, Barber's uncle and confidant. His songs (a possible influence on the young Barber), reveal a tremendous variety and maturity, and were performed by many prominent artists of the time. [Not examined. Based on dissertation abstracts.]

Vladimir Horowitz

490.   Plaskin, Glenn. *Horowitz: A Biography of Vladimir Horowitz.* New York: Morrow, 1983. 607 p. ISBN 0-688-01616-2   ML 417 .H8 P6

In a brief passage (p. 229) Horowitz comments on Barber's Piano Sonata.

491.   Schonberg, Harold C. *Horowitz: His Life and Music.* New York: Simon and Schuster, 1992. 427 p. ISBN 0-671-72568-8   ML 417 .H8 S3

The book contains a few mentions of Horowitz in relation to Barber's Piano Sonata and of a Horowitz recital at the White House, which Barber attended. The recital, however, did not include the Sonata.

Serge Koussevitzky

492.   Leichtentritt, Hugo. *Serge Koussevitzky: The Boston Symphony Orchestra and the New American Music.* New York: AMS Press, reprint of Cambridge Mass: Harvard University Press, 1947. 199 p. ML 422 .K7 L4

The book contains several passages about Koussevitzky's performances of Barber orchestral works during the 1940s.

493.   Smith, Moses. *Koussevitzky.* New York: Allen, Towne, and Heath, 1947. 400 p. ML 422 .K7 S5

Barber is mentioned in connection with the Tanglewood performance of his Violin Concerto and as a recipient of the "Koussevitzky Foundation Award."

Erich Leinsdorf

494.   Leinsdorf, Erich. *Cadenza: A Musical Career.* Boston: Houghton Mifflin, 1976. 321 p. ISBN 0-395-24401-3   ML 422 .L38 A3

In this rather extensive autobiography, the conductor only briefly mentions his rehearsals for Barber's Piano Concerto (pp. 206–207).

Gian Carlo Menotti

495.   Ardoin, John. *The Stages of Menotti,* Chronology, compiled and annotated by Joel Honig, Garden City: Doubleday, 1985. 225 p. ISBN 0-385-14938-7 ML 410 .M52 A85

This work deals almost exclusively with stage works for which Menotti contributed both libretto and music. His textual contributions to Barber's *Vanessa* and *A Hand of Bridge* are mentioned only in passing. Yet when asked about the music for *Vanessa* (p. 104), he implies that some melodic ideas may have actually originated with him.

496.   Gruen, John. *Menotti: A Biography.* New York: Macmillan, 1978. 242 p. ISBN 0-025-46320-9   ML 410 .M52 G8

While no specific chapter is devoted to Samuel Barber, there are many references to him throughout the book, beginning with their student days at the Curtis Institute of Music.

497.   Sbisà, Nicola. *Menotti il duca di Spoleto e il suo amico Barber.* Schena: Fasano, 1995. 96 p. ISBN 8-875-14776-0   ML 410 .M52 S35

A short book devoted primarily to the life and music of Gian Carlo Menotti ("the duke of Spoleto") with a list of his works and a discography. The second half of the book begins with Menotti's friendship with Barber ("Un'amicizia in musica") and is concerned primarily with *Antony and Cleopatra.* The last chapter is about *Vanessa,* and appears to be strictly an Italian translation of Emily Coleman's interview with Barber that appeared in *Theatre Arts Magazine* (see Item 306).

Dimitri Mitropoulos

498. Trotter, William. *Priest of Music: The Life of Dimitri Mitropoulos.* Portland Oregon: Amadeus, 1995. 495 p. ISBN 0-931-34081-0   ML 422 .M59 T76

While the whole book is an excellent biography, chapter 30, entitled *"Vanessa* Hot and Cold," deals very specifically with that opera, especially ideas and concepts leading up to opening night. However, it is disappointing that the views expressed here are the author's, rather than Mitropoulos's views. For that, the reader needs to consult his interview in *Opera News* (see Item 309).

Charles Munch

499. Honegger, Genevieve. *Charles Munch: Un chef d'orchestre dans le siecle.* Strasbourg: Nuée Bleue, 1992. 383 p. ISBN 2-716-50244-7   ML 422 .M9 A4

So far the only significant monograph of the long-time conductor of the Boston Symphony Orchestra is in French. He was responsible for the first performances of Barber's *Die Natali* and *Prayers of Kierkegaard.* [Not examined.]

500. Munch, Charles. *I Am a Conductor.* translated by Leonard Burkat. New York: Oxford University Press, 1955. ML 422 .M9 A3213

Chapters on Munch's life include "The Musician's Life" and "The Conductor's Life." Barber does not figure into the main narrative, but his works, *Adagio for Strings* and the Overture to *The School for Scandal,* are mentioned in the appendix, which lists works played by the Boston Symphony Orchestra during Munch's first five seasons as music director.

NBC Symphony Orchestra

501. Meyer, Donald Carl. "The NBC Symphony Orchestra." Ph.D. diss., University of California, Davis, 1994. 746 p.

The main chapters of this work are devoted to a narrative history of the NBC Symphony Orchestra from its beginnings in the late 1930s to its dissolution in 1953. Barber's name is mentioned only occasionally. One valuable section of this work is the extensive list (as appendix B) of each program performed by the orchestra over its long history, giving the conductor, titles of pieces, etc. By means of this list we can see that the orchestra performed a Barber work nearly every season. *Adagio for Strings* was played seven times during the regular seasons and was also included in the orchestra's South American tour of 1940. Other

Barber performances include the *Essay for Orchestra* (five times), the First Symphony, and the Overture to the *School for Scandal.*

New York Woodwind Quartet

502. Likmar, Amy Louise. "The New York Woodwind Quintet: A Continuing Legacy." D. M. A. document, Ohio State University, 1999. 147 p.

The author gives a history of the group that figured so prominently in the composition and performance of Barber's *Summer Music.* She consulted current and former members of the group and relied on the Samuel Baron Collection of documents at the Library of Congress. She includes concert listings, a discography and a filmography. [Not examined. Based on dissertation abstracts.]

The Philadelphia Orchestra

503. Ardoin, John, ed. *The Philadelphia Orchestra: A Century of Music.* Philadelphia: Temple University Press, 1999. 256 p. ISBN 1-566-39712-X ML 421 .P55

This survey was commissioned by the Philadelphia Orchestra Association as part of the orchestra's centennial celebration. It includes a discography, bibliography, and references. The era of Eugene Ormandy is obviously featured. [Not examined. Based on RILM abstracts.]

Leontyne Price

504. Lyon, Hugh Lee. *Leontyne Price: Highlights of a Prima Donna.* New York: Vantage Press, 1973. 218 p. ISBN 0-533-00606-6   ML 420 .P94 L99

A recounting of the singer's life with a short discography at the end. [Not examined.]

505. Chapin, Schuyler. *Sopranos, Mezzos, Tenors, Bassos, and Other Friends.* Photographs by James-David Radiches. New York: Crown Publishers, 1995. 266 p. ISBN 0-517-58864-1   ML 400 .C466

Leontyne Price is among the sopranos that Chapin knew and dealt with during his tenure at the Metropolitan Opera. In the ten-page section devoted to her, he mentions her performance in *Antony and Cleopatra,* and how it instilled in her a "permanent dislike" for the director, Franco Zeffirelli. There are two excellent photographs of her, one illustrating the "Leontyne look" and the other the "Miss Price look."

Ned Rorem

506. Rorem, Ned. *The Nantucket Diary of Ned Rorem: 1973–1985.* San Francisco: North Point, 1987. 634 p. ISBN 0-865-47259-9   ML 410 .R693 A3

There are frequent but brief references to Barber throughout this book, and
not always very flattering. For example, he refers to Barber's "snide comments,"
and to his "sly and often unpleasant character." On one occasion he was "at his
most ill-mannered." Yet Rorem was upset when he heard the news of Barber's
death: "Rancor drains away in a trice, and his value replaces it."

William Schuman

507. Rouse, Christopher. *William Schuman Documentary.* New York: Theodore
Presser, 1980. 54 p. ML 410 .S386 R7

In this very short book the author presents a concise biography of the composer and includes a list of works, recordings, and a bibliography. There are no
specific references to Barber.

Eleanor Steber

508. Steber, Eleanor. *Eleanor Steber: Autobiography.* with Marcia Sloat. Ridge-
wood, N. J.: Wordsworth, 1992. 268 p. ISBN 0-963-41740-1   ML 420
.S816 A3.

In her autobiography, the singer who commissioned and first performed
Knoxville: Summer of 1915 briefly discusses the work in the chapter named for
the title of the piece (none of the chapters are numbered). Steber also talks about
her title role of *Vanessa* in a chapter called "The Fire Horse." It is very difficult to
find one's way around this book because there is neither a table of contents nor an
index.

Virgil Thomson

509. Tommasini, Antony. *Virgil Thomson: Composer on the Aisle.* New York:
Norton, 1997. 605 p. ISBN 0-393-04006-2   ML 410 .T452 T58

This recent biography of Thomson is very comprehensive on both his life
and music. Barber is mentioned only occasionally.

Franco Zeffirelli

510.   Zeffirelli, Franco. *Zeffirelli: The Autobiography of Franco Zeffirelli.* New York: Weidenfeld & Nicolson, 1986. 358 p. ISBN 1-555-84022-1   PN 1998 .A3 Z4326

Zeffirelli gives his own views about Barber's *Antony and Cleopatra.* He was expecting Barber to compose "something akin to *Aida*" and was all set to "rise to the occasion with mammoth sets, a vast cast and sumptuous costumes" (p. 203). He also mentions that in one scene there was a "vast revolving golden pyramid, six barges, twelve horses, four elephants, one hundred and twenty Romans with a large crowd of other players all milling about to the thin reedy music of two clarinets. The audience giggled and who can blame them, it was ludicrous." He was pleased, however, that the opera was successful "as a chamber work" when it was revived later in Spoleto (pp. 219–220).

Mary Louise Curtis Bok Zimbalist

511.   Viles, Eliza Ann. "Mary Louise Curtis Bok Zimbalist: Founder of the Curtis Institute of Music and Patron of American Arts." Ph.D. diss., Bryn Mawr College, 1983. 249 p.

While much of this dissertation is a biographical study of the founder of the Curtis Institute of Music in Philadelphia, most of it concerns the Institute itself. The study is chronological, with its chapters divided into various periods according to directors: first the years with Josef Hofmann; then the short period with Randall Thompson; the long regime of Efrem Zimbalist; and the short era of Rudolf Serkin. Viles discusses various prominent teachers at the Institute, including Barber's composition teacher, Rosario Scalero. Barber is mentioned from time to time throughout the work, as an early student in the late 1920s, later as director of the "Madrigal Chorus," and his brief stay as a faculty member in 1965. The author also mentions several recitals of his music that were performed at Curtis.

Viles does not discuss much of the personal relationship of Mrs. Bok and Barber, but does mention two interesting facts. In 1934 Mrs. Bok arranged for Carl Engel, then president of G. Schirmer, to hear some of Barber's music, resulting in the publication of *Dover Beach,* the Cello Sonata, and several songs. This was the beginning of a lifelong association of composer and publisher. Also, Mrs. Bok is listed as an "underwriter" for the purchase of "Capricorn," the home Barber and Menotti shared for so many years.

Chapter 4. Historical Discography, Current Videography, and Archival Tapes

A discography printed in a book will most certainly be out of date by the time the book is published. For the most up-to-date list, the logical source to consult is *Schwann Opus,* published four times a year. Therefore, the following list has been designated an "historical discography," i.e. a list of recordings, originally issued on either 78 or 33 RPM, and most are now available in CD format. These are often the first recordings of a given work, recorded shortly after the piece was composed and frequently done by the performer or performers who gave the premiere. Also included are recordings that Barber recommended to the American Academy in Rome for inclusion in their library and recordings found in the Barber file at the American Academy and Institute of the Arts. It is not known whether Barber recommended these last recordings and/or gave them to the Academy, or whether the Academy itself simply purchased whatever recordings were available at the time. In either case it seems to imply that Barber liked or at least approved of the performances.

Not included in the following citations are the record company release dates of the recordings, since they are not often included on the album or mentioned in reviews. The dates, however, may be inferred as being shortly before the dates of the reviews themselves. The CD reissue statements are as complete as they can be at the time of this book's publication. Newer reissues may continue to come out, thus eliminating the "not currently on CD" citation. Also, even a CD is likely to go out of print at some point, even after only a short shelf life. For future CD purchases, it is always a good idea to consult the *Schwann Opus* and/or your local record dealer.

PREVIOUS DISCOGRAPHIES

Discographies, both old and new, may be useful in establishing the general history of specific Barber recordings over a period of years.

Bibliographies of Discographies

512.   *Bibliography of Discographies,* Vol. 1, "Classical Music, 1925-1975."
       Compiled by Michael Gray and Gerald D. Gibson. New York: Bowker,
       1977. 164 p. ISBN 0-835-21023-5   ML 156.2 .B49

513.   *Classical Music Discographies, 1976–1988; A Bibliography.* Compiled by
       Michael Gray. New York: Greenwood, 1989. 334 p. ISBN 0-313-25942-9
       ML 128 .D56 G7

The two volumes together account for various discographies ranging from
the mid-twenties to the late 1980s. Both volumes list two Barber discographies:
Broder [Gray's Item 150; see Items 514] and Salzman and Goodfriend [151; see
Item 525]. In the later volume, Gray lists 5 discographies (p. 15), including
Broder [B-70], Hennessee [B-71/Item 523], and Kozinn [B-69/Item 524]. The
other two are just sections of program notes from New World Records: from
Third Essay for Orchestra [B-68] and *Antony and Cleopatra* [B-72]. The
Salzman-Goodfriend citation is now deleted.

Discographies

The following books list some of the earliest recordings of Barber's works, but
because they might be considered out of date, many libraries may not keep them
on their shelves.

514.   Broder, Nathan. *Samuel Barber.* (For full citation, see Item 254.)

This discography (p. 104–107) contains 28 recordings of 20 Barber works,
arranged according to opus number, up through the Piano Sonata Op. 26.

515.   Clough, Francis F. and G. J. Cuming. *World's Encyclopaedia of Recorded
       Music.* London: Sidgwick and Jackson, 1952. 890 p. Reprinted, New York:
       Greenwood, 1970. ISBN 0-837-13003-4   ML 156.2 .C6

The main publication lists recordings made between 1925 and April 1950,
listing 9 Barber items (similar to the *Gramophone Shop Encyclopedia* list; see
Items 510–513). There is also a first supplement for 1951 (p. 725–890), which
adds 12 new items. A second supplement (1953), covering May 1951-December
1952, adds 6 new items, while a third (1953–1955) adds 20.

516.   Ellsworth, Ray. "Americans on Microgrove, Part II." *High Fidelity* 6
       (August 1956): 60–66.

The second half of a two-part article covers American composers of the twentieth century. The first part, appearing in the same magazine the previous month (pp. 63–66), deals with earlier centuries. Barber is among about 20 composers and receives less than a full column, mentioning various recordings available in the fairly new long playing (33 1/3) format. Twelve Barber works are mentioned, including several recordings listed individually in the remainder of this chapter. These references will be cited as "Ellsworth" among the listings.

517. *The Guide to Long Playing Records*
      Vol. 1, *Orchestral Music,* by Irving Kolodin. ISBN 0-313-20297-4   ML 156.2 G8
      Vol. 2, *Vocal Music,* by Philip Miller. ISBN 0-313-20295-8   ML 156.4 .V7 M5
      Vol. 3, *Chamber and Solo Instrument Music,* by Harold C. Schonberg. ISBN 0-313-202296-6   ML 156.4 .C4 3
      New York: Knopf, 1955. Reprinted Westport, CT: Greenwood Press, 1978.

Barber works appear in all three volumes of this set, a listing of recordings in the fairly new LP technology. Each work is briefly annotated.

518. Darrell, R. D. *The Gramophone Shop Encyclopedia of Recorded Music,* three editions.

519. 1936. 1st edition, New York: Gramophone Shop, 574 p. ML 156 .G83

Barber's name just barely makes it into this edition at the end under the "addenda" category, listing only his own performance of *Dover Beach.*

520. 1942. 2nd edition, New York: Simon and Schuster, 558 p. ML 156 .G83 1942

Now added to the *Dover Beach* citation is Ormandy's recording of the *Essay for Orchestra.*

521. 1948. 3rd edition, revised and enlarged by Robert H. Reid. Crown Publishers. Reprinted, Westport, Conn.: Greenwood, 1970. 639 p. ML 156 .G83 1948

This list now contains the following six items. All are given a more complete annotation later in this current list. *Dover Beach* is now deleted but may still have been in print. The six listed recordings are:

Toscanini's *Adagio for Strings*   [See Item 535.]

Saidenberg's *Capricorn Concerto*   [See Item 539.]

Ormandy's *Essay for Orchestra* (#1)   [See Item 547.]

Janssen's Overture *to The School for Scandal*   [See Item 552.]

Garbousova's Sonata for Cello and Piano   [See Item 578.]

Walter's Symphony No. 1   [See Item 557.]

522.   Hall, David. *The Record Book* (International edition). New York: Smith
       and Durrell, 1948. 1394 p. ML 156.2 .H34 (There are also earlier editions
       in 1940 and 1942.)

The citation for Barber (p. 281–282) is similar to the *Gramophone* listing
(Item 521, 1948), with Barber's own performance of *Dover Beach* included, but
without Garbousova's performance of the Cello Sonata.

523.   Hennessee, Don A. *Samuel Barber: A Bio-Bibliography*. Westport, Conn.:
       Greenwood, 1985, "Discography," pp. 83–129.

Hennessee compiled a very comprehensive list of LP recordings available at
the time of printing, containing 267 items. He does not, however, list any cas-
settes or CDs, a format just emerging at the time. He also attempts to address the
complicated situation of reissues.

524.   Kozinn, Alan. "Samuel Barber: The Recordings." *High Fidelity/Musical
       America,* 31, no. 6 (June 1981): 44–46; 65–68; and 7 (July 1981): 45–47;
       99–89.

After a lively but fairly brief interview with Barber, Kozinn concludes his
article with a discography, starting with an annotated discussion of the merits and
drawbacks of various recordings followed by a list of individual recordings themselves. Orchestral works (25 recordings) are included in the June issue. This is
followed in the July issue by vocal music (10 recordings), choral works (5 recordings), chamber and solo works (16 recordings), and stage works (7 recordings).

525.   Salzman, Eric and James Goodfriend. "Samuel Barber: A Selective
       Discography," in Eric Salzman, "Great American Composers: Samuel Bar-
       ber." *HiFi/Stereo Review* 17 (October 1966): 77–89. [Henn BG115]

The discography section of this article is only two pages long, listing fifteen
orchestral and band works and three chamber works.

526. Simmons, Walter. "A Continuing Reassessment of Samuel Barber." *Fanfare* 20, no. 4 (March-April 1997): 84, 86, 90–91.

While not a comprehensive discography, this article does address the state of Barber's music on compact disc. Simmons reviews several new releases (he has been reviewing records for this magazine since the early 1990s), but also includes comments on Barber's musical style plus the critical response to his music, both past and present.

527. Turner, Charles. "The Music of Samuel Barber." *Opera News* (January 27, 1958): 7; 32–33.

Although the article is basically about *Vanessa,* Turner concludes the discussion with a section called, "What to read and listen to," essentially a miniature bibliography and discography of Barber's works. It contains fifteen recordings that were available at the beginning of 1958.

Record Ratings and Reviews

The following books may be useful in evaluating the recordings. They list various record reviews, the periodicals in which they appear, and a symbol indicating how the reviewer evaluates the recording (e.g. $+$, $-$).

528. Maleady, Antoinette O. *Record and Tape Reviews Index 1971–74.* Metuchen, N. J.: Scarecrow, 1972–75. 4 vols. This is followed by *Index to record and tape reviews, 1976–82.* San Anselmo, CA: Chulainn Press, 1977–1983. ML 156.9 .R32

Using much the same format as the Myers's volume (see Item 529), this series lists Barber recordings with a brief reference to reviews in magazines and newspapers and their evaluations.

529. *Index to Record Reviews Based on Material Originally Published in Notes, the Quarterly Journal of the Music Library Association, between 1949 and 1977.* Compiled and edited by Kurtz Myers. Boston: G. K. Hall, 1978–1980. 5 vols. Supplements, 1985, 1989. Supersedes *Record Ratings: Music Library Association's Index of Record Reviews.* Compiled by Kurtz Myers, edited by Richard S. Hill. New York: Crown Publishers, 1956. 440 p. ML 156.9 .M8

These volumes list various recordings that were issued between 1948 and 1987, with a list of sources of reviews giving the periodical and date, but no author, and includes a system of ratings from excellent to poor. MLA *Notes* published this information until 1997.

530.   *CD Review Digest: The International Indexing Service (Classical).*
       Vorhees, New York: Peri Press. ISSN 1045-0114. Starting in 1987 (vol. 1).

This series is billed as "an annotated guide to English language reviews of all music recorded on compact and video laser discs." It has a similar format to Items 528 and 529, giving the latest compact disc recordings, arranged alphabetically by composer, followed by a list of magazine reviews. Unlike the earlier listings, this one not only states the name of the reviewer but also gives actual quotations from most of the sources.

THE RECORDINGS

The following recordings are listed according to the same categories as the previous chapters, with the original recording listed first followed by reissues. Following each item is a list of reviews of that recording, presented in short bibliographic form, giving: the name of the reviewer; the periodical in abbreviated form; the date (but without the issue number); and the page number. The periodicals are abbreviated as:

AO	*American Organist*
AM	*American Music*
ARG	*American Record Guide*
At	*Atlantic*
CMJ	*Canadian Music Journal*
Et	*Etude*
Fa	*Fanfare*
Fi	*"the magazine of music and sound"*
GR	*Gramophone*
GrS	*Gramophone Shop Supplement*
HF	*High Fidelity*
HSR	*HiFi Stereo Review*
MM	*Modern Music*
M&M	*Music and Musicians*
MQ	*Musical Quarterly*

MR	Music Review
MT	Musical Times
Na	Nation
NR	New Records
NYT	New York Times
ON	Opera News
OQ	Opera Quarterly
RB	Record Book
R&R	Records and Recordings
SR	Saturday Review
StR	Stereo Review
SRG	Stereo Record Guide

Individual Works

Operas and Ballets

Antony and Cleopatra, **Op. 40 complete, revised version.**

531.   New World, LP NW 322–324
Winner at 27th Annual Grammy Awards (Classical): Best New Classical Composition for 1984.
Cast: Cleopatra: Esther Hinds; Antony: Jeffrey Wells; Caesar: Robert Grayson; Enobarbus: Eric Halfvarson; Christian Badea, conductor.
Recorded live at Spoleto Festival, Italy, June 1983. First complete recording.

Reviews

Heyman, Barbara. *AM* 1986, p. 360.

Hunt, Christopher. *OQ* Summer 1985, p. 92.

Page, Tim. *NYT* November 4, 1984, sec. H, p. 25.

Trudeau, Noah André. *Hi Fi/MusAm* February 1985, (*MA:* 41.)

Reissued on CD: New World NW-80322/24

Review

Simmons, Walter. *Fa* September/October, 1988, p. 95.

Two scenes: "Give me some music" and "Give me my robe"

532.   RCA LSC 3062.
New Philharmonia Orchestra, Leontyne Price, soprano; Thomas Schippers, conductor. Recorded June 1–2, 1968.

Reviews

Ericson, Raymond. *NYT* March 30, 1969, sec 2, p. 30.   [Henn B4a]

Kolodin, Irving. *SR* March 29, 1969, p. 52.   [Henn B4d]

Osborne, Conrad L. *HF* June 1969, p. 82.   [Henn B4f]

Porter, Andrew. *Gr* August 1969, p. 302.   [Henn B4g]

Reissued: RCA Gold Seal AGL 1 5221

Reissued on CD: RCA Gold Seal 09026-61983-2; retitled as "Leontyne Price Sings Barber" (with *The Hermit Songs;* and *Knoxville: Summer of 1915*).

Reviews

Loomis, George W. *ARG* September–October, 1994, p. 96.

Simmons, Walter. *Fa* September–October, 1994, p. 132.

"Give me my robe"

533.   RCA Red Seal ARL 1 4856
New Philharmonic Orchestra, Leontyne Price, soprano; Thomas Schippers, conductor. Probably taken from the RCA LSC 3062 album (Item 532).

Review

Fogel, Henry. *Fa* January–February 1984, p. 293.   [Henn B4b]

A Hand of Bridge, **Op. 35**
534.   Vanguard VRS 1065, VSD 2083
Cast: Geraldine: Patricia Neway (soprano); Sally: Eunice Alberts (contralto); Bill: William Lewis (tenor); David: Philip Maero (bass); Symphony of the Air, Vladimir Golschmann, conductor. Recorded c. 1960.

Reviews

Frankenstein, Alfred. *HF* July 1961, p. 49.   [Henn B5c=wrong year]

Hall, David. *HSR* June 1961, p. 61.   [Henn B5e]

Hughes, Allen. *NYT* April 30, 1961, sec. 2, p. 21.   [Henn B5f]

Salzman, Eric. *HSR* October 1966, p. 77.   [Henn B5g]

Reissued on CD: Vanguard Classics OVC 4016

Reviews

Gutman, David. *Gr* August 1992, p. 69.

Simmons, Walter. *Fa* November–December 1991, p. 253.

Reissued on CD: Vanguard VC 123

Medea (Cave of the Heart) **Op. 23.**
535.   Koch International Classics, KIC 7019
        Atlantic Sinfonietta, Andrew Schenk, conductor.
        This is the only currently available recording of Barber's original 15
        instrument orchestration of the work. It is part of the "Music for Martha
        Graham" album.

Reviews

Dickinson, Peter. *Gr* April 1992, p. 43.

Rothweiler, Kyle. *ARG* July–Aug 1991, p. 24.

Salzman, Eric. *StR* January 1991, p. 98.

Simmons, Walter. *Fa* March–April 1992, p. 142.

Teachout, Terry. *MA* May 1991, p. 67–68.

Medea **(Suite)**
536.   Decca LPS 333
        New Symphony Orchestra, Samuel Barber, conductor.

Reviews

ARG May 1951, p. 297.

Berger, Arthur. *SR* May 26, 1951, p. 62.

Canby, Edward Tatnall. *SR* May 12, 1951, p. 36.

F., H. *Gr* June 1951, p. 4.   [Henn B71e]

Gr S May 1951, p. 1.

Kolodin, Irving. *Orchestra Music,* p. 16.

ML June 1951, p. 3.

NR July, 1951, p. 3.

NS June 1951, p. 662.

Reissued: London LLP 1328; CM 9145

Review

NR 5-56, p. 3

Not currently available on CD.

537.   Composers Recording Incorporated CRI 137
       Japan Philharmonic Symphony Orchestra, William Strickland, conductor.
       On file at American Academy and Institute of the Arts

Reviews

Frankenstein, Alfred. *HF* February 1961, p. 64.

Jones, Ralph E. *NR* December 1960, p. 7.   [Henn B66y]

Kolodin, Irving. *SR* December 30, 1960, p. 38.

538.   Mercury MG 50224; SR 90224
       "The Music of Samuel Barber"
       Eastman-Rochester Orchestra, Howard Hanson, conductor.
       On file at American Academy and Institute of the Arts

Reviews

DeMotte, Warren. *HSR* April 1960, p. 54.   [Henn B71c]

Frankenstein, Alfred. *HF* June 1960, p. 58.   [Henn B71f]

Shupp, Enos E. *NR* March 1960, p. 5.   [Henn B71n]

Reissued: Mercury SRI 75012

Review

Davis, Peter G. *NYT* July 4, 1976, p. D-1.

Vanessa **Op. 32.**
539.   RCA Red Seal LM 6138, LSC 6138l; recorded February and April 1958.
       Original cast: Vanessa: Eleanor Steber (soprano); Anatol: Nicolai Gedda
       (tenor); Erika: Rosalind Elias (mezzo-soprano); Old Doctor: Giorgio Tozzi
       (bass); Old Baroness: Regina Resnik (mezzo-soprano); Major Domo:

George Cehanovsky (baritone); Metropolitan Opera Orchestra and Chorus, Dimitri Mitropoulos, conductor.

Reviews

Briggs, John. *NYT* October 5, 1958, sec 2, p. 21.   [Henn B7 l]

Freeman, John W. *ON* April 3, 1965, p. 34.   [Henn B7dd]

Guentner, Francis J. *America* September 13, 1958, p. 629.   [Henn B7hh]

Johnson, David. *HF* November 1958, p. 55.   [Henn B7 vv]

Johnson, David. *HF* December 1958, p. 51.

Kolodin, Irving. *SR* September 27, 1958, p. 53.   [Henn B7 yy]

Olsen, William A. *NR* October 1958, p. 10.   [Henn B7 rrr]

Turner, Robert. *C M J* Winter 1960, p. 44.   [Henn B7rrrr]

Reissued: ARL 2094 (1977); also abridged version: LM 6062, LSC 6062

Reviews

Banfield, Stephen. *M & M* October 1978, p. 39.   [Henn B7d]

Dickinson, Peter. *MT* October 1978, p. 864.   [Henn B7u]

Mann, William S. *Gr* February 1978, p. 1,456.   [Henn B7 jjj]

Thornton, H. Frank. *NR* May 1977, p. 11.   [Henn B7 oooo]

Reissued on CD: RCA Gold Seal 7899-2-RG

Reviews

Desmond, Arthur. *ARG* November–December 1991, p. 23.

Dickinson, Peter. *Gr* July 1990, p. 272.

Simmons, Walter. *Fa* January–February 1991, p. 144.

Vanessa: **Excerpt, "Do not utter a word"**
540.   RCA Victor LM 2898 and LSC 2898
"Great Soprano Arias," Leontyne Price; RCA Italian Opera Orchestra, Francesco Molinari-Pradelli, conductor.

Reviews

Hope-Wallace, Philip. *Gr* May 1967, p. 601.   [Henn B7 qq]

Osborne, Conrad L. *HF* December 1966, p. 113.   [Henn B8a]

Strongin, Theodore. *NYT* December 4, 1966, sect. 2, p. 34.   [Henn B8c]

Vanessa: **Excerpt, "Intermezzo"**
541.   Columbia ML 5347, and MS 6040 (1959)
        New York Philharmonic Orchestra, Andre Kostelanetz, conductor.

Reviews

Frankenstein, Alfred. *HF* April 1959, p. 61.   [Henn B9a]

Miller, David H. *ARG* June 1959, p. 728.   [Henn B9b]

Vanessa: **Excerpt, "Must the winter come so soon"**
542.   RCA Victor SP 33 21
        "Meet the Artist"
        Rosiland Elias, soprano; Metropolitan Opera Orchestra, Dimitri
        Mitropoulos, conductor.

This appears to be an excerpt from the complete recording.

Orchestral Music

Adagio for Strings, **Op. 11.**
543.   Victor V-11 8287 (78RPM)
        NBC Symphony Orchestra, Arturo Toscanini, conductor.
        Recommended by Barber to American Academy of Rome; see letter [12],
        July 17, 1947.

Reviews

Hall, David. *R B* 1948, p. 281.

Kolodin, Irving. *New Guide,* p. 35.   [Henn B61bb]

McNaught, W. *MT* May 1945, p. 149.   [Henn B61ii]

Reed, Peter Hugh. *Etude* January 1943, p. 31.   [Henn B61qq]

Sharp, Geoffrey N. *MR* 1945, p. 123.   [Henn B61vv]

Reissued: RCA Victor Gold Seal 60307

Reissued on CD: CD RCA 09026-60307-2 and PHS 49

544.   Capitol P8245
        "Contemporary American Music"
        Concert Arts Orchestra, Vladimir Golschmann, conductor.
        On file at American Academy and Institute of the Arts

Review

SRG (1963), p. 977.   [Henn B61xx]

Reissued on CD: Vanguard VC 123

545.   Mercury 40002
       Eastman-Rochester Orchestra, Howard Hanson, conductor.

Review

Luten, C. J. *AMG* March 1953, p. 223.

Reissued: Mercury 50075

Reviews

Frankenstein, Alfred. *HF* May 1956, p. 61.

S. *NR* May 1956, p. 5.

Reissued: Mercury 50148

On file at American Academy and Institute of the Arts

Not currently available on CD

Canzonetta, **Op. 48**
546.   Koch International Classics, Phoenix 111
       Scottish Chamber Orchestra, Julia Girdwood, oboe; José Serebrier, conductor; (first recording).

Reviews

Kennedy, Michael. *Gr* April 1991, p. 1,822.

Rothweiler, Kyle. *ARG* March–April 1991, p. 28.

Salzman, Eric. *StR* January 1991, p. 98.

Simmons, Walter. *Fa* November–December 1991, p. 253.

Capricorn Concerto, **Op. 21**

547.   Concert Hall Society CH-A4; 2 12″(78 RPM); Limited Edition 1947 (for subscribers)
       Saidenberg Little Symphony; Julius Baker, flute; Harry Freistadt, trumpet; Mitchell Miller, oboe; Daniel Saidenberg, conductor.

Reviews

Ellsworth, Ray. *HF* 1956, p. 62. (See Item 516.)

Hall, David. *RB* 1948, p. 282.

Gr Sh April 1949, p. 2.   [Henn B85 l]

ARG October 1947, p. 46.

GS April 1949, p. 6.

Reissued: Concert Hall Society CH 1078

S. "Orchestra" *NR* May 1951, p. 3.   [Henn B85m]

Shupp, Enos, E. Jr. *NR* March 1973, p. 7.

Reissued on CD: PHS 49

548.   Mercury MG 50224 and SR 90224;
        "The Music of Samuel Barber"
        Eastman-Rochester Orchestra, Howard Hanson, conductor (with *Medea Suite*).
        On file at American Academy and Institute of the Arts

Reviews

DeMotte, Warren. *HSR* April 1960, p. 54.   [Henn B71c]

Frankenstein, Alfred. *HF* June 1960, p. 58.   [Henn B71f]

Shupp, Enos E. *NR* March 1960, p. 5.   [Henn B71n]

Reissued: Mercury SRI 75012

Review

Davis, Peter G. *NYT* July 4, 1976, p. D-1.

Not currently available on CD

Concerto for Piano and Orchestra Op. 38.
549.   Columbia ML 6038, MS 6638
        Winner at 7th Annual Grammy Awards (Classical): Best Classical Composition by a Contemporary Composer for 1964 Cleveland Orchestra, John Browning, piano; George Szell, conductor. This recording was used for the dance "Configurations" (see Items 606 and 615).

Reviews

Flanagan, William. *HSR* January 1965, p. 78.   [Henn B65 j]

Kammerer, Rafael. *ARG* January 1965, p. 392.   [Henn B65y]

Klein, Howard. *NYT* November 1, 1964, sec. 2, p. 23.

Kolodin, Irving. *SR* October 31, 1964, p. 70.   [Henn B65aa]

Kupferberg, Herbert. *At* February 1965, p. 134.   [Henn B65cc]

MacDonald, Malcolm. *Gr* July 1965, p. 55.   [Henn B65ee]

Rich, Alan. *HF* December 1964, p. 80.   [Henn B65ii

Reissued: CBS Classics 61621 (paired with the Stern performance of the violin concerto)

Reviews

Layton, Robert. *Gr* March 1975, p. 1,639.   [Henn B65dd]

Rayment, Malcolm. *R&R* April 1975, p. 21.   [Henn B65hh]

Reissued on CD: Sony SMK 60004

Concerto for Violin and Orchestra, Op. 14
550.   Concert Hall E8 12″ (78RPM) 1951 (for subscribers)
       Winterthur Orchestra, Louis Kaufman, violin; Walter Goehr, conductor.

Review

ARG September 1953, p. 56.

Reissued: Orion ORS 79355

Reviews

Moore, David. *ARG* May 1980, p. 16.   [Henn B66jj]

Moore, J. S. *NR* February 1980, p. 4.   [Henn B66kk]

Reissued on CD: Music and Arts 667

Reviews

Bauman, Carl. *ARG* November–December 1991, p. 26.

Nelson, David K. *Fa* September–October 1991, p. 251.

551.   Composers Recordings Incorporated CRI 137
       Imperial Philharmonic, Wolfgang Stavonhagen, violin; William Strick-
       land, conductor. On file at American Academy and Institute of the Arts

Reviews

Jones, Ralph E. *NR* December 1960, p. 7.   [Henn B66y]

Frankenstein, Alfred. *HF* February 1961, p. 64.

Kolodin, Irving. *SR* December 31, 1960, p. 38.

552.   Columbia ML 6113 and MS 6713
        "Two Twentieth-Century Masterpieces"
        New York Philharmonic, Isaac Stern, violin; Leonard Bernstein, conductor.
        See letter [Bern 5] (chapter 6) where Barber considers Bernstein's record-
        ing "such a moving performance."

Reviews

Flanagan, William. *HSR* July 1965, p. 65.   [Henn B66n]

Frankenstein, Alfred. (under Hindemith) *HF* June 1965, p. 70.   [Henn B66r]

Klein, Howard. *NYT* April 18, 1965, sect. 2, p. 15.   [Henn B66cc]

Kolodin, Irving. *SR* May 29, 1965, p. 54.

Mellers, Wilfrid. *MT* November 1965, p. 867.   [Henn B66hh]

Shupp, Enos, E. Jr. *NR* July 1965, p. 7.   [Henn B66uu]

Reissued: CBS 61621 (with Browning's performance of the piano concerto)

Reviews

Dickinson, Peter. *MT* November 1976, p. 913.   [Henn B66i]

Layton, Robert. *Gr* March 1975, p. 1639.   [Henn B66ee]

Rayment, Malcolm. *R&R* April 1975, p. 21.   [Henn B66qq]

Reissued on CD: Sony Classics SMK 64506 and SMK 60004

Reviews

Lehman, Mark. *ARG* November 12, 1995, p. 78.

Nelson, David K. *Fa* January–February, 1996, p. 315.

Valin, Jonathan. *Fi* September 1996, p. 17.

Concerto for Violoncello and Orchestra, **Op. 22**
553.   Decca LPS 332
        New Symphony Orchestra, Zara Nelsova, cello; Samuel Barber, conductor.
        Recorded Dec 10, 1950.

Reviews

Berger, Arthur. *SR* May 26, 1951, p. 62.   [Henn B67b]

Canby, Edward Tattnal. *SR* May 12, 1951, p. 36.

Ellsworth, p. 62.

Kolodin, p. 16.

Gr S May 1951, p. 1.

Not currently available on CD

Die Natalie: Chorale Preludes for Christmas, Op. 37
554.   Louisville LS 745
         Louisville Orchestra, Jorge Mester, conductor.

Review

Brown, Royal S. *HF* December 1975, p. 85.

Reissued on CD: Albany Records Troy 021-2

Reviews

Miller, Karl. *ARG* July–August 1990, p. 63.

Simmons, Walter. *Fa* May–June 1990, p. 110.

Essay for Orchestra (No. 1), Op. 12
555.   Victor-18062, 78 RPM (12″)
         Philadelphia Orchestra, Eugene Ormandy, conductor; recorded 1941.
         Recommended by Barber to American Academy in Rome; see letter [12],
         July 17, 1947.

Reviews

Hall, David. *RB* 1946, p. 764.   [Henn B68f]

Reed, Peter Hugh. *ARG* August 1941, p. 435.   [Henn B68j]

Taubman, Howard. *NYT* August 19, 1941, sec. 9, p. 6.   [Henn B68k]

Reissued on CD: PHS 49

556.   Mercury 400014
         Eastman-Rochester Orchestra, Howard Hanson, conductor.

Reviews

Frankenstein, Alfred. *HF* May 1956, p. 61.

S. *NR* May 1956, p. 5.

Reissued: Mercury 50148

On file at American Academy and Institute of the Arts

Not currently available on CD

"Horizon" *(no opus no.)*
557.   Koch International Classics KIC 7206 (CD)
         San Diego Chamber Orchestra, Donald Barra, conductor.
         The first recording of a work written in the 1940s.

Review

Raymond, David. *ARG* September–October 1995, p. 101.

Music for a Scene from Shelley, **Op. 7**
558.   American Recording Society ARS 26
         "200 Years of American Music"(for subscribers), 1953.
         American Recording Society Orchestra, Walter Hendl, conductor.

Reviews

Ellsworth, p. 62.

Kolodin, Irving. *SR* April 25, 1953, p. 60.

Schonberg, Harold C. *NYT* May 3, 1953, sec. 2, p. 9.

Not currently available on CD

Night Flight, **Op. 19a** (Second movement of Symphony No. 2)
559.   RHS 342
         London Symphony Orchestra, David Measham, conductor.

Reviews

Brown, Royal S. *HF* March 1977, p. 95.

Layton, Robert. *Gr* September 1976, p. 409.

Reissued on CD: Unicorn-Kanchana UK CD 2046

Overture to *The School for Scandal,* Op. 5
560. Victor-11-8591 12″
  Janssen Symphony of Los Angeles, Werner Janssen, conductor.

Reviews

Hall, David. *RB* 1948, p. 282.

McPhee, Colin. *MM* November–December 1944, p. 47. [Henn B76p]

Reissued: RCA Camden CAL 205

Reissued on CD: CD PHS 49

561. Mercury 40002
  Eastman-Rochester Orchestra, Howard Hanson, conductor.

Review

Luten, C. J. *AMG* March 1953, p. 223.

Reissued: Mercury 50075

Reviews

Frankenstein, Alfred. *HF* May 1956, p. 61.

S. *NR* May 1956, p. 5.

Reissued: Mercury 50148

On file at American Academy and Institute of the Arts

Reissued: Mercury SRI 75012

Review

Davis, Peter G. *NYT* July 4, 1976, p. D-1.

Reissued on CD: PHS 49

***Second Essay for Orchestra,* Op. 17**
562. Vanguard VRS 1065 and VSD 2083
  Symphony of the Air, Vladimir Golschmann, conductor.

Reviews

Finkelstein, Alfred. *HF* July 1961, p. 49.

Hall, David. *HSR* June 1961, p. 61. [Henn B5e]

Harvey, Trevor. *Gr* August 1968, p. 272.

Hughes, Allen. *NYT* April 30, 1961, sect. 2, p. 21.

Salzman, Eric. *HSR* October 1966, p. 77.   [Henn B5g]

Reissued on CD: Vanguard Classics OVC 4016

Reviews

Gutman, David. *Gr* August 1992, p. 69.

Simmons, Walter. *Fa* November–December 1991, p. 253.

Currently on CD: Vanguard VC 123

***Serenade for String Orchestra* Op. 1**
563.   Vanguard VRS 1065 and VSD 2083
        Symphony of the Air, Vladimir Golschmann, conductor.

Reviews

Finkelstein, Alfred. *HF* July 1961, p. 49.

Hall, David. *HSR* June 1961, p. 61.   [Henn B5e]

Harvey, Trevor. *Gr* August 1968, p. 272.

Hughes, Allen. *NYT* April 30, 1961, sect. 2, p. 21.

Salzman, Eric. *HSR* October 1966, p. 77.   [Henn B5g]

Reissued on CD: Vanguard Classics OVC 4016 (1991)

Reviews

Gutman, David. *Gr* August 1992, p. 69.

Simmons, Walter. *Fa* November–December 1991, p. 253.

Reissued on CD: Vanguard VC 123

***Souvenirs,* (orchestral version) Op. 28**
564.   Capitol G7 146
        Philharmonia Orchestra, Efrem Kurtz, conductor.
        On file at American Academy and Institute of the Arts

Reviews

Frankenstein, Alfred. *HF* May 1959, p. 49.   [Henn B78e]

Jones, Ralph E. *NR* June 1959, p. 3.

Not currently on CD

Symphony No. 1 in One Movement, Op. 9 (rev. 1944)
565.   Columbia CX 252, two 12" records
Philharmonic-Symphony Orchestra of New York, Bruno Walter, conductor.
Recorded January 23, 1945.
Recommended by Barber to American Academy in Rome; see letter [12],
July 17, 1947.

Review

Hall, David. *RB* 1948, p. 282.

ARG September 1945, p. 19.

Gr June 1948, p. 9.

Gr Sh October 1945, p. 1.

Reissued: Columbia 1218/90

Reissued on CD: Sony Classical SMK 64466 and PHS 49

566.   Mercury 400014
Eastman-Rochester Orchestra, Howard Hanson, conductor.

Reviews

Frankenstein, Alfred. *HF* May 1956, p. 61.   [Henn B79j]

S. *NR* May 1956, p. 5.   [Henn B79z]

Reissued: Mercury 50148

On file at American Academy and Institute of the Arts

Not currently available on CD

Symphony No. 2, Op. 19
567.   London (Decca) LPS 334 (1950)
New Symphony Orchestra, Samuel Barber, conductor.

Reviews

Berger, Arthur. *SR* May 26, 1951, p. 62.

Canby, Edward Tatnall. *SR* May 12, 1951, p. 36.

Kolodin, p. 16

Reissued: London LLP 1328; CM 9145

Review

NR May 1956, p. 3

Reissued: Everest 3282 (1970)

Not currently available on CD

***Third Essay for Orchestra,* Op. 47**
568.   New World Records NW 309
          "Recorded Anthology of American Music"
          New York Philharmonic Orchestra, Zubin Mehta, conductor.

Reviews

Davis, Peter G. *NYT* April 12, 1981, p. D-29.

Freed, Richard. *SR* May 1981, p. 56.   [Henn B81b]

Kozinn, Alan. *HF* April 1981, p. 77.

Lange, Albert. *ARG* October 1981, p. 21.   [Henn B81c]

Reissued on CD: NW 80309-2

Reviews

Herman, Justin. *Fa* September 10, 1994, p. 173.

Oliver, Michael E. *Gr* May 1988, p. 1578.

Simmons, Walter. *Fa* January–February 1988, p. 82.

***Toccata Festiva,* Op. 36**
569.   Columbia Col. ML 5798 MD 6398;
          E. Power Biggs, organ, Philadelphia Orchestra, Eugene Ormandy, conductor. On file at American Academy and Institute of the Arts

Reviews

Bronkhorst, Charles Vary. *AO* February 1963, p. 22.   [Henn B82b]

Jones, Ralph E. *NR* March 1963, p. 12.   [Henn B82e]

Salzman, Eric. *HF* April 1963, p. 88.   [Henn B82i]

Reissued: CBS BRG 72364

Reviews

Aprahamian, Felix. *Gr* May 1966, p. 552.   [Henn B82a]

Not currently available on CD

Band

Commando March (no opus no.)

570.   Mercury SRI 75086

> **Reissued** Mercury MG 40006; "American Concert Band Masterpieces"
> Eastman Symphonic Wind Ensemble, Frederick Fennell, conductor.

Reviews

Grunfeld, Frederic V. *HF* October 1954, p. 82.   [Henn B83d]

Lyons, L. *ARG* February 1954, p. 200.   [Henn B83e]

NR February 1954, p. 15.

Schonberg, Harold C. *NYT* February 21, 1954, sec. 2, p. 9.

Reissued: Telarc 10043

Reviews

Bauman, John. *Fa* July–August 1979, p. 129.   [Henn B83a]

Payne, Ifan. *ARG* September 1979, p. 53.   [Henn B83f]

Not currently available on CD

Choral Music

The Lovers, Op. 43

571.   Koch International Classics KIC 7125

> Winner at 35th Annual Grammy Awards (Classical): Best Contemporary
> Composition for 1992.
> Dale Duesing, baritone; Chicago Symphony Orchestra and Chorus;
> Andrew Schenk, conductor. (With *Prayers of Kierkegaard,* same orches-
> tral and choral forces, but with Sarah Reese as soprano soloist.)

Reviews

Headington, Christopher. *Gr* March 1992, p. 92.

Linkowski, Allen. *ARG* July–August 1992, p. 88.

Luten, C. J. *ON* January 30, 1993, p. 36.

Salzman, Eric. *StR* June 1992, p. 97.

Simmonds, Walter. *Fa* July–August 1992, p. 110.

Prayers of Kierkegaard, **Op. 30**
572.   Louisville LS 763
         Gloria Capone, soprano; Chorus of the Southern Baptist Theological Sem-
         inary, Richard Lin, director; Louisville Symphony Orchestra, Jorge
         Mester, conductor.

Reviews

Hall, David. *StR* January 1979, p. 94.   [Henn B20h]

Simmons, Walter. *Fa* November–December 1978, p. 16.   [Henn B20v]

Reissued on CD: Albany Troy 021-2

Reviews

Miller, Karl. *ARG* July–August 1990, p. 63.

Simmons, Walter. *Fa* May–June 1990, p. 110.

Reincarnations, **Op. 16**
573.   Cook Laboratories 1092
         On file at American Academy and Institute of the Arts
         "Sounds of Our Times" Hufstader Singers, Robert Hufstader, conductor.

Reissued: Cook 11312

Reviews

LJ October 1, 1953, p. 1,676.

A Stopwatch and an Ordnance Map, **Op. 15**
574.   Vanguard VRS 1065 and VSD 2083
         Symphony of the Air, Vladimir Golschmann, conductor; with Robert
         Decormier Chorale.

Reviews

Finkelstein, Alfred. *HF* July 1961, p. 49.

Hall, David. *HSR* June 1961, p. 61.   [Henn B5e]

Harvey, Trevor. *Gr,* August 1968, p. 272.

Hughes, Allen. *NYT* April 30, 1961, sect. 2, p. 21.

Salzman, Eric. *HSR* October 1966, p. 77.   [Henn B5g]

Reissued on CD: Vanguard Classics OVC 4016 (1991)

Reviews

Gutman, David. *Gr* August 1992, p. 69.

Simmons, Walter. *Fa* November–December 1991, p. 253.

Currently on CD: Vanguard VC 123

Vocal Music

Complete Songs of Samuel Barber

575. Deutche Gramophone DG 435 867-2
"Secrets of the Old" Cheryl Studer, soprano; Thomas Hampson, baritone; John Browning, piano.

Reviews

Ashby, Arved. *ARG* September 10, 1994, p. 132.

B., L.S. *ON* August 1994, p. 51.

Simmons, Walter. *Fa* January–February 1994, p. 133.

Andromache's Farewell, **Op. 39**
576. Columbia Col. ML 5912 and MS 6512
Martina Arroyo, soprano; New York Philharmonic, Thomas Schippers, conductor.
Recorded April 9, 1963.

Reviews

Ericson, Raymond. *NYT* November 10, 1963, sect. 2, p. 14.   [Henn B26d]

Flanagan, William. *HStR* February 1964, p. 86.   [Henn B26e]

Shupp, Enos, E. Jr. *NR* January 1964, p. 3.   [Henn B26j]

Reissued on CD: Sony Masterworks Portrait MPK 46727

Review

Gutman, David. *Gr* May 1994, p. 88.

Dover Beach, **Op. 3**
577. Victor 8898 (78 RPM)
Samuel Barber, baritone; The Curtis String Quartet, Jascha Brodsky, Charles Jaffe, violins; Max Aronoff, viola; Orlando Cole, cello. Recorded May 13, 1935.

Reviews

Ellsworth, p. 62.

Hall, David. *RB* p. 282.

Reissued: RCA Victor LCT 1158

Review

Hinton, James Jr. *HF* January 1956, p. 128.   [Henn B86h]

Reissued: New World Records, NW 229

Reissued on CD: PHS 49

Reviews

Guttman, David. *Gr* October 1991, p. 152-3.

Harrison, Max. *Gr* June 1983, p. 128.   [Henn B86g]

578.   Columbia Masterworks CSP/CKS 7131 (1968)
          Dietrich Fischer-Dieskau (baritone), The Juilliard String Quartet: Robert
          Mann and Earl Carlyss, violins; Raphael Hillyer, viola; Claus Adam, cello.
          Recorded April 8, 1967.

Reviews

Clark, Robert. *HSR* October 1968, p. 109.   [Henn B86a]

Jones, Robert. *NYT* August 18, 1968, sec. 2, p. 24.   [Henn B86j]

Kolodin, Irving. *SR* July 27, 1968, p. 108.   [Henn B86m]

Osborne, Conrad L. *HF* November 1968, p. 108.   [Henn B86n]

Reissued: CBS 61898

Reissued on CD: Sony Masterworks Portrait MPK 46727

Reviews

Gutman, David. *Gr* October 1991, p. 152-3.

Tuska, Jon. *Fa* November–December 1992, p. 114.

Hermit Songs, **Op. 2**
579.   CD RCA Gold Seal 09026-61983-2
          Leontyne Price, soprano; Samuel Barber, piano.
          Live performance of Library of Congress concert, October 30, 1953; not
          released until 1992.

Reviews

Loomis, George W. *ARG* September–October 1994, p. 96.

580.   Columbia Col ML 4988
       Leontyne Price, soprano; Samuel Barber, piano.
       Recorded November 19, 1954; first professional recording

Reviews

Berger, Arthur. *SR* August 27, 1955, p. 39.   [Henn B33d]

Broder, Nathan. *MQ* October 1955, p. 551.   [Henn B33e]

Ellsworth, p. 62.   [Henn B33g]

Frankenstein, Alfred. *HF* September 1955, p. 57.   [Henn B33i]

Haggin, B. H. *Na* August 8, 1955, p. 122.   [Henn B33k]

Schonberg, Harold C. *NYT* July 10, 1955, sec. 2, p. 12.   [Henn B33v]

Reissued: Odyssey 32 16 0230

Reviews

Davis, Peter G. *HF* November 1968, p. 122.   [Henn B33f]

Miller, Philip L. *ARG* December 1968, p. 282.   [Henn B33q]

Schonberg, Harold C. *NYT* July 10, 1955, sec. 2, p. 12.   [Henn B33v]

Reissued on CD: Sony Masterworks Portrait MPK 46727 and Sony 60899

Reviews

Gutman, David. *Gr* October 1991, p. 132.

Loomis, George W. *ARG* September–October 1994, p. 96.

Luten, C. J. *ARG* November–December 1999, p. 90.

Knoxville: Summer of 1915, Op. 24

581.   Columbia ML-2174 (with Firkusny *Excursions)*
       Eleanor Steber, soprano; Dumbarton Oaks Orchestra, William Strickland,
       conductor.
       Recorded November 7, 1950.

Reviews

Canby, Edward Tatnall. *SR* May 12, 1951, p. 36.

Ellsworth, p. 62.   [Henn B36g]

Kolodin, Irving. *The Guide* Vol. 1, *Orchestral Music,* p. 17.

Miller, Philip L. *The Guide* Vol. 2, *Vocal Music,* p. 29.

"Vocal," *NR* May 1951, p. 13.   [Henn B36oo]

Reissued: Columbia Col ML 5843

On file at American Academy and Institute of the Arts

Reviews

Daniel, Oliver. *SR* September 29, 1962, p. 47.   [Henn B36b]

Flanagan, William. *HSR* July 1963, p. 56.   [Henn B36k]

Haggin, B. H. *New Rep* June 29, 1963, p. 26.   [Henn B36q]

Kolodin, Irving. *SR* May 25, 1963, p. 50.   [Henn B36t]

Kupferberg, Herbert. *At* July 1962, p. 121.   [Henn B36u]

Osborne, Conrad L. *HF* November 1963, p. 82.   [Henn B36z]

Reissued: "Legendary Performances." Odyssey 32 16 0230 (1968)

Reviews

Davis, Peter G. *HF* November 1968, p. 122.   [Henn B36c]

Miller, Philip L. *ARG* December 1968, p. 282.   [Henn B36x]

Reissued on CD: Sony Masterworks Portrait MPK 46727 and Sony 60899

Reviews

Danker, Laura. *AM* Spring 1995, p. 120–124.

Gutman, David. *Gr* October 1991, p. 152.

582.   RCA LSC 3062
       Leontyne Price, soprano; New Philharmonia Orchestra, Thomas Schip-
       pers, conductor. Recorded June 1–2, 1968.

Reviews

Ericson, Raymond. *NYT* March 30, 1969, sect. 2, p. 30.   [Henn B36h]

Flanagan, William. *StR* June 1969, p. 76.   [Henn B36j]

Osborne, Conrad L. *HF* June 1969, p. 82.   [Henn B36bb]

Porter, Andrew. *Gr* August 1969, p. 302.   [Henn B36cc]

Reissued on CD RCA Gold Seal 09026-61983-2

"Leontyne Price Sings Barber"

Reviews

Loomis, George W. *ARG* September–October 1994, p. 96.

Schillaci, Daniel. *New West* April 1981, p. 118.   [Henn B36jj]

Mélodies passagères

583. New World Records NW 229
      "Songs of Samuel Barber and Ned Rorem"
      Pierre Bernac, baritone; Francis Poulenc, pianist.
      Originally recorded February 15, 1952, a few days after their Town Hall
      performance.
      Not currently available on CD

Nuvoletta

584. RCA Gold Seal 09026-61983
      Leontyne Price, soprano; Samuel Barber, piano.
      Live performance of Library of Congress concert, October 30, 1953; not
      released until 1992.

585. Lyrichord LL83
      "Songs to Texts of James Joyce"
      Patricia Neway, soprano; Robert Colston, piano.
      On file at American Academy and Institute of the Arts

Reviews

Miller, Philip L. *ARG* June 1960, p. 857.

Salzman, Eric. *NYT* June 19, 1960, sect. 2, p. 16.

Starkie, Walter. *SR* March 26, 1960, p. 47.   [Henn B46g]

Not currently available on CD

Chamber Music

Sonata for Violoncello and Piano, **Op. 6**

586. Concert Hall Society CH-B1 (4 78 RPM)
      Raya Garbousova, cello; Erich-Itor Kahn, piano.

Reissued: Concert Hall Society CH 1092

Reviews

"Chamber Music," *NR* August 1951, p. 6.   [Henn B90e]

Ellsworth, p. 62.

Frankenstein, Alfred. *HF* Spring 1952, p. 55.   [Henn B90j]

Reed, Peter Hugh. *ARG* January 1948, p. 154.   [Henn B90u]

Schonberg, Harold C. *Guide* Vol. 3, *Chamber and Solo,* p. 22.

Reissued on CD: PHS 49

587.   Orion ORS 7297
       Lucille Greco, cello; Mary Mark Zeyen, piano.
       On file at American Academy and Institute of the Arts

Review

Shupp, Enos, E. *NR* March 1973, p. 7.   [Henn B90x]

588.   Stradivari STR 602
       George Ricci, cello; Leopold Mittman, piano.
       On file at American Academy and Institute of the Arts

Reviews

Berger, Arthur. *SR* January 26, 1952, p. 54.

H[arman] C[arter], *NYT* November 18, 1951, sec. 2, p. 6.

Schonberg, Harold C. *Guide to LP* Vol. 3, p. 21-22.

"Some Chamber Works." *ARG* December 1951, p. 107.

String Quartet, **Op. 11**

589.   Stradivari STR 602
       Stradivari String Quartet: Arnold Eidus, Louis Graeler, violins; David
       Mankowitz, viola; George Ricci, cello.
       On file at American Academy and Institute of the Arts

Reviews

Berger, Arthur. *SR* January 26, 1952, p. 54.

H[arman] C[arter], *NYT* November 18, 1951, sec. 2, p. 6.

Schonberg, Harold C. *Guide to L P* Vol. 3, p. 21-22.

"Some Chamber Works." *ARG* December 1951, p. 107.

Summer Music, Op. 31
590. Concert-Disc CM 2161 and CS 216
      New York Woodwind Quintet: Samuel Baron, flute; Jerome Roth, oboe; David Glazer, clarinet; Arthur Weisberg, bassoon; John Barrows, French horn.

Reviews

Bookspan, Martin. *HSR* March 1960, p. 99.   [Henn B92b]

Frankenstein, Alfred. *HF* January 1960, p. 68.   [Henn B92e]

Salzman, Eric. *NYT* December 13, 1959, sec. 2, p. 18.   [Henn B92p]

Reissued on CD: Boston Skyline BSD137

591. Columbia Col ML5441 and MS 6114
      Philadelphia Woodwind Quintet: Robert Cole, flute; Anthony Gigliotti, clarinet; John de Lancie, oboe; Sol Schoenbach, bassoon; Mason Jones, French horn.
      On file at American Academy and Institute of the Arts

Reviews

Cohn, Arthur. *ARG* May 1960, p. 714.   [Henn B92c]

Hall, David. *HSR* May 1960, p. 65.   [Henn B92g]

Kolodin, Irving. *SR* March 26, 1960, p. 52.   [Henn B92h]

O., W. A. *NR* April 1960, p. 7.   [Henn B92m]

Salzman, Eric. *NYT* June 19, 1960, sect. 2, p. 16.   [Henn B92o]

Piano Music

592. Musicmaster 67122-2-C
      "Complete Solo Piano Music," John Browning, piano.
      Reissued on CD: Helios CDH 88016

Ballade, Op. 48
593. VAIA 1146
      "Van Cliburn Retrospective Series"
      Stephen de Groote, piano.
      Recorded in 1977, but not issued until early 2000.

Excursions, **Op 20**
594.   RCAV (Red Seal) 62644 (The Private Collection, Vol. 2.)
        Vladimir Horowitz, piano.
        Live performance, March 28, 1945 (never before released)
        Reissued on CD: Enterprise (Piano Library Series) ENT PL 239

595.   Columbia ML 2174
        Rudolf Firkusny, piano (with Steber's *Knoxville*).

Reviews

Canby, Edward Tatnall. *SR* May 12, 1951, p. 36.

Gr Sh May 1951, p. 1.   [Henn B94ml

Richie, Donald. *ARG* April 1951, p. 280.   [Henn B94n]

Schonberg, Harold C. *Guide to LP* Vol. 3, *Chamber and Solo,* p. 21.

"Vocal." *NR* May 1951, p. 13.   [Henn B94r]

Not currently available on CD

596.   Col ML5639, MS 6239
        Andre Previn, piano.
        On file at American Academy and Institute of the Arts

Reviews

Ericson, Raymond. *NYT* May, 28, 1961, sec. 2, p. 15.

Frankenstein, Alfred. *HF* August 1961, p. 57.   [Henn B94h]

Hall, David. *HSR* August 1961, p. 60.

Kolodin, Irving. *SR* May 27, 1961, p. 44.

Shupp, Enos, E. Jr. *NR* May 1961, p. 15.

Interlude (no opus no.)
See Browning, "Complete Solo Piano Music," Item 592 above; previously unrecorded.

Nocturne, **Op. 33**
597.   Golden Crest CR 4065
        "American Encores from a Russian Tour" (1963)
        Grant Johannsen, piano.
        On file at American Academy and Institute of the Arts

Review

Rich, Alan. *NYT* August 18, 1963, sec. 2, p. 10.

Piano Sonata, Op. 26
598.   RCA Victor LM 1113
         Vladimir Horowitz, piano.
         Recorded, May, 15, 1950.

Reviews

Ellsworth, p. 62

Schonberg, Harold C. *Chamber and solo,* p. 22.   [Henn B98sss]

Schonberg, Harold C. *Gr* March 1951, p. 219.   [Henn B98uuu]

Reissued: RCA Red Seal ARM 1 2952 and "The Horowitz Collection" RCA VLD 7021

Reviews

Ericson, Raymond. *NYT* August 18, 1963, sec. 2, p. 11.

Goldsmith, Harris. *HF* October 1963, p. 145.   [Henn B98aa]

Kagan, Susan. *Fa* May–June 1979, p. 126.

Kammerer, Rafael. *ARG* September 1963, p. 15.

Offergeld, Robert. *HSR* November 1963, p. 57.

Salter, Lionel. *Gr* December 1963, p. 282.   [Henn B98qqq]

Shupp, Enos E., Jr. *NR* October 1963, p. 12.

Reissued on CD: RCA Gold Seal 60377-2-RG

Review

Rabinowitz, Peter J. *Fa* January–February 1991, p. 278.

Gr 7/91 p. 54

599.   Artia MK 1513
         Daniel Pollack, piano.
         On file at American Academy and Institute of the Arts

Reviews

Frankenstein, Alfred. *HF* January 1961, p. 11.   [Henn B98v]

Hall, David. *HFS* February 1961, p. 62.   [Henn B98dd]

Lancaster, J. B. *ARG* December 1960, p. 303.   [Henn B98ccc]

Reissued on CD: Naxos 559015

Review

Young, John Bell. *ARG* September-October 1999, p. 101.

Souvenirs, **Op. 28 (two-piano version)**
600.   Columbia 4855
        Arthur Gold and Robert Fizdale, pianos.
        Recorded August 15, 1952.

Reviews

Berger, Arthur. *SR* April 24, 1954, p. 57.   [Henn B78b]

Ericson, Raymond. *HF* July 1954, p. 54.   [Henn B78d]

Luten, C. J. *ARG* May 1954, p. 284.   [Henn B78j]

Schonberg, Harold, C. *Chamber and Solo,* p. 22.   [Henn B78p]

Schonberg, Harold, C. *NYT* May 2, 1954, sec. 2, p. 9.   [Henn B78q]

NR May 1954, p. 15.

VIDEOGRAPHY

Commercially Available Videotapes

The following is a list of videotapes that may have been produced for network television broadcast, but have been packaged for commercial release. As with audio recordings, one or more of them may go out of print at any time and may be re-released under a different label. The categories remain the same as in all previous chapters, even though many works are now choreographed as dances.

Operas and Ballets

Medea (Cave of the Heart): **complete**
601.   **An evening of dance and conversation with Martha Graham**
        Video Arts International, 1984.
        Originally telecast as part of PBS *Great Performance Series:* "Dance in America," December 14, 1984. (Same as Item 611.)
        85 minutes, color

Includes complete performance of *Cave of the Heart,* with Takako Asakawa as Medea, Donlin Foreman as Jason, Jacqulyn Buglisi as victim, and Jeanne Ruddy as chorus. Set design by Isamu Noguchi. As part of her introduction, Graham discusses her interpretation of the Medea legend. The other two dances are: *Errand into the Maze* and *Acts of Light.*

Medea: **Excerpt "Medea's Dance of Vengeance"**
602.   **Martha Graham Dance Company**
       nonesuch Recording
       90 minutes, color
       Originally telecast on PBS *Great Performance Series:* "Dance in America," on April 7, 1976. Same as Item 612 at the Museum of Television and Radio.
       Danced by Takako Asakawa as Medea; other dances include: *Diversion of Angels, Lamentation, Frontier, Adorations,* and *Appalachian Spring.* Recorded February 1976 in Nashville, Tennessee.

603.   **American Masters: Martha Graham: The Dancer Revealed**
       Kultur International Films, Ltd., c. 1994.
       Originally telecast, May, 5, 1994 on PBS as part of the *American Masters* series.
       60 minutes, color

"Medea's Dance of Vengeance" from *Cave of the Heart* danced by Takako Asakawa as Medea; (same excerpt as Item 602); Same program as Item 613 at Museum of Television and Radio.

604.   *Vanessa*
       Lyric Distribution Video, 1978.
       Originally telecast on PBS on January 31, 1979. Co-production of South Carolina Educational Network and WNET 13, New York; Taped at the Spoleto Festival U.S.A. in the summer of 1978.
       Cast: Johanna Meier as Vanessa; Catherine Ciesinski as Erika; Henry Price as Anatol; Orchestra of the Spoleto Festival U.S.A., Christopher Keene, musical director and conductor.

Orchestral

Adagio for Strings
605.   **The Maryinsky Ballet St. Petersburg mixed bill**
       Kultur International Films Ltd., video, 1991.

Among the several ballets presented by the former Kirov Ballet company is a dance version of Barber's *Adagio for Strings*, with choreography and costumes by Oleg Vinogradov, the orchestra conducted by Victor A. Feotov. The dancers are not named.

Concerto for Piano

606.   **The Dancer and the Dance: Baryshnikov**
       Kultur International Films Ltd., Video, c. 1983.
       Originally produced for British Television's "The South Bank Show" for
       London Weekend Television (LWT).
       82 minutes, color

       "Configurations" is a dance set to Barber's *Piano Concerto,* with choreography by Choo San Goh, featuring Mikhail Baryshnikov and Marianna Tcherkassky as principle dancers, with the National Ballet of Washington. See also Item 615.

"Intermezzo" from *Vanessa*

607.   **Great Music from Chicago: Andre Kostelanetz Conducts the Chicago
       Symphony Orchestra**
       Facets Music on Video VHS SO5519

       Andre Kostelanetz conducts the "Intermezzo" from Barber's opera, *Vanessa* (along with Borodin's *Polovetsian Dances,* Chabrier's *Rhapsody Espagña* and Ravel's *Mother Goose Suite).*

Vocal Music

"Sure on this shining night"

608.   **Thomas Hampson: I hear America Singing**
       Kultur International Films Ltd., Video, 1997.
       Facets Music on Video VHS 30879
       Originally produced by WNET for PBS *Great Performances Series,* 1997.
       90 minutes, color

       All the songs on this program are by American composers, performed by various American singers. Thomas Hampson sings Barber's "Sure on this shining night," with John Browning at the piano (55 minutes into the program).

Archival Videotapes

The following items are television programs that are not, for the most part, commercially available for purchase but can be viewed as library material in the institutions listed below.

General

609. New York City: Museum of Television and Radio: T84:0079
      Camera Three: "Happy Birthday, Samuel Barber!" telecast on CBS, March 3, 1977, produced and directed by Roger Englander.

The program begins with the "Two-Step" from *Souvenirs,* played by James Tocco and Gilan Akbar Tocco, followed by a interview with Barber by James Tocco. Then there is a brief biography of Barber who discusses *Dover Beach* and plays an audiotape of his recording. Tocco plays the fugue from the Piano Sonata. The American String Quartet plays the "Adagio" movement from the String Quartet, Op. 11; Esther Hinds sings "Sleep Now," Op. 10, #2 accompanied by Barber at the piano; Barber and Tocco conclude the program with the "Tango" from *Souvenirs.*
      Also available at the Library of Congress.

Opera and Ballet

610. ***Antony and Cleopatra***
      New York City: Museum of Television and Radio: T 77:0548
      The Bell Telephone Hour: "The New Met: Count Down to Curtain," telecast on NBC, November 20, 1966.

Pre-opening activity at the new Metropolitan Opera House, culminating in the opening night premiere of *Antony and Cleopatra,* narrated by Joseph Julian. Included are production activities of Rudolph Bing; Leontyne Price works on her role; Barber and Schippers discuss the latest cuts and edits; Schippers rehearses Act III, scene 3; Zeffirelli works on the set; a brief conversation with Leontyne Price. The program concludes with the following excerpts: "Give me some music," a chorus of Antony's soldiers, and the final scene: "Give me my robe."

Medea (Cave of the Heart)

611. Library of Congress
      An Evening of Dance and Conversation with Martha Graham
      Originally telecast as part of PBS *Great Performance Series:* "Dance in America," December 14, 1984.
      The same as Item 601.

Medea's Dance of Vengeance

612. New York City: Museum of Television and Radio: T80:0271
Great Performances: "Dance in America," telecast on PBS, April 7, 1976.
The same as Item 602. Also available at the Library of Congress.

613. New York City: Museum of Television and Radio: T32:903
American Masters: "Martha Graham: The Dancer Revealed," telecast on
PBS, May 13, 1994.
Same as Item 603.

Orchestra

Concerto for Piano and Orchestra, Op. 38

614. New York Public Library: **Alvin Ailey American Dance Theater**
Videotape of rehearsal (rehearsal clothes), December 19–23, 1969; 24
minutes, black and white.

Poem (c. 8 minutes), a ballet, choreographed by Pauline Koner, to the second
movement of the Barber Piano Concerto, danced by "a man and a woman."
Although these roles are uncredited, the two dancers are likely to be George Faison and Linda Kent.

615. New York City: Museum of Television and Radio: T88:0168
South Bank Show: "Baryshnikov: The Dancer and the Dance, Part 2."
Created for London Weekend Television (LWT), telecast on PBS, Decem-
ber 12, 1983.
Same as Item 606.

Vocal Music

"Bessie Bobtail"

616. Boston Conservatory, Alphin Library.
An eclectic program of dance includes a work entitled "Prayers Don't
Help" choreographed by Lee U. Speno to Samuel Barber's song, "Bessie
Bobtail," with Ross Neill, singer, and Elizabeth Brant, pianist.

Piano

Excursions, **Op. 20**

617. New York City: Museum of Television and Radio: T82:0338

Westinghouse Presents (first in a series): "The Sound of the Sixties," hosted by John Daly, produced and directed by Dore Schary; telecast on NBC, October 9, 1961.

Among a great number and variety of segments, Andre Previn plays the fourth of Barber's *Excursions* (which he had recently recorded, see discography Item 596).

Souvenirs

618. New York City: Museum of Television and Radio: T90:0031
Bell Telephone Hour: "Adventures in Music" (premiere special), telecast on NBC, January 12, 1959.

The New York City Ballet dances to Barber's *Souvenirs,* adapted for television by Todd Bolender from his original ballet (see Item 68) with Gold and Fizdale, duo-pianists. It appears on the program after the Baird puppets, and soprano, Renata Tebaldi.

ARCHIVAL AUDIO TAPES

Orchestra

Adagio for Strings

619. New York City: Museum of Television and Radio: R84:0030
NBC Symphony Orchestra with Arturo Toscanini
Broadcast on NBC Radio, December 13, 1941.

Essay for Orchestra (No. 1)

620. New York City: Museum of Television and Radio: R84:0009
NBC Symphony Orchestra with Arturo Toscanini
Broadcast on NBC radio, January 24, 1942.

Third Essay for Orchestra, Op. 47

621. New York City: Museum of Television and Radio: R84:37
New York Philharmonic Concert, Pt. 1
Broadcast on September 14, 1978. Zubin Mehta, conductor; Martin Bookspan, commentator.

Vocal

Knoxville: Summer of 1915

622. New York City: Museum of Television and Radio: R84:92
New York Philharmonic Concert

Broadcast on CBS Radio, November 14, 1959, from Carnegie Hall (excerpt). The program includes Barber's Knoxville: Summer of 1915, with

Thomas Schippers, conductor, and Leontyne Price, soprano. It also contains an intermission interview with Samuel Barber and James Fassett. Also available at the Library of Congress: Motion Picture, Broadcasting, and Recorded Sound Division.

Archival Tapes at the Library of Congress

From 1945 through the 1990s there have been numerous concerts given at the Library of Congress, mainly chamber music programs, that have featured works by Barber. Because many of the performers have not recorded these works commercially, these tapes provide the only opportunity to hear their performances. The following tapes may be listened to in the Library of Congress's Recorded Sound Reference Center (Madison, LM113).

Library of Congress Concert Series

All concerts in this series were performed and recorded in the Coolidge Auditorium and are arranged in chronological order, with the featured Barber work listed. October 4, 1945

623. **Budapest String Quartet**
        2 sound tape reels
        Given under the auspices of Gertrude Clarke Whittall Foundation.
        String Quartet, Op. 11
        February 9, 1950

624. **Boston String Quartet**
        2 sound tape reels
        Presented under the auspices of the Elizabeth Sprague Coolidge Foundation.
        String Quartet, Op. 11
        October 25, 1951

625. **Budapest String Quartet**
        1 sound tape reel
        Presented under the auspices of Gertrude Clarke Whittall Foundation.
        String Quartet, Op. 11
        October 3, 1952

626. **New Music String Quartet**
        1 sound tape reel
        Presented under the auspices of Gertrude Clarke Whittall Foundation.
        String Quartet, Op. 11
        November 28, 1952

627. **Hufstader Singers**
     1 sound tape reel
     Given under the auspices of the Elizabeth Sprague Coolidge Foundation.
     Robert Hufstader, conductor. The concert of vocal chamber music by
     American Composers is in honor of the Conference of the American Stud-
     ies Association.
     Reincarnations, Op. 16
     March 6, 1953

628. **Leonard Rose, cellist**
     1 sound tape reel
     Presented under the auspices of the Gertrude Clarke Whittall Foundation.
     Sonata for Violoncello and Piano, Op. 6
     March 1, 1957

629. **New York Woodwind Quintet**
     1 sound tape reel
     Given under the auspices of Gertrude Clarke Whittall Foundation.
     Summer Music, Op. 31
     March 11, 1960

630. **Philadelphia Woodwind Quintet**
     1 sound tape reel
     Presented under the auspices of the Gertrude Clarke Whittall Foundation.
     Summer Music, Op. 31
     April 21, 1961

631. **Budapest String Quartet**
     2 sound tape reels
     Given under the auspices of the Gertrude Clarke Whittall Foundation.
     String Quartet, Op. 11
     December 10, 1976

632. **Cleveland Quartet**
     2 sound tape reels
     Presented under the auspices of Elizabeth Sprague Coolidge Foundation.
     String Quartet, Op. 11
     March 10, 1978

633. **Emerson String Quartet**
     2 sound tape reels
     Given under the auspices of the Elizabeth Sprague Coolidge Foundation.

Dover Beach, Op. 3 with Thomas Beveridge, baritone.
August 8, 1980

634. **Concert Soloists of Wolf Trap**
2 sound tape reels
Concert given under the auspices of the McKim Fund in the Library of Congress.
Barber's Sonata for Violoncello and Piano Op. 6 (1932), with Charles Curtis, cello, and Earl Wild, piano.
October 8–9, 1981

635. **Julliard String Quartet**
4 sound tape reels
Edited for broadcast of October 9, 1981
Performed under the auspices of the Gertrude Clarke Whittall Foundation.
Barber's *Dover Beach*, Op. 3, with the Julliard String Quartet and William Parker, baritone.
June 25, 1982

636. **Library of Congress Music Division Concert**
2 sound tape reels
Songs sung in English and German
The program is part of the Library of Congress Summer Chamber Festival, 1982. "Three Songs" for voice and piano, Op. 45 with Barbara Shuttleworth, soprano, William Black, piano.
March 10, 1984

637. **Henry Herford, song recital**
2 sound tape reels
Performed under auspices of the Da Capo Fund and the Gertrude Clarke Whittall Foundation.
Mélodies passagères, with Robin Bowman, pianist.
May 11, 1984

638. **Festival of American Chamber Music, Paul Sperry recital**
2 sound tape reels
Performed under the auspices of the Elizabeth Sprague Coolidge Foundation, the Da Capo Fund, the McKim Fund, the Norman P. Scala Memorial Fund, and the Gertrude Clarke Whittall Foundation.
Barber's *Despite and Still* is part of a recital called "An American Sampler: Then, Now and In Between." Later broadcast in 1992 by American Public Radio as a program entitled "Friends of Dr. Burney," part of the

"Americana" Series, program 23, part 1.
April 28, 1984

639. **Library of Congress Music Division Concert: "The Saturday Series"**
2 sound tape reels
Under the auspices of the Elizabeth Sprague Coolidge Foundation, the
Gertrude Clarke Whittall Foundation, the McKim Fund, and the Da Capo
Fund in the Library of Congress.
Dover Beach, Op. 3, with Sanford Sylvan, baritone; Isodore Cohen, Mei-
Chen Lioa, violins; Ah Ling Neu, viola; Robie Brown Dan, cello.
May 2, 1986

640. **Alexander String Quartet**
2 sound tape reels
Under the auspices of the Elizabeth Sprague Coolidge Foundation, the Da
Capo Fund, the Serge Koussevitzky Music Foundation, the Norman P.
Scala Memorial Fund, and the Gertrude Clarke Whittall Foundation. Part
of the Festival of American Chamber Music, May 2, 1986. String Quartet,
Op. 11

641. **Dawn Upshaw (Naumburg Award Winner)**
2 sound tape reels
Under the auspices of the Da Capo Fund and the Naumburg Foundation.
"Sure on this shining night," with Margo Garrett, piano.
December 10, 1988

642. **1991–1992: Chamber Music by Samuel Barber, Program I, part 2**
1 sound tape reel (58 minutes, 39 seconds)
Produced by Anne McLean for the Music Division and the Recording Lab-
oratory of the Library of Congress for broadcast in 1992 by American Public Radio.

The program features various performances of Barber's works, collected
from earlier programs in the Library of Congress series: "O waly waly," with
Samuel Barber, voice and piano (recorded late 1930s); String Quartet, with the
Budapest String Quartet, (recorded October 25, 1951; see Item 625); an excerpt
from Barber interview with James Fassett (recorded by CBS in June of 1949; see
Item 622); A performance of *Excursions* (solo piano arrangement) with James
Tocco, pianist (recorded October 30, 1987); excerpts from another Barber inter-
view; a performance of *Nuvoletta,* with Leontyne Price, soprano, Samuel Barber,
piano (recorded October 30, 1953; see Item 584); *Summer Music,* with the New
York Woodwind Quintet (recorded March 1, 1957; see Item 629).

Marlboro Music Festival

Four concerts performed at the Marlboro Music Festival during the 1990s, all of which feature performances of Barber's *Dover Beach,* have been recorded and are available for listening at the Library of Congress. Taped in Marlboro, Vermont, from 1991 to 1996.

643. July 7, 1991
      Sound cassette RGA 5088
      With Paul Rowe, baritone; Kerry McDermott, Renée Jolles, violins; Daniel Foster, viola; and Peter Wiley, cello.

644. July 28, 1993
      Sound cassette RGA 5544
      With André Solomon-Glover, baritone; Miranda Cuckson, Catherine French, violins; Caroline Coade, viola; and David Soyer, cello.

645. August 10, 1994
      Sound cassette RGA 3822-3833
      With Vincent Stringer, bass-baritone; Leila Josefowicz, Andrew Kohji Taylor, violins; Susan Dubois, viola; and Judith Serkin, cello.

646. July 31, 1996
      Sound cassette RGA 4891-4892
      With Robert Sapolsky, baritone; Yoon-Kyung Kwon, Hilary Hahn, violins; Philip Naegele, viola; and Kristina Reiko Cooper, cello.

America in Concert

Several programs from the radio series "America in Concert" feature performances of works by Barber. The program, a nationally syndicated one-hour program, is described as "a sampler of chamber and symphonic music as it is being performed in communities throughout the United States."

647. Program #3
      RWA 5367 (1979): one tape reel 7 1/2 ips.
      Medea's Meditation and Dance of Vengeance performed by the Arkansas Symphony Orchestra, Kurt Klippstatter, conductor.

648. Program #27
      RWA 5391 (1979): one tape reel 7 1/2 ips.
      Knoxville: Summer of 1915 performed by the Midland Symphony Orchestra, Charlene Peterson, soprano, Don Jaeger, conductor.

649. Program #112
      RWA 5476(c. 1980): one tape reel 7 1/2 ips.
      Adagio for Strings performed by the Community Arts Symphony, Gordon Parks, conductor.

650. Program #161
      RWA 8101 (1980s): one tape reel 7 1/2 ips.
      Concerto for Violin performed by the Midland-Odessa Symphony and Chorale, Mark Peskanov, violin; Thomas Hohstadt, conductor.

651. Program #210
      RWB 0319 (1980s): one tape reel 7 1/2 ips.
      Medea's Meditation and Dance of Vengeance performed by the Fort Lauderdale Symphony Orchestra, Emerson Buckley, conductor.

Chapter 5. Holographs and Other Manuscripts

Most of Barber's manuscripts are housed in the Library of Congress, but the original copies are no longer available to the general public. However, copies of these manuscripts (of published works at least) are now contained on microfilm. Manuscripts of unpublished works are still uncatalogued and not yet on microfilm. Other manuscripts and copies are housed at the Sibley Library of the Eastman School of Music, which are on loan to them from G. Schirmer publishers. These are copies that Barber sent to the Schirmer editors to make the final printed versions, and may be somewhat different from the versions found at the Library of Congress. The University of Pennsylvania also has an archive of scores in its Eugene Ormandy collection—printed scores with bowings, notes, etc., written in by Ormandy and some of the players in the Philadelphia Orchestra. While not as significant, perhaps, as original manuscripts, these nevertheless might be of interest to future Barber scholars. Manuscripts from Barber's youth can be found at the Chester County Historical Society. A few other sources are the New York Public Library, Curtis Institute of Music (not really accessible), the Marian Anderson Collection at the University of Pennsylvania, and the Pierpont Morgan Library (accessible with written permission). I have made no attempt to list and/or describe some of the manuscripts that are in private collections, because most scholars would not usually be allowed access to them.

The following list is meant as a general inventory only, giving the name of the work, the item number, and a brief description of the contents. I have not attempted to compare, contrast, or give an historical chronology of these documents. Barbara Heyman promises such a study in her forthcoming thematic catalogue.

LIBRARY OF CONGRESS

Music 1907

(unless otherwise listed) This is the collection of Barber manuscripts now photographed on four reels of microfilm. What the microfilm gains in accessibility it loses, however, in some details, e.g. various additional markings in color pencil.

Items in this set are alphabetical by title, up through item 33 after which the list seems to have no logical organization. When a facsimile exists in accessible format, e.g. book or dissertation (usually the ones by Heyman: Items 257 [diss.] and 258 [book]), it is listed after the item.

Reel 1

Item 1   *Ad bibinem cum me rogaret ad cenam* (c. 1943)
Holograph score, in pencil, for chorus SATB. Text adapted from Venantius Fortunatis. The composer's note about alterations in the words (p. 6).

Composed as a tribute to Carl Engel and published in the *Festscrift: A birthday gift for Carl Engel* (New York, Schirmer, 1943). Gift of G. Schirmer, Jan. 10, 1944.

Item 2   *Adventure* 1954
Score, 17 pages. In pencil on transparent paper; at end: Nov. 25 '54.

Facsimile of the first 14 measures are in Heyman, p. 346; see also Heyman diss., p. 535 for facsimile of mm. 36–44. At bottom of cover: gift of Samuel Barber, Dec. 29, 1965.

Item 3   *Andromache's Farewell*
A.   Score, in pencil, 33 pages.

B.   Preliminary sketches, 28 pages.

C.   Sketches for a piano-vocal score, 16 pages. Page of typed text with the note: "still to be composed." Gift of the composer, Dec. 23, 1966.

Item 4   *Capricorn Concerto*
A.   Score, holograph in pencil, on transparent paper. Pages 7–10 are missing. At end: Sept. 8, 1944.

B.   Holograph sketch in pencil, 11 pages.

Gift of the composer, Dec. 29, 1955. On the verso of the last page is a sketch for the golden anniversary canon for Sidney and Louise Homer.

Item 5   **Concerto for Violoncello**
Holograph score, 107 pages, in pencil. I: pp. 1–49; II: 50–60; III: 63–107. At end: Nov. 27, 1945. Capricorn. Gift of the composer, Dec. 28, 1954.

Item 6   *Excursions* 1944
A.   Holograph in ink on transparent paper. I: 4 pages; II: 3 pages; III: 4 pages, IV: 4 pages.

B.   Holograph sketches of 1st, 2nd, and 4th pieces, in pencil, 12 pages.

Dated at end: June 16, '44

Item 7 *Hermit Songs*
Holograph sketches in pencil, 42 pages. One page has the text "Do not say a word, Anatol," from *Vanessa*.

Item 8 *Hermit Songs*
Black-line print from copyist's manuscript with [composer's] additions and corrections in pencil, but does not say "composer's." The rhythm for "pity" is corrected from two equal eighths to a sixteenth and a dotted eighth-note. Tempos are added in pencil; fingerings in the third song and other performer indications suggest that this was the copy Barber played from to accompany Leontyne Price for their performance in Washington, D.C. at the Library on Oct. 30, 1953.

Item 9 *Knoxville: Summer of 1915*
A. Full score in pencil, 61 pages; At end: April 4, 1947.

B. Holograph in pencil of incomplete score without the words; with a few corrections and tempo indications added in a different hand. Gift of the composer, Dec. 28, 1956.

Item 10 *Knoxville: Summer of 1915*
Short (piano vocal) score in pencil, 20 pages, with some corrections. At end: April 4, 1947. Gift of the composer, Dec. 28, 1956. Facsimile starting at m. 146 in Heyman, p. 292.

Item 11 *Let down the bars, O death*
Holograph in pencil; in portfolio with the composer's *Reincarnations*. At end: Wolfgang June 25, '36. The beginning of a choral work on verso of leaf; unidentified, but likely to be "Mary Ruane" on a text by James Stephens.

Item 12 *Medea:* **Ballet Suite** ("Suite from the ballet" is crossed out)
Holograph score in pencil, 101 pages. Contains some corrections, often written above the staff. Gift of the composer, Dec. 30, 1957.

Item 13 *Medea's Meditation and Dance of Vengeance*
Holograph score in pencil, 52 pages. Tempo markings added in different color (?); some notes in margins. At end: "Rome, August '53." Gift of the composer, Dec. 23, 1966.

Item 14 *Mélodies passagères*
Holograph in pencil; 5 items; a few sketches appear between the songs.
At the end of each item:1: Jan. '50; 2: April 21 '51; 3: April 26 '51; 4: Feb. 16, '52; 5: Feb. 10, '58

Item 15   *Die Natali*
Holograph in pencil, called "first draft," but more like sketches. Many passages are crossed out. At end: Sept. 16 '60.

Item 16   *Silent Night*
For organ, arranged by the composer from *Die Natali.*
Holograph, in pencil, with pencil sketches included.

Item 17   *Nuvoletta*
Holograph in pencil, 8 pages. Almost like final copy. At end: Oct. 17 '47.

Item 18   *Prayers of Kierkegaard*
Holograph sketches. Also contains passages by and about Kierkegaard; quotes from the choral music of Handel *(Dettinger Anthem),* some sketches for *Hermit Songs,* and a note about the origins of *Souvenirs.*

Item 19   **Quartet, Strings Op. 11 Adagio movement**
Holograph in pencil, 14 pages. Still the second movement of the String Quartet; At end: Sept. 19 '36. St. Wolfgang. Gift of the composer, Dec. 28, 1954.

Item 20   *Adagio for Strings* **(arr.)**
Holograph in ink, 7 pages, now officially entitled *Adagio for Strings.* According to the typewritten copy of composer's letter (included) to Harold Spivacke (dated July 28, 1943), the red pencil markings on p. 5 were made by Arturo Toscanini. Gift of the composer, July 29, 1943. Facsimile in Heyman, p. 169.

Item 21   *Reincarnations*
Score (3 items) in ink on transparent paper. At end of

1.   St. Wolfgang. Aug. 8 '37 ("Mary Hines"): with some corrections

2.   Dec. 17 '40 ("Anthony O'Daly")

3.   Nov. 10 '40 ("The Coolun")

Also holograph sketches, in pencil (3 items). Items are usually in both Barber's hand and in copyist's hand. In portfolio with "Let down the bars, O death." Two facsimiles, both early and late versions, of "Coolin" mm. 14–20 in Heyman, p. 187.

Item 22   **Sonata for Piano**
Holograph in pencil, 31 pages. At end: June 1949. Also two copies of a black-line print edition of the work, with composer's additions and corrections in colored pencil (37 pages) and composer's penciled corrections for the holograph (1 page).

Barber suggests changing the meter from common time to cut time. In second movement he changes Presto to Allegro vivace e leggiero; and in third movement he changes Adagio to Adagio mesto. Facsimile of passage starting at m. 97 in Heyman, p. 305, with Barber's instruction to "insert the following." After this is the copyist's version with Barber's corrections incorporated.

Item 23   Songs (four orchestrated songs)
Holograph in pencil; 5 pages, without the words. "Nocturne," 2 pages; "Sure on this shining night," 4 pages; "I hear an army," 12 pages; "Monks and Raisins."

Item 24   Songs Op. 2
Holograph in ink of "With rue my heart is laden," 3 pages. At end: Jan. 25, 1928. (See also "The Daisies," Item 38.)

Item 25   Songs Op. 10
Three songs to poems from *Chamber Music* by James Joyce; 5 items, holograph in ink. Two versions of No. 1: the first with a one-measure introduction and the second with a four-measure introduction. No. 2 has an old ending crossed out and a new one added, There are two versions of No. 3, the first in pencil. At end of each item: 1: Nov. 21 '35 Rome; 2: Nov. 29 '35 Rome; 3: July 13 '36 St. Wolfgang.

Item 26   Songs Op. 13
Four songs for voice and piano, holograph in ink, on transparent paper. Corrections might be in Barber's hand, but it doesn't quite look like it. At end of: No. 1: 1937; No. 2: Sept. 1938; No. 3: Sept. 1938; No. 4: Feb. 11, 1940. Also holograph sketches of all four songs, in pencil.

Item 27   Songs Op. 18
"The queen's face on the summery coin."
In ink, on transparent paper; At end: Nov. 1942
Also holograph sketch, in pencil, 4 pages.

Item 28   *Souvenirs* Op. 28
A.   Holograph sketch, 1 page in pencil.

B.   Score in pencil.

C.   Black-line print with Barber's additions and corrections in colored pencil, 37 pages.

Reel 2

Item 29   *Souvenirs* Op. 28 arr. for orchestra
First a sketch, then a score (88 pages) in pencil, with corrections in red ink. One measure crossed out in "Schottische." The remaining movements are in the order III, V, and IV.

Item 30   *A Stopwatch and an Ordnance Map*
A.   Holograph score in pencil, 5 pages.

B.   Second version, with the addition of four horns, three trombones, and tuba.
       The score consists of the original printed score cut up and taped below; addi-
       tions, in pencil and ink. 7 pages.

Item 31   Symphony No. 2
Full score: I: 41 pages; II: 9 pages; III: 31 pages; in pencil on transparent paper.
Some pages are missing in Movement II. There are notes in margins of Move-
ment III. At end: Feb. 3, 1944

Item 32   *Summer Music*
Holograph in pencil with irregular pagination with corrections in red pencil or
ink. Dated November 5, 1955.
Facsimile in Heyman, p. 368; 4 mm. before [26]; also facsimile of later passage
[31] to [33] in Heyman diss., p. 564 and mm. 1–4, Heyman diss., p. 574.

Item 33   Three choruses "arranged by me from my songs"
Pencil manuscript of "Sure on this shining night" for SATB, 7 pages.
Pencil manuscripts of "Heaven-Haven"

a. SATB piano for rehearsal only, 3 pages.

b. for men's chorus a cappella, 3 pages.

c. for women's chorus a cappella, 3 pages.

Pencil manuscript for "Under the Willow Tree," SATB 10 pages.

Item 34   Concerto for Violin
Holograph in pencil; first page missing
I: p. 1–38; II: p. 39–53; III: p. 54–58.

Item 35   Sonata for Cello
Holograph; first three pages are missing; p. 5 scratched out. At end: Dec. 9, '32
       Facsimile of passage around m. 128, Heyman, p. 112 (ex. 51a), and second
movement, starting at m. 10, the first two measures of which is also in Scedrov
(Item 429), Appendix A, p. 79 as ex. 2.1. Scedrov, Appendix A, also contains the
following brief excerpts from the holograph score: p. 80 (ex. 2.6) first movement,
mm. 156–171; p. 82 (ex. 2.10) third movement, m. 35; p. 82 (ex. 2.11) third
movement, mm. 85–86; p. 83 (ex. 2.13) third movement, mm. 67–71; p. 83 (ex.
2.15) first movement, mm. 82–84; p. 84 (ex. 2.17), third movement, mm. 91–93;
and p. 85 (ex. 2.20) third movement, mm. 166–170. In his interview with Orlando

Cole, Scedrov explains the relationship between these passages and the eventual published score.

Item 36   *Serenade* for String Quartet
Holograph in pencil, 14 pages. At end: Jan. 1, 1929

Item 37   *The Virgin Martyrs*
A.   Holograph sketches, in pencil.

B.   Full copy, 5 pages.

Item 38   *The Daisies*
Holograph in pencil, one page: dated July 20, 1927.
Facsimile in Heyman, p. 48, is from the personal collection of Katherine Homer Fryer, not from the Library of Congress.

Item 39   *Dover Beach*
Holograph in pencil (or possibly in ink), 7 pages. Dated May 7, 1931
Facsimile of first page in Heyman, p. 97 (ex. 4.1); later passages, pp. 100 and 101.
Other, more extensive passages in Heyman diss., pp. 151–154 (ex. 4.4–4.7).

Item 40   *Toccata Festiva*
First draft, dated Feb. 13, 1960; short score, in pencil, 52 pages.
Some passages crossed out.

Item 41   *Second Essay*
Holograph, short score; first draft, incomplete; some passages crossed out.

Item 42   *Night Flight*
Holograph of first draft, short score; some passages crossed out.

Item 43   An Old Sketchbook, from c. 1933
Fragments and preliminary drafts of both later published compositions and abandoned pieces. Kreiling (Item 386) discusses some of these items in her dissertation, pp. 50–62. Much of the sketchbook is difficult to read and sort out.

pp. 5–10.   sketch: fragment later used in "Music for a Scene from Shelley." Heyman, p. 126 calls it "extensive material." Mm. 1–82, trumpet parts, mm. 34–42.

pp. 11–17.   sketches for songs: "I seize the sphering harp" (fragment from Blake's "Four Zoas") sketch: on Meleager's "Cold blows the winter wind" (J. A. Symond's translation = Kreiling, p. 56) and "Sadly, sadly, I passed the maid."

pp. 18–19. sketch for Symphony in One Movement

p. 20. "Earth, the air, the sun, the sea"

p. 23. "King David was a sorrowful man" sketch for a song on Walter de la Mare's poem, "King David" (10 measures, words and melody only)

p. 24–25. sketch for "Bessie Bobtail"

pp. 26–33. sketch: fragment later used in *First Essay* (this is probably for second essay, Heyman, p. 205), or this might be another sketch; three sketches: one called Essay II, another with the tempo "in quartet allegro." Also fragments of the Violin Concerto, Heyman, p. 205.

p. 34. "cover us with your"

pp. 36–37. sketch for passacaglia, Symphony in One Movement

p. 38. chart of themes in Sibelius's Seventh Symphony. Facsimile in Heyman, p. 141.

p. 44–51. Night Wanderers, crossed out

p. 53. draft: a song on Joyce's poem, "Strings in the earth and air" =Kreiling, pp. 78–79.

p. 56. fragments later used in Violin Concerto; mm. 1–9; facsimile, Heyman, p. 198.

pp. 58–61. "Good people keep the holy day" song on William Henry Davies's "The Beggar's Song"; facsimile in Heyman, p. 138.

p. 64. "come with me under my coat" sketch for "The Coolin' "

pp. 66–72. short score and draft of *Second Essay*

p. 72. sketch: fragment later used in *Vanessa*

p. 76. sketch for the new scherzo movement of Symphony in One Movement, four measures

pp. 79–88. blank

On the front lining paper and adjoining pages are various poems, including "Chinese poem by Croc-cki/X dynasty" and a German folk text. Also included are lists of books and music that Barber wanted to purchase.

Item 44   *Vanessa*
Pencil sketches, 345 pages. In different sets of manuscript notebooks in differing formats; Earlier version of "Must the winter come so soon" begins with the line, "Will the winter never end." See Menotti original libretto, Item 47.

Item 45   *Vanessa*
Short (piano vocal) score. Barber specifically calls for eighth notes in the vocal line to be beamed together "not in the old conventional way" (i.e. with separate flags). He emphatically states, "Please copy *as I have it*." For triplets, use bracket but not with a "3" under it. Some passages crossed out and some notes are in the margin. No date at the end. Act I: pp. 1–56; Act II: 1–77; includes "skating aria;" very little crossed out; no date at end; Act III: 1–47; no orchestral introduction because it is "not ready yet." At end: Summer, Sept. '56. Act IV: no Intermezzo. For the quintet, some notes to printer, indicating doublings for rehearsal. At end: Capricorn, April 7 (9?) '57.

Reel 3

Item 46   *Vanessa*
Reproduction of copyist's short (piano-vocal) score, c. 251 pages; with composer's corrections and additions; 2 leaves of holograph data; "I prefer lobster with oysters" crossed out. Stage directions added later. No "skating aria" in Act II; Act III, still no orchestral introduction. In a passage near the end of Act III, a correction in Barber's hand is taped over the copyist's measures. In the passage, "He will not be born," the "He" is crossed out, and "It" is added. A note at the end, saying something about 28 minutes on each side are possible, implies plans for a recording.

Item 47   *Vanessa*
First draft of Menotti's libretto, 40 leaves typed, mainly single spaced. Contains corrections and changes by both composer and librettist (often double spaced) e.g. "I shall dismiss him if he got lost" is changed to "I shall have him dismissed if they are lost." A few passages are handwritten. There is a whole new page of monologue for the doctor. Very few changes in Acts III and IV.

Item 48   *Vanessa*
Holograph, full score, in pencil c. 476 pages; p. 247 numbered twice, and two extra pages are inserted between 245 and 246. Tempo markings (in different color?) added; Act II: ice skating aria is present; some notes are written in the margin. Act III: orchestral introduction has been added. Act IV: now has the "Intermezzo" between the two scenes.

Item 49   Piano Concerto
Holograph sketches, 47 pages, beginning with slow movement. Then more complete versions of movements I (p. 25), III, (p. 29) and II (p. 37). Includes a list of recordings of works by Schoenberg, Berg, and Boulez.

Item 50   Piano Concerto
Short score, in pencil; I: 1–27; II: 1–15; one passage crossed out; note to copyist: reduce 2 staves to 1; III: 1–20.

Item 51   Piano Concerto
Full score; first two pages are missing; some pages are in copyist's hand; I: 1–64; II: 65–?; III: new pagination, 1–57. Facsimile in Heyman, p. 417.

Item 52   Chorale for Brass Choir
Holograph score, in pencil, 3 pages, brass score only; no words.
Later to become "Easter Chorale." It appears that Pack Browning's words needed to fit already existing melodic line.

Item 53   *Canzone* for flute and piano
Pencil manuscript, 4 pages, no corrections; Original title "Elegy" erased and "Canzone" (for Manfred) added. See Heyman, p. 413.

Item 54   *Mutations from Bach*
Holograph score, 11 pages; words from the original chorale are often inserted with the chorale melody. At end: 1967

Item 55   "Under the willow tree" from *Vanessa*
Full score, 20 pages.

[a] pencil manuscript, with piano accompaniment, 10 p.

[b] pencil manuscript; here called "Country Dance, from *Vanessa*" 17 numbered leaves, for orchestra only, no words; but a note indicates, "This may be performed with the addition of a mixed chorus."

Reel 4 (starts with a copy of item 55 above)

Item 56   *Antony and Cleopatra*
Short (piano-vocal) score, in pencil, a few pages bearing excerpts taken from proof sheets on which the composer made extensive corrections. Some passages are crossed out. Each scene has its own pagination. Act I: passage from printed score taped in at the end of the act. II: notes to Paul W. (copyist?); III: parts of printed score taped in.

Item 57   *Antony and Cleopatra*

Possibly a holograph, full score of Act I, in pencil; irregular paging with some pages missing.

Item 58   *Antony and Cleopatra*

Full score of Acts II and III. Old page 18 is crossed out with a new page to be inserted; after the two acts is an aria for Caesar ("What would you more?") in a different hand and in short score. At end: Capricorn Aug. 29 '66

Item 59   *Antony and Cleopatra*

A six-page orchestral passage using many of the motives presented throughout the opera.

Item 60   **"Give me some music" from** *Antony and Cleopatra*

Act I, scene 4, full score, concert version; in pencil; incomplete. The beginning looks like Barber's hand. The 18 pages are reproductions of holographs with annotations; also included is the Schirmer published score.

Item 61   **Symphony No. 1 in one movement**

Holograph score in pencil, 55 pages. Tempos and rehearsal numbers are in different pencil (possibly different color); The caption: "To Gian Carlo Menotti." At end: "Roquebrune Feb. 24–26, '36." Facsimiles of the endings of the allegro and scherzo sections in Heyman diss., p. 225.

Items 62   *Despite and Still*

Holograph of first draft, in pencil; some passages crossed out. At end: Santa Christina: I: June 1968; II: July 20; III: Aug. 3; IV: no date; V: Aug. 14.

Item 63   *Despite and Still*

Second draft, in pencil, with the dedication "To my friend Leontyne Price."
Second holograph, dated June 1968, of "A Last Song," transposed a half tone higher.

Item 64   *Despite and Still*

Pencil manuscript, 13 pages, for medium voice, but without "Solitary Hotel;" also includes published score.

Item 65   *Despite and Still*

Publisher's proofs, for both high and medium voices, 21 pages, with corrections and additions by the composer. Some fingerings are included.

Item 66   *Twelfth Night*

First holograph sketches, then a manuscript of the first draft, in pencil, 11 pages. Dated "Xmas '68."

Item 67   *Twelfth Night*
Holograph score, in pencil; 7 pages. Also includes published score. At end: Christina, '68.

Item 68   *To Be Sung on the Water*
Score of first draft, in pencil, 3 pages. At end: Dec. 14, '68.

Item 69   *To Be Sung on the Water*
Pencil manuscript, 6 pages, dated December 14, 1968.

Item 70   *Wondrous Love*
Holograph score, in pencil, 7 pages. With preliminary statement, "hymn was published in the 'Original Sacred Harp' Atlanta, Georgia, 1869." [This is not true, see Heyman, p. 401.] Gift of Samuel Barber, Dec. 29, 1966.

Item 71   *Nocturne* **for Piano**
Holograph score, in pencil, 4 pages.

Item 72   *A Hand of Bridge*
Holograph sketches (but more complete than the term "sketch" would imply), in pencil, 15 pages. Some passages are added. At end: Feb. 19, '59

Item 73   *A Hand of Bridge*
Holograph of short score, in pencil, 7 pages. At end: Feb. 19, '59

Item 74   *A Hand of Bridge*
Holograph of full score, in pencil, 51 pages, with some pages crossed out. At end: March 13 (?) '59

Music 1811

Manuscripts in the Koussevitzky Foundation Collection

Items 1–14   Contains autograph manuscripts of various composers, arranged alphabetically; Barber works are items 2–4.

Item 2   *Die Natali*
Holograph score, in pencil, 67 pages. On title page: Commissioned in celebration of the 75th season of the Boston Symphony Orchestra, Charles Munch, Music Director. Dedicated to the memory of Serge and Natalie Koussevitzky. Note: all instruments in the score are written in C. Some measures are crossed out. At end: Santa Christina. Sept. 3, '60.

Item 3   *Prayers of Kierkegaard*
Holograph orchestral score in pencil, 59 pages. No corrections, but rehearsal numbers are added in darker [blue?] pencil.

Item 4   *Prayers of Kierkegaard*
Holograph piano-vocal score in pencil, 31 pages. In caption: To the memory of Serge and Natalie Koussevitzky. At end: Jan. '54
Barber provides notes to editor: e.g. tenor clef must be changed to treble, throughout; at two places: reduce these 5 staves to 3.

Music 1571

only 1 item: *Hermit Songs*

Score in pencil, the title page in ink, 36 pages. Pages 2, 6, 10, 18, 22, 24, and 32 are blank. A few measures are crossed out in "Heavenly Banquet."

> On p. 3: To Elizabeth Sprague Coolidge
>
> On p. 4: I. At St. Patrick's Purgatory, Nov. 17, '52
>
> On p. 5: II. Church Bell at Night, Nov. 3, '52
>
> On p. 9: III. St. Ita's Vision, Jan. 9, '53
>
> On p. 14: IV. The Heavenly Banquet, Nov. 13, '52
>
> On p. 17: V. The Crucifixion, Oct. 26, '52
>
> On p. 21: VI. Sea-snatch, Jan. 6, '52
>
> On p. 23: VII. Promiscuity, Jan. 15, '53
>
> On p. 28: VIII. The Monk and his Cat, Feb. 16, '53
>
> On p. 31: IX. The Praises of God, Jan. 27, '53
>
> at end: X. The Desire for Hermitage, Jan. 15, '53

The following volumes have not yet been converted to microfilm and are not normally available to the public. An updated and more complete inventory will be in Heyman's thematic catalogue.

Earliest Compositions

1917–1919 (leather-bound volume), a bequest to the Library of Congress in 1984 from the Estate of Samuel Barber. See Heyman, p. 11; the volume includes the following:

> "Isabel" a song on a text by John Greenleaf Whittier. Facsimile in Heyman dissertation, p. 14.
>
> "Sadness" (for piano) in C minor, called Op. 1, No. 1. Facsimile in Broder, after p. 16.

"Melody in F" (for piano)

"Sometime" a song on a text by Eugene Field

"War Song" (for piano) Op. I, No. V; Facsimile in Heyman, p. 14.

"In the Firelight," a song on a text by Eugene Field; Facsimile in Heyman, p. 15.

"At Twilight"

"Lullaby"

"Largo"

"My Fairyland" Op. XIV

Box 1, **Libretto of *Antony and Cleopatra***
Working manuscript as devised by Barber and Franco Zeffirelli.
Box 3, **Manuscripts of Sam Barber, 1917–1927**
Includes "Three Essays for Piano"

School Compositions, 1927–1928

"Rounds for Three Voices," 1927.

Title	Author of text
"A Lament"	Percy Bisshe Shelley
"To Electra"	Robert Herrick
"Dirge: Weep for the world's wrong"	anon.
"Farewell"	Robert Louis Stevenson
"Not I"	Robert Louis Stevenson
"Of a rose is al Myn Song"	anon.
"Sunset"	Stevenson
"The Moon"	Shelley
"Sun of the Sleepless"	Lord Byron
"The Throstle"	Lord Alfred Tennyson
"When day is gone"	Robert Burns
"Late, late, so late"	Tennyson
"Three Chorale Preludes and Partitas" for organ	

Also includes various two- and three-voice fugues and assignments for the study of fugues by Mozart, Brahms, and Beethoven.

Barber's Orchestration Book c. 1930

Includes:

"Interludes for Piano" (1931–32). Facsimiles of parts of No. 1 (1931) in Heyman, p. 79, and Heyman diss., p. 117. Facsimile of parts of No. 2 (1932) in Heyman, p. 80, and Heyman diss., p. 118.

Fragment of a Piano Concerto (1930). Facsimile in Heyman diss., p. 114.

Various comments on jazz (for several quotations, see Heyman, p. 238).

Miscellaneous

Fadograph of a Yestern Scene

Facsimiles in Heyman diss., p. 750 (ex. 12.9) of mm. 1–5; p. 751 (ex. 12.10) of mm. 10–12 and 17–19; p. 75 (ex. 12. 11) of mm. 8–9; and p. 753 (ex. 12.12) of mm. 26–28.

Fantasie for Two Pianos in the Style of Joseph Haydn

Mentioned in Heyman, pp. 26, 30. Derived from his earlier "Allegretto in C" in Themes, 1920. See also "Sonata in Modern Form" at the Chester Country Historical Society.

A discussion in Heyman's dissertation, including two examples showing the first 18 measures of the first section (2.3/ 2.4) and two examples showing two passages from the andante con moto section (2.5/ 2.6).

"Horizon"

A positive photocopy of the manuscript, 10 numbered leaves; holograph in Heyman, p. 362 (ex. 13.2a) mm. 1–8; and p. 364 (ex. 13.3) 2 mm. after [18]

"Mother Goose Rhymes Set to Music."

"The Old Man from Jamaica"

"The Rockabye Lady"

"I love Little Pussy" [facsimile, Heyman, pp. 20–21]

"The Rose Tree" (Act I)

plus "Gypsy Dance" arranged for violin and piano. Facsimile of holograph, Heyman, pp. 22–23 (ex. 1.4)

"There's Nae Lark"

A song from 1927 on a text by Swinburne. Facsimile of mm. 1–15 in Heyman, p. 51.

LIBRARY OF CONGRESS HOLOGRAPHS BY ACQUISITION

Several manuscripts donated by Barber to the Library of Congress are listed in the *Quarterly Journal of Current Acquisitions,* and annotated in several short citations usually just called "Music." The first is by Richard S. Hill (1954 volume) and all the later ones are by Edward N. Waters, with the last reference being called, "Harvest of the Year."

November 1954   Vol. 12, p. 46

Autograph score of set of 10 *Hermit Songs* (Music 1907, Item 8). "Added to the list of works commissioned by the Coolidge Foundation during the founder's lifetime."

November 1955   Vol. 13, p. 26

Two autograph scores "of two of his best works": *Adagio for Strings* (Music 1907, Item 20) and the Concerto for Violoncello (Music 1907, Item 5). The cello concerto is described as being "well on its way to becoming a standard work in the limited repertoire available to cellists."

November 1956   Vol. 14, p. 10

The library received five holographs: *Capricorn Concerto* (Music 1907, Item 4) and four songs from different opus numbers. "A nun takes the veil" Op. 21; "The secrets of the old," Op. 13, no. 1 (Music 1907, Item 26); "Sure on this shining night," Op. 13, no. 2 (Music 1907, Item 26); and "With rue my heart is laden," Op. 2, no. 2 (Music 1907, Item 24). "These are highly significant additions to the collection of manuscripts of American composers."

November 1957   Vol. 15, p. 15

Three versions of *Knoxville: Summer of 1915.* (Music 1907 Items 9 and 10), "an important and popular work." The three versions together "form a highly significant unit in the output of one of America's major composers."

November 1958   Vol. 16, p. 9

"Pursuing a practice initiated some years ago, Samuel Barber . . . gave the library" the following four autographs: *Medea* Op. 23 (Music 1907, Item 12); *Nuvoletta* Op. 25 (Music 1907, Item 17); "Nocturne" Op. 13, No. 4 (Music 1907, Item 26); and "The Queen's face on the Summery Coin" Op. 18, No. 1 (Music 1907, Item 27).

November 1959   Vol. 17, p. 19

"As gifts from Samuel Barber," two autographs of songs: "Rain has fallen" Op. 10, No. 1 (Music 1907, Item 25) and "Sleep Now" Op. 10, No. 2. Both are a "welcome addition to a growing collection of this composer's holographs."

November 1960   Vol. 18, p. 15

A miscellaneous group of pieces: "Let down the bars, O death" (Music 1907, Item 11), quotations from Rilke and Melville; sketches for a melody; and another sketch for unaccompanied chorus with the words, "The Skylike girl whom we knew" (i.e., "Mary Ruane"). Also the manuscript of "I hear an army marching" (Music 1907, Item 25). Barber had already presented the other two songs of Op. 10; Nov. 1959, above.

January 1966   Vol. 23, p. 21

Full score for *Prayers of Kierkegaard* (Music 1811, Item 3). The score "enriches the collection of holographs of Samuel Barber."

January 1967   Vol. 24, pp. 54–55.

A donation of six manuscripts: *Adventure* (Music 1907, Item 2), which is "aptly titled," calling for an "extraordinary orchestra," including "a number of exotic instruments from the Museum of Natural History;" the *Hermit Songs* copyist's manuscript (Music 1907, Items 7 and 8, described as "an extremely important document"); "Monks and Raisins" Op. 18, No. 2; Piano Sonata, Op. 26 (Music 1907 Item 22), which has received "great and deserved acclaim;" two versions of *Souvenirs* Op. 28: for piano duet (Music 1907, Item 28) and full orchestra (Music 1907, Item 29); and two versions of *A Stopwatch and Ordnance Map* Op. 15 (Music 1907, Item 30).

G. SCHIRMER COLLECTION ON LOAN TO
EASTMAN SCHOOL OF MUSIC

This collection contains several boxes of manuscript material of several composers whose music was published by G. Schirmer, including Samuel Barber. The files are arranged alphabetically by composer.
Barber material is in Box 1, M2A 1, 4–2, 3

Folder 1/6   *Adagio for Strings,* 5 pages
In black ink on Schirmer Style 5 manuscript paper, with the name, Samuel Barber added, printed in green ink and signed in black ink. On adjacent (facing) page: First performance Nov. 5, 1938, by the National Broadcasting Company Orchestra, Arturo Toscanini, conductor at New York. Slurs, phrasing marks, and notes to the engraver are added in red pencil.
Parts: 2 pages each for the two violins, viola, and cello, but 1 page only for double bass; stamped Feb. 25, 1939 and initialed C. D. Bow markings are added in regular pencil with ties and slurs in regular and blue pencil.

Folder 1/7   *Andromache's Farewell*
Note from Barber: "Don't forget: Dear Hans [Heinsheimer]: please keep this to engrave from." A piano reduction of the introduction is included, called the "only

copy;" also included are program notes for the New York Philharmonic premiere. Introduction: 3 pages, in regular pencil, up to [5], i.e. the voice entry. Natural sign added in red ink.

Reduction for voice and piano: notation in regular pencil, but text is printed. Additions in red pencil; also at [12] in red pencil: "Engrave other pages;" see attached sheet= 3-page addition in regular pencil for substitution. After [20] is a new left hand part, written in pencil. There is also a new ending.

Folder 1/8   Concerto for Violoncello and Orchestra
Piano reduction; in pencil; solo part edited by Raya Garbousova.

> pp. 1-23   First Movement: added rehearsal numbers in blue pencil; notes, slurs, and accents in red pencil. Some measures of the printed score are taped over the manuscript copy.
>
> pp. 24-28   Second Movement: printed score with corrections in blue pencil; some measures of pencil score are taped in, and some corrections have been added in the margin.
>
> pp. 29-47   Third Movement: suggestions are in regular and red pencil; questions, in red pencil, probably by the engraver; Barber's answers in blue pencil. Some measures of pencil score taped in.

Cello part: 23 pages; printed score with corrections in blue pencil; Some places with manuscript in regular pencil taped in. The final page (of third movement) in regular pencil.

Folder 1/9   *Dover Beach,* 7 pages
Piano reduction: in black ink with corrections and rehearsal letters added in red. A few notes of the bassline near the end are changed in blue pencil.

Folder 1/10   *Dover Beach,* 9 pages
Full score in black ink on Carl Fischer manuscript paper. At end: May 7, 1931. Corrections in red pencil.

Folder 1/11   *Excursions*
All four items are dated 12/5/44 in red pencil.
The confusion of the number of each movement seems to show that Barber once considered having these pieces presented in the reverse order of their later publication.

First movement: number I is added in blue pencil with IV crossed out; 4 pages with black ink on maestro manuscript paper and corrections in red pencil.

The meter signature is often changed from a large 5/4 covering two staves to two smaller 5/4's, one on each staff.

Second movement: number II is added in blue pencil with III crossed out. 3 pages.

Third movement: number III added in blue pencil with II crossed out. 4 pages. The last 5 measures are crossed out, with three new ones, in regular pencil to replace it.

Fourth movement: number IV added in blue pencil with I crossed out. 4 pages. With some slight changes made.

Engraved by Edward Weiss (in red ink).

Folder 1/12   *Knoxville: Summer of 1915,* 21 pages
The phrase, "reduction for piano by the composer," is added in regular pencil. Added in blue pencil: the SB monogram and the dedication: In memory of my Father.

The score is in good ink manuscript by the copyist, with rehearsal numbers and other additions in blue and red pencil. The original instruments are indicated by green ink. Some modifications: a cut is indicated before [16]; a new accompaniment is taped in (in regular pencil) from [16] to [19]; a new vocal line is added after [23]; and new final measures are added.

Folder 1/13   *Let down the bars, O death,* 1 page
Manuscript in black ink is dated 6–30–42 by the copyist, WJW, but the date 9/18/42 is added in red pencil. Designation, "for four-part chorus of mixed voices, a capella," is added in red pencil. A few "anticipatory" meter changes are added at the ends of some lines, in red pencil.

Folder 1/14   *Mélodies passagères*
Manuscript is in black ink with red pencil corrections. Includes the signature SB and Barber's full name signed. Dated 2/15/52 RCS (presumably a copyist). A small sheet of corrections laid in, averaging one correction per song.

pp. 2–3 I: Jan. 1950

pp. 4–7 II: black ink (but looks like different hand from I) with corrections in regular and red pencil. April 21, 1951

pp. 8–9 III: black ink (looks like yet another hand), no corrections; April 26, 1951

New pagination:

pp. 2–5 IV: black ink (more like hand I). The melody altered at "Valaisan" next to last two times. Feb. 16, 1950

New pagination:

pp. 2–3 V: Black ink; natural signs added in red pencil with small grace
               notes added in regular pencil. Feb. 10, 1950

Folder 1/15   *Monks and Raisins,* 3 pages
Black ink on Maestro manuscript paper with a few corrections in red pencil;
dated: 7/20/43. At the bottom of first page: text from "Have Come, Am Here,"
used by permission.

Folder 1/16   *A Nun Takes the Veil,* 2 pages
Manuscript in black ink. For the sweeping 32-notes in the accompaniment, a note
in red is added: "as close as possible." At the end is the date, 1937; A question in
red asks: Is this wanted? [The engraver wants to know if he should include the
date in the final printed copy.]

Folder 1/17   *Nuvoletta,* 10 pages
Manuscript in ink in copyist's hand. There are many textual corrections in regular
pencil and a slight musical change in the cadenza. A question, in red pencil, asks
about the rest in unmetered measure: what value? (double whole note?) The
answer (presumably by Barber) in blue pencil: yes. Dated: Oct. 17, 1949.

Folder 1/18   *The Queen's Face on the Summery Coin,* 4 pages
Manuscript in black ink, in Barber's hand; dated: 7/20/47. Only a few corrections
are added in red pencil. At end: Nov. 1942.

Folder 1/19   *Reincarnations*
Manuscript in black ink, Barber's hand.

1. "Mary Hines," 5 pages.

    A few changes in red pencil. At end: St. Wolfgang Aug. 8, '37 (but crossed
out; probably not to be included in printed score).

2. "Anthony O'Daly" 4 pages.

    Only a few minor corrections in red pencil. At end: Dec. 17, '40 (crossed
out).

3. "Coolun" 3 pages.

    The "un" in the title is crossed out and replaced by "in." Minor corrections in
red pencil. At end: Nov. 10, '40 (crossed out).

Folder 1/20 *Secrets of the Old,* 3 pages
Manuscript in black ink, Barber's hand with ties and slurs in red ink. "con ped." crossed out; with "Ped." added in blue pencil.

Folder 1/21 **Sonata for Piano,** 37 pages
A good ink manuscript, copyist's hand, engraved by Harry Dieser. Corrections and suggestions and questions in red pencil with Barber's (?) replies in magenta ink. At end: June 1949.

Folder 1/22 *A Stopwatch and an Ordnance Map,* 10 pages
Manuscript in black ink in Barber's hand with corrections in red ink (or red pencil?) Written in green ink at the bottom of p. 1: the kettledrums may be doubled by a piano in octaves, thus (example given) if and where necessary for support. A few text clarifications are given in green ink and an indication for a solo tenor in green pencil. At end: Jan. 20, '40

Folder 1/23 *The Daisies,* 2 pages
All three songs of the eventual Opus 2 are in black ink, in Barber's hand. The phrase, "con pedale" is added in red pencil with other changes in red and green pencil. At end: The Windmill, Rogers Park, July 20, 1927.

"With rue my heart is laden," 2 pages
Dated E. S. 12 /27/35. Is this the copyist date? Some corrections in green pencil, with a reminder to "mark slurs plainly," written in red pencil. The first letter of each line of text is underscored three times in purple pencil. At end: Jan. 25, 1928.

"Bessie Bobtail," 3 pages
The meter sign, C with slash (i.e. "cut time") is changed to 2/2 in red pencil. Other corrections in green pencil. An attention engraver reads: "all the text on this page is to be in Italics." At end: Camden, Maine Aug. '34.

Folder 1/24 **Violin Concerto,** 31 pages
A photocopy of a pencil draft, a reduction for piano and violin (with no attribution). There are almost no corrections; some added fingerings.

Folder 1/25 *The Virgin Martyrs,* 4 pages
Manuscript in black ink with the phrase "copyright by G. Schirmer" added in regular pencil at the bottom of the first page. Textual changes are in green ink and a few marks are in red ink. No date at the end, but stamped "Apr 3 1939" at beginning.

Box 26M2A **1.4-2, 3 Oversized manuscripts**
Folder 26/1 *Commando March,* 25 pages
Manuscript in regular pencil on King Brand Brass Band manuscript paper, 32 staves; the pages are cut in the middle then taped back together. Some printed

instrument names are crossed out and others are inserted. Various corrections are in red, brown, regular (lead), and blue pencil. On p. 22 there is a large insert of p. 23. At the end is a single sheet of manuscript paper with additional corrections in regular pencil.

Folder 26/2   Overture to *The School for Scandal*
Arrangement for band by Frank M. Hudson. Manuscript in black ink on Professional Band manuscript paper. Opposite the first page is the following typed note: "This transcription is dedicated in sincerest admiration and gratitude to the Ohio State University concert Band and its conductor Dr. Donald E. McGinnis." [Strangely, "in sincerest admiration and gratitude" is crossed out!] Also on this page, written in blue pencil, is the following: "Use flexible layout, listing all instruments only on first page. Only playing instruments to be engraved" [on remaining pages]. This is followed by 15 specific corrections in red pencil. Throughout score changes are made in regular, red, blue, and green pencil.

BARBER MATERIALS AT THE CHESTER COUNTY HISTORICAL SOCIETY

West Chester, Pa.

This list is based on Kreiling's (Item 386) classification and annotations presented in the appendix to her dissertation, pp. 332–335. Used with permission of the author. A very brief list also appears in Hennessee, p. ix.

Vocal manuscripts

1. "The Rose Tree" (opera). Score in pencil, only the first act is complete. A libretto in pencil; typewritten; a score of "My Dream," in pencil with type-written words. Hennessee lists individual parts: "Gypsy Dance, "Gypsy Song," "Dialogue for Act 1, scene 1," and Serenade, Act 1, scene 2."

2. "Christmas Eve—a trio with solos, Op. XIII—S. O. Barber." Two scores, in pencil; three soprano parts, two first alto parts and two second alto parts. The melody for the "Shepherd's Solo" (hand copied, not a facsimile) is in Kreiling, p. 38.

3. "Invocation to Youth," a song, for voice and piano, score in pencil; text by Lawrence Binyon, with the first line: "Come, then, as ever."

4. "Music When Soft Voices Die," a song, for voice and piano; score in pencil; on a text by Percy Bysshe Shelley.

5. "October Mountain Weather," a song, for voice and piano; score in pencil; text by Barber.

6. "An Old Song," a song for voice and piano; score in ink, dated 1921; with a text by Charles Kingsley. Hand copy (not facsimile) of the entire song is in Kreiling, pp. 39–41. First line: "When all the world is young, and all the trees are green."

7. "Thy Will Be Done," a song for voice and organ; score in ink, dated 1924; [Hennessee says 1923;] Op. V, No. 1; a revised version of "The Wanderer."

8. "The Wanderer," eight-measure sketch, in pencil. (1920)

9. "Hunting Song," a song, with part for cornet, score in ink; text by John Bennett.

10. "Let down the bars O death," for chorus, score in ink, and dedicated "To the Chester County Historical Society, June 1944, Samuel Barber." Facsimile of the beginning in Heyman, p. 178.

Keyboard Manuscripts

1. "Co-ed Music Book" containing a four-measure sketch for piano and a two-page "Menuetto" for piano.

2. "Three Sketches for Pianoforte" signed "Samuel O. Barber 2nd."
    The following dates are according to Heyman, p. 25.
    "Love Song" dedicated "to Mother"(April 1924)

Published in *American Composers of the Twentieth Century* (Schaum Publications, 1969), and listed in Maurice Hinson's *Guide to the Pianist's Repertoire,* Bloomington: Indiana University Press, 1979. An expanded version printed privately in 1924; reprinted in Heyman, pp. 28–29. In a brief article barely two columns long ["Three Musical Discoveries." *Keyboard Classics* (July–August 1986), pp. 4–5.], Bennett Lerner mentions how he discovered this piece in the Schaum collection. He devotes one paragraph to "interpretation" of the piece and includes three measures of the score. He thinks it has the "character of a slow waltz." The other two works discussed are Marc Blitztein's *Variation II* and Paul Bowles' *Orosí.*
"To My Steinway" dedicated "to Number 220601" (June 1923)
"Minuet" dedicated "to Sara" (Barber's sister)
Not in Barber's hand, possibly a "professional calligrapher."

3.   "Main Street" score in ink, no text.

4.   "Themes, Op. X, No. 2, Samuel O. Barber 2nd" [all in ink]
     "Minuetto," April 1923
     "Andante Religioso"
     "Allegretto in C"

5.   "Sonata in Modern Form Piano II/XVI"
     (includes part for Piano I; in ink). A later version entitled, "Fantasie for Two
     Pianos Written in the Style of Joseph Haydn" (1924), Library of Congress.

6.   Various untitled pieces and sketches, in ink and pencil. [Hennessee calls
     them, "sketches, fragments, juvenilia."]

7.   "Petite Berceuse"
     Not listed in Kreiling but mentioned by Heyman, p. 26; facsimile, Heyman
     diss., p. 36.

   Also included are various pieces of music from Barber's personal collection:
Beethoven sonatas, pieces by Chopin, Gluck, Goddard, Mozart and Tchaikovsky;
plus piano exercise books, including Hanon, and concert programs.

MANUSCRIPTS AND COPIES AT THE CURTIS INSTITUTE OF MUSIC

The following items are not usually accessible to the public and should therefore
be treated as a private collection.

"With rue my heart is laden"

Holograph score in ink; at end: Jan. 25, '28; a presentation copy given by the
composer to Gama Gilbert, to whom the song is dedicated.

Reincarnations
Marked "24 copies;" probably used for Curtis Madrigal Chorus performance in
1940.

String Quartet (parts) in the Orlando Cole Collection

Ozalid print of copyist's manuscript for the discarded original third movement,
"Andante mosso, un poco agitato—Allegro molto, alla breve." Facsimile of first
page in Heyman, p. 159.

"Song for a New House"

Holograph manuscript, with a dedication to Mrs. Zimbalist, presented to her in
1940 on the occasion of her move from Merion to her new home in Philadelphia.

Dover Beach

1. 1 score, 9 pages. A photocopy of the manuscript, a fair copy in the hand of Ella Saile; with title page and some annotations in the composer's hand.

2. The voice part, 4 pages; a photocopy of the manuscript; vocal line with instrumental cues in Saile's hand; includes revisions and the composer's cover note to Rose Bampton prior to the work's London performance on June 30, 1935.

3. Orlando Cole's cello part

Music for a Scene from Shelley
1 holograph manuscript score, 15 pages with a quotation from Shelley's "Prometheus Unbound." At end: Aug. '33

"Under the Willow Tree" from *Vanessa*

Pencil manuscript version of the song, arranged for SATB chorus and orchestra; presented to Mrs. Zimbalist in 1956 and inscribed: "For Mary—souvenir of wonderful waltzes! Philadelphia." At end: Oct. 8, 1956.

Variations on Happy Birthday: for Eugene Ormandy

Reproduction of the manuscript (see University of Pennsylvania, Rare Manuscript Collection).

MARIAN ANDERSON COLLECTION OF MUSIC MANUSCRIPTS (UNIVERSITY OF PENNSYLVANIA)

Anderson evidently wanted copies of Barber's songs to perform before Schirmer published them. Either Schirmer or Barber himself must have sent her these copies. She must have admired Barber's music because she performed "I hear an army" in Carnegie Hall in January 1939. According to Heyman (p. 203), she performed both "Nocturne" and "A Nun Takes the Veil," on her tour in 1942. Schirmer did not copyright the songs until 1941, which may have been too late for her to learn them from the published score. However, she never mentions Barber or his songs in her autobiography, *My Lord What a Morning*, New York: Viking, 1956.

MSS Coll 199

Songs Op. 13
Ozalid reproduction of holograph scores

Folder 52   "Nocturne"
1 manuscript, 4 pages; at end: Feb. 11, 1940

Folder 53   "A Nun Takes the Veil"
1 manuscript, 2 pages; at end: 1937

Folder 54   "Secrets of the Old"
1 manuscript, 3 pages; at end "Sept. 1938"

Folder 55   "Sure on this shining night"
1 manuscript, 2 pages, at end: "Sept. 1938"

HOLOGRAPHS AT THE NEW YORK PUBLIC LIBRARY

Edith Evans Braun Collection
Series S: Box 1: MAI 20074 Holograph sketches

This file contains discarded pages from Barber's Symphony No. 1 and may be of interest to those concerned with the history of the work, "later withdrawn and repudiated by the composer." [This seems like an odd statement. It's not clear whether this is from Symphony No. 2, or No. 1.]

Toscanini Memorial Archive

ZBT 227

The file contains only one page: the beginning of "To leave, to break," from *Vanessa* (p. 444). It is a microfilm of the holograph page owned by the Metropolitan Opera Guild.

JPB 86-2 R.S. A. 4

Antony and Cleopatra, one score in three volumes, reproduced from the holograph and signed by the composer. At end: Capricorn; Aug. 29 '66

JPB 96-1

Another copy of *Antony and Cleopatra,* with annotation: "Elizabeth Ostrow, New World Records, recording, editing, mixing score, June 1983."

JNG 96-145

Third Essay (for orchestra) Op. 47. One score, 51 pages, reproduced from the holograph. It also includes the recording engineer's emendations for the issue of the work on New World Records, with an attached note for the percussion layout, dated 4/17/78.

ANTON BREES CARILLON LIBRARY AT THE BOK TOWER GARDENS, LAKE WALES, FLORIDA

Pieces for Carillon (1931–32); published by Schirmer in 1934; also unpublished: "Legend" (dated II, 1931); "Round," "Dirge," and "Allegro."

PIERPONT MORGAN LIBRARY, NEW YORK CITY: MARY FLAGLER CARY MUSIC COLLECTION

1. Holograph of a version of *Adagio for Strings*, entitled "Essay for Strings." It is inscribed "To my friend Henry-Louis La Grange, Souvenir of Capricorn, April 7, 1947." This is obviously not the date of the music itself, the "Adagio" having been converted to its orchestral form about a decade earlier.

2. Sketches for the third movement of the Piano Sonata.

3. Sketches for Medea, 4 pages.

VAN PELT LIBRARY, RARE BOOK AND MANUSCRIPT COLLECTION (UNIVERSITY OF PENNSYLVANIA)

MS. Coll 60

This collection contains various works by Barber, either photocopies of the manuscripts or printed scores, with notations by Ormandy and/or Barber.

Box 17   *Adagio for Strings*
With markings by Ormandy, bowings marked in the parts by members of the orchestra.

Second Essay for Orchestra
With bowings and slight alterations; some manuscript lines are inserted; some parts are marked.

Box 191   *Andromache's Farewell*
Score, 53 pp. with marks by Ormandy, including alterations and bowings.

Piano Concerto
1 score, 137 leaves; includes alterations.

Box 192   *Die Natali*
Includes alterations and bowings.

Violin Concerto
With bowings and indication of durations.

Box 193   *The Lovers*
Short score; inscribed by Barber to Ormandy: "Dear Eugene, missed you today! This score is more or less complete, more to follow for the orchestra as I orchestrate."

Box 194   *Prayers of Kierkegaard*
Three scores:

1.   with markings, including durations.

2.   with extensive markings, and indications of instrumentation.

3.   Schirmer rental copy; with extensive markings and bowings.

Symphony No. 1
With bowings, indication for doublings, and minor alterations.

Toccata Festiva
Called "final version," spiral bound, with markings, bowings, and indications for doubling.

Box 309   *Capricorn Concerto*
Inscribed: "To Eugene with friendliest greetings, Capricorn, Sept. '51"

First Essay for Orchestra
Inscribed: "To Eugene Ormandy in appreciation and with friendly greetings, Sept. 1941."

Medea's Meditation and Dance of Vengeance
Includes bowings and markings by Ormandy.

Music for a Scene from Shelley
2 copies:

1.   with additions and changes.

2.   with a few markings.

Overture to *The School for Scandal*
Contains Ormandy's markings, with bowings, and indications for doubling.

Box 800   Variations on Happy Birthday
Holograph dated Jan. 24, 1970, for Ormandy's 70th birthday and the concert and ball for the 113th anniversary of the Philadelphia Orchestra. 39 leaves. For a facsimile of Barber's contribution, see Heyman, p. 464.

Chapter 6. Letters and Other Correspondence

This chapter is devoted to letters, usually written by Barber to colleagues, conductors, and friends. This correspondence may sometimes seem entirely one-sided, but that is because the letters are in the collections of the recipients who seldom made copies of their replies. Occasionally there will be replies, as in the letters from William Schuman. He (or his secretary) would usually type the letter with a carbon copy to keep in Schuman's records. It is in this series of letters that we sense a real ongoing conversation, and a good rapport between two colleagues.

These letters are primarily housed in the Library of Congress and the New York Public Library, which are easily accessible to the public. Letters housed at Yale University, The University of Pennsylvania, the Academy of Rome (the New York office), and the American Academy and Institute of the Arts are somewhat less accessible, but a letter or phone call can often make them available for research. This chapter does not include those letters in private collections, because they will not normally be available for study. However, Barbara Heyman did have access to many private collections and she quotes many of them in both her dissertation (Item 257) and book (258). Especially revealing is the long correspondence Barber had with his uncle, Sidney Homer. Heyman promises to edit a volume of many of Barber's letters in the near future.

Correspondence is in the form of letters unless otherwise stipulated (e.g. postcard or telegram). Annotations are brief and do not attempt to capture the essence of Barber's witty and often acerbic writing style. The origin of the letter is presumed to be from and to the homes, vacation homes, or offices of the correspondents unless stipulated (e.g. Rome). The passages in brackets are an editorial attempt to define or clarify statements that may not be immediately apparent by the content of the letter alone. If a passage of a letter is quoted in a published source (usually Heyman), it is also cited along with the page number. It will quickly become apparent to the reader that some letters are far more interesting than others. However, in the interest of trying to present a somewhat complete list, even the most mundane letters are included along with the most informative ones.

LETTERS TO INDIVIDUALS

Leonard Bernstein

Bernstein (1918–1990) was a renowned composer, pianist, and conductor. Barber and he had an on-and-off friendship over a period of several decades.

Library of Congress, Music Division:
Bernstein Collection

Box 3 Folder 65
All letters are from Barber to Bernstein

Dated letters

[Bern 1]   August 24, 1941
The letter concerns the performance of his Violin Concerto at the Berkshire Music Festival, which Barber considers "one of the most exciting evenings of my life." (This work had just been performed there earlier in August, by Koussevitzky and Ruth Posselt. [See Kouss 6]). Barber hopes that the two of them may continue their brief acquaintance. He also hopes the army "will not get" him [Bernstein]. There are too few conductors who can beat legato; anyone can "hurl sfs [sforzandos] at brass instruments."

[Bern 2]   Monday (the only date given, but possibly the Monday after August 24, 1941)
Barber extends an invitation to visit and mentions that Menotti is working on a new opera [probably *Ilo E Zeus*].

[Bern 3]   October 2, 1958   Telegram
Barber says he will be there [New York] tonight to cheer [referring to the opening concert of Bernstein's first season as musical director of the New York Philharmonic].

[Bern 4]   February 10, 1961   Telegram
Barber congratulates Bernstein and the New York Philharmonic. He says that Bernstein's schedule should allow him time to compose.

[Bern 5]   April 29, 1965
Barber thanks Bernstein for his recording of the Violin Concerto [on Columbia with the New York Philharmonic and Isaac Stern; see Item 552], calling it "such a moving performance."

[Bern 6]   February 8, 1968
This is the same as the letter sent to Copland, a generic recommendation for Orazio Orlando as "musical and literary assistant." See Cop [19].

Undated letters

[Bern 7]   No date but probably close in time to letter [Bern 1], c. 1940.
A question of the draft into the army; Barber thinks that Bernstein ought to be able to develop an "impassioned asthmatic wheeze" to avoid service. He mentions reading some works of Baudelaire.

[Bern 8]   No date but probably close in time to letter [Bern 1].
Barber is sorry that Bernstein couldn't come to the Pocono house. He suggests that the combination of "ragweed and cats," may have been too much for him.

[Bern 9]   No date; from Capricorn; a reference to "khaki" implies that Barber was still in the army at the time.
Barber mentions *Peter Grimes*, the Benedictine, and a pleasant evening he spent with Bernstein. He encloses a review of his "favorite critic." [The critic is unnamed, but is someone who evidently reviewed one of Bernstein's performances. The word "favorite" is probably meant to be ironic.]

Katherine Garrison Chapin Biddle

Georgetown University Library, Washington, D.C.
Special Collections Division: Francis and Katherine Biddle papers
    Most of the correspondence is from Samuel Barber to Katherine Garrison Chapin Biddle (1890–1977), an American poet, and her husband Francis Biddle, the United States attorney general for Franklin D. Roosevelt's last term, 1941–1945.

Dated letters

Box 28, folder 13
[Bid 1]   February 13, 1940, to Katherine
Barber returns some of her poems and hopes to set some of them to music [which seems not to have happened]. He mentions the completion of his *Stopwatch and an Ordnance Map* and the song "Nocturne."

Box 41, folder 1
[Bid 2]   June 2, 1940, to Mr. Biddle
Barber thanks Biddle for the invitation to hear "And they lynched him on a tree" on June 24; he is leaving NYC for the summer and probably cannot get back; he is glad Rodzinsky will perform it. [No specific mention of the composition. Is *it* "And they lynched him on a tree?"]

Box 48, folder 11
[Bid 3]   February 8 (no year given but probably 1942), postcard to Katherine Barber mentions finishing a "new essay" for Bruno Walter for a performance in April. With a new publication of Biddle's poems, he senses an "increasing deepness" in her work. Menotti's new opera goes on next week at the Met. [This is undoubtedly *Ilo e Zeus*, a work that Menotti repudiated shortly after the Met debut. He attempted to have all copies of the score destroyed.]

Box 28, folder 13, item 1
[Bid 4]   March 22, 1942
Barber mentions Toscanini's recording of *Adagio for Strings*; He has had to turn down an offer from the Metropolitan Opera because [Christopher] La Farge's libretto was "uninspiring." He has finished a new *Essay* that Bruno Walter will perform with the New York Philharmonic and Serge Koussevitzky with perform later with the Boston Symphony. [This is undoubtedly the *Second Essay for Orchestra.*]

Box 28, folder 13, item 2
[Bid 5]   March 31, 1942
Concerns his draft status. He is 1A and the condition of his eyes makes him "OK for non-combatant service."

Box 28, folder 13, item 3
[Bid 6]   November 14, 1942, U.S. Army letterhead
Many different items in this letter include: Toscanini's recording of his *Adagio for Strings;* the Army music school's performance of *Stopwatch and an Ordnance Map;* and Koussevitzky's performance of the *Second Essay* (which he thinks is better than Walter's). He mentions that Shostakovitch requested copies of his music. (Quoted in Heyman, p. 213.)

Box 28, folder 13, item 4
[Bid 7]   November 30, 1942, U.S. Army letterhead
The letter concerns his *Second Essay.* Barber says that although it has no program, one might hear that it "was written in war-time." He mentions setting Biddle's "Between Dark and Dark" to music. [But see letters Bid 9 and Bid 10.]

Box 28, folder 13, item 5
[Bid 8]   December 16, 1963
Barber is sorry that he missed seeing Biddle in Washington and thanks her for the letter; he "loved what she said."

Undated letters

Box 28, folder 13, item 6
[Bid 9]   Dated only February 27 (likely to be 1950), Biddle to Barber
She reminds Barber that he played and sang his setting of her poem, "Between Dark and Dark" in her house; she liked it but he "discarded it." (See reply [Bid 10]).

Box 28, folder 13, item 7
[Bid 10]   Dated March 26 (likely to be 1950), Barber's reply to [Bid 9]
The letter concerns the Dumbarton Oaks concert of April 1, 1950 when Rudolf Firkusny performed the Piano Sonata and Eileen Farrell sang *Knoxville: Summer of 1915*. He thanks her for her new poems. He says that he never "got" "Dark and Dark" into music. [This statement conflicts with his earlier letter [Bid 4]. He either doesn't remember writing it, or he tried to compose the song and didn't "get it." In any event the music is lost.]

John Bitter

Curtis Institute of Music; typescript, signed; gift to the Institute, 1997
Bitter was a flautist and a classmate of Barber's.

[Bit 1]   July 24, 1980, from Barber [New York] to John Bitter [probably Miami Beach, Fla.]
Barber plans to visit Gian Carlo Menotti's home in Scotland before going on to Paris for a concert of *Antony and Cleopatra,* and invites Bitter to visit him in New York.

Edith Evans Braun

Edith Evans Braun (1887–1976) was a longtime friend and colleague of Barber and Mary Curtis Bok Zimbalist. Like Barber, she studied composition with Rosario Scalero and both had compositions performed on a recital at the Curtis Institute in 1930. She also played piano for Rose Bampton's performance of Barber's songs (eventually becoming Op. 2) at the Curtis Institute in 1937. She was married to John Braun, once Barber's voice teacher. "Bessie Bobtail" is dedicated to them. In his letters he often addresses her as "Gnädige," "Dearest Gnädige," or "Dearest Edie."

New York Public Library, Performing Arts Division:
Edith Evan Braun Collection
All letters are from Barber to Braun.

Folders 4–14; JPB 91–96

Folder 4

[Braun 1]   March 18, 1950
Barber talks about the reception of Menotti's *The Consul.* He mentions a book about Stravinsky and finds him to be "an unsympathetic figure."

Folder 5

[Braun 2]   January 15, 1951
Barber says that his work is going well; Gian Carlo is totally exhausted; and that Kinch [Robert Horan] tried to commit suicide.

Folder 6

[Braun 3]   January 7, 1952
Barber mentions reading Melville [he was considering *Moby Dick* as a possible opera subject], and thanks her for the *Carmen* score, which he considers a "model of orchestration." He is concerned about a "horrid ASCAP showdown" meeting on Thursday. He has written another "fast sort of two-step," for the ballet suite [*Excursions*]. He, who never could write "light things," now "cannot get stopped."

Folder 7

[Braun 4]   April 7, 1952
Barber says that he is writing from the new desk she sent him. What follows is an incredible 22-line description of her! (e.g., "ever ready for an orgy or a memorial service".)

Folder 8

[Braun 5]   July 25, 1953
Barber laments the recent death of his uncle, Sidney Homer. His letters gave "wise words of counsel, caution and encouragement and general thoughts about music and life." He considers incorporating them into a book. [Quotations from nearly all of the letters between Barber and Homer appear throughout the Heyman book.]

Folder 9

[Braun 6]   September 24, 1953
Barber says he is busy working with Leontyne [Price] and loving it [presumably on the *Hermit Songs*]; he is nearly finished with *Prayers of Kierkegaard.* Menotti

is working on a new opera, probably *The Saint of Bleecker Street*, which was performed in December of 1954.

Folder 10

[Braun 7]   March 15, 1957
Barber mentions that the Boston Symphony Orchestra is recording *Adagio for
Strings* and *Medea*. He hopes to finish the final scene of *Vanessa* in a matter of
weeks and has just finished a quintet "in the form of a circular canon" for the
final act.

Folder 11

[Braun 8]   August 29, 1960? (probably 1968, misread and out of sequence),
from Santa Christina, Val Gardena, Italy
Barber has not seen much of Menotti this year but is glad for the success of his
opera *Help, Help, the Globolinks.*

Folder 12

[Braun 9]   October 6, 1960
Since Charles Munch will do *Die Natali* in Boston in December, Barber says that
he needs to "orchestrate FAST." Robert Shaw is doing *Prayers of Kierkegaard*
and *Knoxville: Summer of 1915* in Cleveland.

Folder 13

[Braun 10]   August 2, 1968
He mentions Menotti's various productions in Israel *(The Consul),* Spoleto, and
Hamburg (possibly *Help, Help, the Globolinks*). Barber has written four new
songs [probably four of the five of *Despite and Still*]. He calls Peter Serkin "a bit
of a nut," with his long hair and beads.

Folder 14

[Braun 11]   April 11, 1971
Barber mentions that he is working on the Girard [bank] commission [*The
Lovers*], and is halfway through the orchestration. He has accepted a commission
for the Pittsburgh Symphony [the work that eventually becomes *Fadograph of a
Yestern Scene*], but has not started it yet.

Leonard Burkat

Burkat (1943–1981) was a music librarian, arts administrator, and program anno-
tator during the 1950s. He was artistic administrator of the Boston Symphony
Orchestra and assistant to Charles Munch.

Yale University, Music Library, Archival Papers:
The Leonard Burkat papers established in 1979
MSS 25   4 boxes, arranged alphabetically by correspondent, c. 130, including
Barber

Box 1, Folder 1/9

[Burkat 1]   Undated letter, autumn 1954, Barber to Burkat
Concerning the Boston and New York performances of *Prayers of Kierkegaard,*
Barber stresses that the soprano and tenor soloists should be first rate. He also
suggests the placement of the bells used in the score and is reassured about the
xylophone part. [Entire letter in Heyman, p. 354.]

Burkat 2]   March 29, 1955, Barber to Burkat
Barber says that the French translation [probably of *Prayers*] can wait; Schirmer
will publish a score with English-German, and will do an English-French score
next year. He mentions that a performance [of what?] in Chicago went well.

Burkat 3]   June 29, 1955, Barber to Charles Munch
Barber comments on the London and Vienna performances of *Prayers of
Kierkegaard* and hopes that Munch will be able to schedule a performance of it
sometime for Paris. Von Karajan has scheduled performances of the work for
Rome and Berlin. He gives a list of corrections. [Quoted in Heyman, p. 359, with
a facsimile of most of the letter, p. 360.]

[Burkat 4]   February 10, 1958, postcard from Barber to Burkat and Munch
Barber is touched to receive the kind [note] about *Vanessa*. Once the recording
process is over he will start on the piece for Munch [presumably *Die Natali*]. He
is eager to hear the recording of *Medea.*

[Burkat 5]   February 18, 1958, carbon copy of letter from Burkat to Barber
Burkat tells Barber that the *Medea* recording is due out in April. He also asks him
to let him know about the piece for the Boston Symphony Orchestra. What shall
it be? [Again, this is presumably *Die Natali.*]

[Burkat 6]   June 25, 1959, Barber to Burkat
Barber thanks him for his "kind word about Harvard." [Barber had just received
an honorary doctorate there earlier in June.]

Elizabeth Sprague Coolidge

There are several letters between Barber and Elizabeth Sprague Coolidge
(1864–1953), patroness of the arts who was responsible for the commissions of
many new American musical compositions, including Barber's own *Hermit
Songs* in the early 1950s. These letters, however, are all from the 1930s, when he

first became acquainted with her. They are primarily about *Dover Beach* and the Cello Sonata.

Library of Congress, Music Division: Elizabeth Sprague Coolidge Collection

[Cool 1]   September 1933, Barber to Coolidge
In their first correspondence, Barber mentions the premiere of *Dover Beach,* which he calls, "a horribly scholastic affair." [This refers to the first public performance at a League of Composers' concert the previous March.] [Quoted in Heyman, pp. 100–101.]

[Cool 2]   no date; but probably close in time to [Cool 1]
Barber says he "is taking the liberty" of sending her a copy of his Cello Sonata and of *Dover Beach.* [Quoted in Heyman, p.118]

[Cool 3]   c. September/October 1933, Barber to Coolidge
With this letter, Barber includes the score of *Dover Beach* and says that the Cello Sonata will be sent later.

[Cool 4]   October 29, 1933, Coolidge's reply [Cool 3]
Coolidge thanks Barber for sending her the manuscript, but has been too busy to look it over.

[Cool 5]   May 12, 1934, Barber to Coolidge
Barber says that he is looking forward to hearing the Toscanini concert in Paris.

[Cool 6]   May 15, 1934, telegram from Coolidge to Barber
She does not understand his note and has not received the letter to which he has referred.

[Cool 7]   May 16, 1934, Barber to Coolidge
He asks if she would be interested in hearing some of his music. He would be "delighted and honored" if he and "a very good cellist" could perform the Cello Sonata for her.

[Cool 8]   May 18, 1934, Coolidge to Barber
Coolidge thanks Barber for his offer but must refuse because she is too busy now, and will be away later.

Aaron Copland

Library of Congress, Music Division: Copland Collection
Box 246/Folder 26 (19 leaves) 1944–1975
All letters are from Samuel Barber to Aaron Copland (1900–1990).

Very little material in the biographies of either composer deals with their relationship. In his biography, *Aaron Copland: The Life and Works of an Uncommon Man* (Item 478), Howard Pollack only occasionally mentions Barber, and then it is usually only as a part of a generic list of American composers. He cites and quotes from two of the following letters. Copland himself refers to Barber fairly often in his own book (with Vivian Perlis) *Copland Since 1943* (Item 480). He quotes from three of the following letters. Heyman refers to Copland fairly often, but cites no letters simply because they had not yet been donated to the Library of Congress at the time of her publication.

Dated letters

[Cop 1]   September 16, 1944
Barber has just finished the *Capricorn Concerto* (a "rather tooting piece") for Daniel Saidenberg. [Saidenberg was the head of the Music Department of the Office of War, and the founder and conductor of the Saidenberg Sinfonietta. For a brief biography, see Heyman, p. 237.] Barber saw [Stravinsky's] *Danse Concertantes* and Copland's *Rodeo,* which he liked. He hopes Copland will "knuckle down" to a good symphony: "We deserve it of you, and your career is all set for it." [Quoted in Copland-Perlis, p. 64.] [As it happens, Copland was indeed working on his Third Symphony at the time of this letter. This may be a coincidence, or perhaps Barber knew that Copland had received the commission for this work from the Koussevitzky Music Foundation the previous year.] Barber mentions that he recently had dinner with Koussevitzky, who looks "very well and rested." [Koussevitzky, in fact, may have told Barber about Copland's new symphony project during the course of this dinner.]

[Cop 2]   August 24, 1948
Barber says that he has heard "nothing striking" in Europe. In Italy, he finds the music of [Luigi] dalla Piccola [sic] "interesting but difficult." He asks Copland if he is composing.

[Cop 3]   July 30, 1951
This letter concerns the "Happy Birthday" Album for Mrs. Mary Curtis Bok Zimbalist for her 75th birthday on August 6. Twenty composers contributed variations on the tune. [This is an exact copy of a letter sent to Schuman on the same date; see [Schu 9 and 10]. Both letters are similar to one Barber sent to his former teacher, Rosario Scalero on June 12. Scalero was among the other composers from whom he requested a musical tribute.]

[Cop 4]   October 23, 1951
Menotti is ready to resign [from ASCAP?], but Douglas [Moore] is already implicated officially in ASCAP in its present unsatisfactory state. [The reference is to the inequity of royalties that ASCAP paid composers during the early 1950s. See also Barber's letter to Sidney Homer on this subject, in Heyman, pp. 320–321.]

[Cop 5]   November 26, 1951, postcard
Barber says that Virgil [Thomson] has asked them for a 12:30 lunch "chez lui" next Friday.

[Cop 6]   February 19, 1952, postcard
Barber suggests they give ASCAP "a little prod." He is off to Paris and perhaps Italy.

[Cop 7]   August 2, 1953
Chuck [Charles Turner] and Barber would love to come up for the weekend of the 7th. [Presumably a reply to a Copland invitation.]

[Cop 8]   August 12, 1953
Barber thanks Copland for a "corking wonderful time." [Clearly a thank-you note for the weekend they spent together.] He asks if they have become friends: "It would be nice." [Quoted in Copland-Perlis [Item 480], p. 207 and Pollack [Item 481], p. 193.] Chuck is off to see F. Granger [perhaps actor Farley Granger].

[Cop 9]   May 6, 1955, from Rome
Barber is delighted to hear that Copland plans to play *Summer Music* at Tanglewood, he hopes by the New York Woodwind Quintet. He has been to Spain, and "hopped on" the [ocean liner] Andrea Doria in Gibraltar. [It was fortunate that he did not "hop on" the Andrea Doria a year later, because it was struck by the liner, *Stockholm,* on June 25, 1956, causing it to sink.]

[Cop 10]   July 26, 1956
Barber asks Copland to visit; He has just finished the second act [of *Vanessa*]. Apparently *Summer Music* [at Tanglewood?] was not too bad.

[Cop 11]   February 10, 1958
Barber thanks Copland for the wire about *Vanessa* and hopes he can hear the end sometime. [Did Copland attend some of the early rehearsals?]

[Cop 12]   March 16, 1960
Barber says "if you have all the youth of the U.S. at your feet, at least I have a great following among retired secretaries, janitors, et al." [Quoted in Copland-Perlis, p. 283.] P. S. At a small concert in N.Y. Chuck's new violin piece got a rave review from Flanagan. [Charles Turner was an excellent violinist, having performed Barber's Violin Concerto in the early fifties, but was also a composer. The piece in question is likely to have been his *Serenade for Icarus,* for violin and piano, which Schirmer published in 1961. The reviewer must be William Flanagan, a frequent contributor to *Hi/Fi Stereo Review*.]

[Cop 13]   June 17, 1960, from Munich
Life (in Munich) is "heavenly." [Quoted in Pollack [Item 481], p. 193.] Barber says that he has finished "that very loud piece" for organ and orchestra [the *Toccata*

Festiva]. He and Manfred [Ibel] are off to Villa Capriolo. [Manfred Ibel is a young man that Barber had met in Europe in 1958, and who eventually moved into a small cottage on the Capricorn grounds. For a brief biography, see Heyman, p. 412.]

[Cop 14]   Postcard from Mexico; postmark date unclear (but filed between 1960 and 1966 items)
Barber says that he and Manfred [Ibel] have been driving about, and have settled by the sea in a remote fishing village. It is signed "affectionately Sam;" added above the first line is "with love, Manfred." [In a different hand, presumably Manfred's.]

[Cop 15]   April 1966, postcard
Barber tells him, "My God, how much work!" [probably from the extensive and exhausting work on *Antony and Cleopatra*.]

[Cop 16]   August 28, 1967, from St. Christina
John Browning ("my" pianist) played "your" variations splendidly at Spoleto—still "a ripping piece." "Stephen Sp was there and we all admired." [perhaps Stephen Spender]

[Cop 17]   October 29, 1975
Barber is delighted to hear that Copland conducted his *Capricorn Concerto* in Norway. He remembers with pleasure that it is "one of my things that you like."

Undated letters

[Cop 18]   No date, but mentions that he will be back at Capricorn Sept. 26; a letter in thick pencil from Donaueschingen
addressed to: Hochverehrter—Aaron—carissimo! [dearest, highly-adored Aaron]
Barber is here for rehearsals (6 weeks) [of what?] investigating the Grundsymptomatischetonalitatsveranlegungsmöglichkeit der Zeitgenössischten—Ton—Konkret*-Kreationen.*concretinismo. This incredible, satirical, pseudo-Germanic expression is almost impossible to translate, but one possible guess is: the possibility of fundamental, symptomatic tonality require-ments in contemporary composition of "concrete" music. *Musique concrète* is an avant-garde technique of early electronic music [e.g., Pierre Schaefer, et al.] The footnote indicates "very concrete" with the emphasis on "cretin" indicating Bar-ber's disdain for anything "experimental" or "avant-garde."

[Cop 19]   Samuel Barber letterhead, no date but probably February 8, 1968, because this is an exact copy of a letter sent to Bernstein on that date. See Bern [6]. This is a formal, generic recommendation for Orazio Orlando, "who has come to my attention as a musical and literary assistant." This is in "immigrationese." [The score of *Antony and Cleopatra* is dedicated to Orlando.]

Walter Damrosch

Damrosch (1862–1950) was a composer, conductor (sometimes with the NBC Symphony Orchestra), and educator. There are three letters from Barber to Damrosch and one reply from Damrosch's secretary.

New York Public Library, Performing Arts Division: Damrosch Collection

[Dam 1]   April 3, 1939, Barber to Damrosch
Barber sends Damrosch a copy of *Music for a Scene from Shelley.* He suggests that *Essay for Orchestra* may be "too intimate and tenuous" to include in a program for the world's fair; he suggests that the Overture to *The School for Scandal* might make a better opening.

[Dam 2]   February 27, 1944, Barber to Damrosch
The Symphony dedicated to the Army Air Force [later to be called Symphony No. 2] will be performed this Saturday with Koussevitzky and the Boston Symphony Orchestra and on radio the following week in Carnegie hall. He asks Damrosch if he could wire General Matthew Arnold after the performance.

[Dam 3]   March 14, 1944, Damrosch's secretary to Barber
She tells Barber that Damrosch has indeed sent a telegram to General Arnold telling him that the symphony was "received with great enthusiasm."

[Dam 4]   March 21, 1944, Barber to Damrosch
Barber tells Damrosch that he was delighted to see him at Carnegie Hall for the performance of his Symphony No. 1 and to know that he also heard his Symphony No. 2. He tells him that he is "just getting into my stride as a composer."

Leonard Ellinwood

Ellinwood (1905–1994) worked at the Library of Congress, primarily as a cataloguer, from 1939 to 1975.

Library of Congress, Music Division: Ellinwood Collection

[Ellin 1]   April 7, 1956, Barber to Ellinwood
Barber tells Ellinwood that he is disappointed that he cannot attend the performance of *Prayers of Kierkegaard,* but needs to "rush off" to Spain. He gives his best wishes to Paul Callaway and hopes that a tape can be made of the performance. [Callaway was organist and choir director at Washington Cathedral, where the work was presented. He eventually premiered Barber's *Toccata Festiva.*]

Lehman Engel

Engel (1910–1982) was a composer and a major figure in American musical theater.

Yale University Library, Archival Papers: The Papers of Lehman Engel
MSS 39   (not yet catalogued)

[Eng 1]   September 17, 1934, from Barber to Mme Carlos Salzedo (wife of
the composer and harpist)
Mme. Salzedo conceived of an all-Barber program for the NBC Music Guild with
Werner Janssen conducting. In this letter Barber responds favorably to such a
project. He mentions that many of his manuscripts are in the hands of his publisher, but some of his vocal works are available. He also would be willing to sing
on the program. [Heyman, p. 121]

Ross Lee Finney

Finney (1906–1997) was a composer and teacher, primarily at the University of
Michigan from 1949 to 1973. He served in the Office of Strategic Services during
World War II, which may explain the context of the typed form that follows.

Library of Congress, Music Division: Finney Collection

[Fin 1]   a typed form rather than a letter
Includes a list of works composed and performed in 1942, such as the *Second
Essay* (with Bruno Walter and the New York Philharmonic). Barber states that
"due to military duties" he cannot compose anything "for a civilian use." Signed
by Barber.

Vladimir Horowitz

Russian born pianist (1903–1989) known for performances of the music of
Chopin and many Russian composers. He premiered Barber's Piano Sonata.

**Yale University Music Library, Archival Papers: The Vladimir and Wanda
Toscanini Horowitz papers**
Established by Mr. and Mrs. Horowitz, beginning in 1986
MSS 55   164 boxes, in 9 series documenting the lives of the legendary pianist
and his wife through their correspondence (Series I) with family members, performers, agents, recording companies, and composers, including Barber. [not
listed in Heyman]

[Horo 1]   October 19, 1949, Barber to Horowitz
Barber wishes he could have heard Horowitz's Chopin concert in New York. He
asks him to contact Hans Heinsheimer [at G. Schirmer] about a preview concert
[of the Piano Sonata] and asks if it is "ok" for Rudolf Firkusny to play the Sonata
at the Bliss house at Dumbarton Oaks. [This performance indeed took place; see
Item 138.]

[Horo 2]   April 23, 1951, telegram Barber to Horowitz
Barber says the performance was "absolutely wonderful." [The performance in question is probably, but not necessarily Barber's Piano Sonata.]

[Horo 3]   June 30, 1951, Barber to Wanda
Barber expresses sympathy to Mrs. Horowitz at her "great loss" [i.e. the death of her mother, Mrs. Arturo Toscanini]. She helped many people get through red tape and other "little things."

[Horo 4]   March 17, 1965, Barber to Horowitz
Barber is "thrilled" that Horowitz will "play for people again" instead of that "ghastly machine" [i.e. the phonograph]. Hurray from your "old fashioned but affectionate admirer."

[Horo 5]   Undated note to Wanda
Barber encloses a letter from Martha Graham saying she is pleased that he can be present at a ceremony on May 25, 1978 at which Alice Tully will be presented the "Martha Graham Medal." Could Volodya [Vladimir] play?

[Horo 6]   June 7, 1979, Barber to Horowitz
Barber is happy that Horowitz's "splendid performance" of his Piano Sonata has been reissued. He says that his treatments [probably chemotherapy for cancer] are going well but they leave him "a bit fatigued." Yet he still seems to have plans to "write something good" for the piano.

Serge Koussevitzky

Koussevitzky (1874–1951) was conductor of the Boston Symphony Orchestra from 1924 to 1951 and was responsible for programming many American orchestral works. He also commissioned new works under the Koussevitzky Music Foundation.

Library of Congress, Music Division: Serge Koussevitzky Collection

The collection of letters between Barber and Koussevitzky is extremely extensive: over 60 correspondences in nearly 15 years. While the topics vary, most letters tell us something about the difficulties encountered by a young composer who is trying to get his orchestral music performed. This is particularly relevant for the years of World War II. In addition to the letters between Barber and Koussevitzky, this collection contains one letter between Barber and Richard Burgin, Koussevitzky's concertmaster and assistant conductor of the orchestra; a short exchange of letters between Koussevitzky and Generals Yount and Arnold; one letter from Howard C. Bronson, chief of the Music Section of the Special Services Division of the Army to Koussevitzky; a brief exchange of letters between Koussevitzky and the cellist Raya Garbrousova; and a few letters between Barber and Mrs. (Olga) Koussevitzky.

Folder: 1938–44

[Kous 1]   December 16, 1938, Barber to Koussevitzky
In his first letter, Barber mentions his admiration for Koussevitzky and hopes that someday he will conduct one of his works. He asks if he might send copies of his *Symphony in One Movement, Adagio for Strings,* and *Essay for Orchestra.* [The entire letter is quoted in Heyman, p. 145.]

[Kous 2]   December 19, 1938, Koussevitzky to Barber
In reply, Koussevitzky says he is interested in seeing the score of *Adagio for Strings.* He would like to have a new and larger score for a possible performance next season. [The entire letter is quoted in Heyman, p. 145.]

[Kous 3]   January 6, 1939, Barber to Koussevitzky
Barber says that he has asked Schirmer to send Koussevitzky a copy of *Adagio for Strings,* and will try to have a new work ready for the following season.

[Kous 4]   November 10, 1940, Koussevitzky to Barber
Koussevitzky invites Barber to attend rehearsals of The Overture to *The School for Scandal* with the Boston Symphony Orchestra the following week. [This letter is mentioned but not quoted in Heyman, p. 93.]

[Kous 5]   April 30, 1941, Barber to Koussevitzky
Barber mentions that three of his works have been played at the Berkshire Music Festival.

[Kous 6]   July 30 1941, Barber to Koussevitzky
Barber tells Koussevitzky that he is looking forward to the performance of his Violin Concerto at the Berkshire Festival and would like to attend rehearsals. [The performance took place on August 14. See [Bern 1] for Barber's enthusiastic reaction to this performance.]

[Kous 7]   November 10, 1941, Koussevitzky to Barber
Koussevitzky hopes that Barber can attend the rehearsals and performance of The Overture to *The School for Scandal* on November 15 and 16.

[Kous 8]   Dec. 16, 1941, carbon of letter, unsigned, but likely to be Mrs. (Olga) Koussevitzky
"Dr. K" has returned from his Western trip. The *Essay for Orchestra* was a success wherever it was played.

[Kous 9]   March 20, 1942, Barber to Koussevitzky
Barber recommends *A Stopwatch and an Ordnance Map* for a performance at Tanglewood that summer because it is "appropriate for the times." [Koussevitzky chose not to perform it then.] He also hopes that Koussevitzky might perform the *First Essay.* [Heyman, pp. 189 and 209.]

[Kous 10]   Sept. 14, 1942, Barber to Koussevitzky
Barber mentions being inducted into the army. He hopes that Koussevitzky will perform his *Second Essay*. He congratulates him on this summer's Berkshire Festival. Barber had hoped to compose an opera with Dylan Thomas as librettist [in response to a commission from the Koussevitzky Foundation], but this will have to be postponed. [Heyman, pp. 209, 211, 375.]

[Kous 11]   October 5, 1942, Koussevitzky to Barber
Koussevitzky says that he will perform the Overture to *The School for Scandal* in Boston later in October, and will do the *Essays* in New York this season. He is sorry that Barber has to put off the completion of his opera. [Heyman, p. 209.]

[Kous 12]   October 16, telegram from Barber to Koussevitzky
Barber hopes to be able to come to the concert tomorrow and asks for two tickets.

[Kous 13]   January 4, 1943, Barber to Koussevitzky
This letter contains a list of minor corrections for the *Second Essay*. He says that the revised version of the First Symphony is just about ready and is "a better work now." [See Heyman, p. 147, 209.]

[Kous 14]   February 24, 1943, Barber to Koussevitzky
The score and parts for the [First] symphony are being copied. He hopes Koussevitzky will like it and that it is not too late for it to be included in the current season. [Heyman, p. 147.]

[Kous 15]   August 16, 1943, postcard from Barber to Koussevitzky
Barber says that he has orchestrated the *Commando March* and will send it to him as soon as it is copied. [Koussevitzky had requested that Barber score the work for orchestra as well as band.]

[Kous 16]   November 8, 1943, Barber to Richard Burgin
Barber suggests some minor changes in the *Commando March* and asks that he pass them along to Koussevitzky and the performers. [Heyman, p. 215.]

[Kous 17]   November 11, 1943, Koussevitzky to Barber
Due to scheduling difficulties, Koussevitzky regrets that he could not include the *First Symphony* in the first half of the 1943 season, but is eager to do it in the second half. He tells Barber that the audience was enthusiastic about the *Commando March*. [Heyman, pp. 148, 215.]

[Kous 18]   November 11, 1943, Barber to Koussevitzky
Barber tells Koussevitzky that his "little March" [*The Commando March*] sounded "very well indeed" over the radio. [Heyman, p. 215.]

[Kous 19]   November 16, 1943, Barber to Koussevitzky
Barber would like Koussevitzky to perform both of his symphonies. The Air

Force wants the Second Symphony to be performed this season and hopes that Koussevitzky will do the premiere. Barber, Copland, and Schuman were photographed for the *March of Time* news reel. [Heyman, pp. 148 and 218.]

[Kous 20]   November 29, 1943, General Yount to Koussevitzky
General Yount says that the Office of the Commanding General of the Army Air Forces would like Koussevitzky to premiere Barber's Second Symphony in Boston, New York, and on the radio. [Heyman, p. 219.]

[Kous 21]   December 16, 1943, Koussevitzky to General Yount
Koussevitzky replies that, if the *Flight Symphony* [The Second Symphony] is finished by March 1944, he would introduce it in his concerts and radio performances in Boston and New York.

[Kous 22]   January 17, 1944, telegram from Koussevitzky to Barber
Koussevitzky urges Barber to complete and prepare the orchestra parts for the Second Symphony for performances on March 3 and 4.

[Kous 23]   January 19, 1944, telegram from Barber to Koussevitzky
Barber assures Koussevitzky that the Second Symphony will be ready on time. The third movement is nearly completed. The electrical instrument [a tone synthesizer] is being constructed at the Bell Telephone laboratories. [For a description of this device, see Heyman, p. 219.]

[Kous 24]   January 31, 1944, Barber to Koussevitzky
The Second Symphony is finished and orchestrated. He asks if Koussevitzky would care to look over the third movement with him. [Heyman, p. 220.]

[Kous 25]   February 2, 1944, Koussevitzky to Barber
Koussevitzky tells Barber that he would be pleased to look over the third movement with him.

[Kous 26]   February 15, 1944, telegram from Barber to Koussevitzky
Barber says that the score [of the Second Symphony] was mailed today and that he will arrive with the electrical instrument in time for rehearsal on the 28th.

[Kous 27]   February 18, 1944, telegram from Koussevitzky to Barber
Koussevitzky tells Barber that he is worried because he has not yet received a copy of the symphony.

[Kous 28]   February 23, 1944, Barber to Koussevitzky
Barber is glad that Koussevitzky now has the score of symphony [it must have arrived shortly after the previous telegram] and "awaits the magic" he will bring to it. He hopes that it can be performed more than once, because many officers might miss it if there was only a single performance. [Heyman, p. 220, 225.]

[Kous 29]   March 4, 1944, Koussevitzky to General Arnold
Koussevitzky praises Barber's *Flight Symphony* as a work "of lasting importance and creative value," and urges the general to give Barber more opportunities to compose. [Heyman, p. 226.]

[Kous 30]   March 6, 1944, Koussevitzky to General Yount
This is identical to the letter to General Arnold [Kous 29]. See also Damrosch's letter [Dam 3].

[Kous 31]   March 18, 1944, General Yount to Koussevitzky
Yount tells Koussevitzky that he heard the first radio performance of the symphony and thought it was "magnificent." He says that Barber is both a great musician and a "patriotic citizen," and that he will be given "a suitable assignment." [Heyman, p. 226.]

[Kous 32]   March 21, 1944, Barber to Koussevitzky
Barber thanks Koussevitzky for the "inspired interpretation" of his performances of the Second Symphony. [Heyman, p. 225.]

[Kous 33]   March 24, 1944, Howard C. Bronson to Koussevitzky
Bronson, the chief of the Music Section of the Special Services Division, wants the *Flight Symphony* to be recorded so that other soldiers can hear it. The symphony "marks another milestone for the music of the Army of the United States." [Heyman, p. 227.]

[Kous 34]   March 31, 1944, General Arnold to Koussevitzky
The general considers the *Flight Symphony* to be "one of the most outstanding contributions to musical literature that has come out of this war era." Yount has placed Barber on "detached service." [Heyman, p. 226.]

[Kous 35]   April 18, 1944, Barber to Koussevitzky
Barber is waiting to hear of his future in the military, but is hopeful, due to Koussevitzky's "wonderful letter" on his behalf. [Heyman, p. 227.]

[Kous 36]   October 20, 1944, Barber to Koussevitzky
Barber mentions that George Szell gave him a few conducting lessons to help him conduct the *Capricorn Concerto* [with members of the Chicago Symphony at the University of Chicago]. He hopes to begin an opera soon [in fulfillment of a commission from the Koussevitzky Foundation]. [Heyman, p. 312.]

[Kous 37]   October 30, 1944, Koussevitsky to Barber
Koussevitzky wishes Barber good luck in his "new venture" of conducting. He also encourages him to compose an opera. [Heyman, pp. 312, 376.]

[Kous 38]   November 27, 1944, Barber to Koussevitzky
This letter contains a number of unrelated musical thoughts. Barber says that both

George Szell and Eugene Ormandy have scheduled performances of the *Second Essay* for the same week in New York. Valdimir Horowitz is playing the *Excursions* beautifully. His own conducting venture went well with the Chicago Symphony players in *The Capricorn Concerto*. He is still hoping for a suitable libretto for an opera [but the project was later abandoned]. [Heyman, pp. 210, 312, 375, 376, 409.]

[Kous 39]   December 8, 1944, Koussevitzky to Barber
Koussevitzky agrees that "Horowitz does play the *Excursions* beautifully." He hopes to see Barber conduct sometime soon.

Folder: 1945-55

[Kous 40]   January 28, 1945, Barber to Koussevitzky
Barber tells Koussevitzky that he has started work on the Cello Concerto, which he had commissioned, and has discussed the technical aspects with Raya Garbousova. He has been listening to the radio about Russian victories. [Heyman, p. 249.]

[Kous 41]   March 5, 1945, Garbousova to Koussevitzky
She hopes that Barber's concerto will be ready in May and thinks that performing it will "help her career enormously." [Heyman, p. 249.]

[Kous 42]   April 21, 1945, Barber to Koussevitzky
Barber has had to abandon his opera plans since he did not like the libretto. However, the Cello Concerto is progressing. [Heyman, p. 376.]

[Kous 43]   July 28, 1945, Barber to Olga Koussevitzky
Barber tells Mrs. Koussevitzky that the first two movements of the Cello Concerto are finished and Garbousova seems enthusiastic about it. [Heyman, p. 250.]

[Kous 44]   July 31, 1945, Olga Koussevitzky to Barber
Mrs. Koussevitzky tells Barber that Mrs. Anne Brown is interested in his new Cello Concerto. [Even though Koussevitzky had commissioned the work, her husband, John Nicholas Brown, had actually paid for it.] [Heyman, p. 251.]

[Kous 45]   April 21, 1945, Barber to Koussevitzky
Barber tells Koussevitzky that he regrets that he was never able to study conducting with him at the Berkshire Music School. He says that he will conduct some of his music on the CBS radio program, "Invitation to Music." [Heyman, pp. 243, 312.]

[Kous 46]   August 3, 1945, Barber to Olga Koussevitzky
Barber tells Mrs. Koussevitzky how much he wishes to be a civilian again and that a "strong letter" from her husband might help him gain an early discharge. [Heyman, p. 250.]

[Kous 47]   August 8, 1945, from Koussevitzky "To whom it may concern"
This generic letter is an immediate response to Barber's above request. He states that Barber is an "outstanding" American composer; only as a civilian can his "creative gifts and powers be fully exploited for effective cultural propaganda and the benefit of high artistic aims."

[Kous 48]   September 28, 1945, Barber to Koussevitzky
Barber thanks Koussevitzky for his letter, which contributed to his "demobilization." He says how wonderful it is to be "completely free" to work on his music again. The Cello Concerto is finished and he will soon begin working on the instrumentation. [Heyman, pp. 250–51.]

[Kous 49]   June 11, 1946, a long letter, typed, from Rome and addressed to "Gus."
Barber finds excellent musicians here [in Rome]; conductors are "crazy" to know about American music; they liked Bernstein's concert. Barber conducted concerts in Prague of the *Capricorn Concerto* and *Adagio for Strings*. He extends his love to Ann. [So far, the identity of Gus and Ann are unknown; the reason the letter is in the Koussevitzky file is also a mystery.]

[Kous 50]   October 16, 1946, Barber to Koussevitzky
Barber tells Koussevitzky that he arrived back at Mt. Kisco after five wonderful months abroad. He admits, however, that during that time he "didn't compose a note."

[Kous 51]   February 7, 1947, Barber to Olga Koussevitzky
Barber tells Mrs. Koussevitsky that Assisi was wonderful. He has been working hard and has finished a suite for full orchestra derived from the ballet for Martha Graham [his *Medea Suite* from *Cave of the Heart*]. Eleanor Steber, "a sincere and intelligent artist," asked for something for her with orchestra. [This, of course, will become *Knoxville: Summer of 1915*]. He has asked Thornton Wilder to write an opera libretto. [Nothing ever comes of this.]

[Kous 52]   April 9, 1947, telegram from Barber to Koussevitzky
Barber tells Koussevitzky that he has finished the work for soprano and orchestra and would like to play it for him [*Knoxville: Summer of 1915*].

[Kous 53]   April 10, 1947, telegram from Koussevitzky to Barber
In reply, Koussevitzky tells Barber that he would be delighted to see him tomorrow.

[Kous 54]   April 22, 1947, Barber to Koussevitzky
Eleanor Steber ("the best possible choice") has commissioned *Knoxville: Summer of 1915*. Barber hopes that she will be able to sing it for Koussevitzky, whenever he has the time, and that he will conduct it. [Heyman, p. 288.]

[Kous 55]   April 26, 1947, telegram from Koussevitzky to Barber
Koussevitzky says that he expects to communicate with Barber by the middle of May.

[Kous 56]   Summer 1947 Barber to Koussevitzky
Barber says that he has finished teaching and that his students were enthusiastic. [Barber taught Arthur Honneger's students at the Berkshire Music Center after Honneger had a heart attack and was unable to return there to teach.]

[Kous 57]   October 11, 1947, Barber to Olga Koussevitzky
Barber has problems with the scheduling of *Knoxville: Summer of 1915* and asks Mrs. Koussevitzky to check on her husband's schedule for availability. [Heyman, p. 288.]

[Kous 58]   October 22, 1947, telegram from Koussevitzky to Barber
Koussevitzky says that he is unable to change the performance date [*Knoxville: Summer of 1915*], but could possibly postpone the work until the following season. [Heyman, p. 288.]

[Kous 59]   October 28, 1947, Barber to Koussevitzky
Barber agrees to the original premiere date of *Knoxville: Summer of 1915* for next April, and says that he hopes he can be back from Europe by then. [Heyman, p. 289.]

[Kous 60]   Apr. 1, 1948, Barber to Koussevitzky
Barber says that he is still at the Academy in Rome, and is "bitterly disappointed" that he cannot return in time to hear the premiere of *Knoxville: Summer of 1915*. [Heyman, p. 289.]

[Kous 61]   April 26, 1948, Barber to Koussevitzky
Barber commends Koussevitzky on his "wonderful" performance of *Knoxville: Summer of 1915,* and praises his twenty-five years of work with The Boston Symphony Orchestra. [Koussevitzky had just announced his retirement.] [Heyman, p. 290.]

[Kous 62]   January 8, 1949, telegram from Barber to Koussevitzky
Barber says he is sorry that he had to miss tonight's performance [of his Violin Concerto played by Ruth Posselt, Boston Symphony Orchestra, with Koussevitzky conducting].

[Kous 63]   March 15, 1949, Barber to Koussevitzky
Barber says that he has asked Schirmer to send Koussevitzky a copy of the revised version of his Second Symphony. He is happy with the improvements. [Heyman, p. 230.]

[Kous 64]   June 29, 1955, Barber to Olga Koussevitzky
Barber tells Mrs. Koussevitzky of the "quite exceptional success" in the

performances of *Prayers of Kierkegaard* in London and Vienna. [The work is dedicated to the Koussevitzkys.] The choir in London gave it a "dramatic effect." [Heyman, p. 359.]

William Miller

William Miller is evidently a family friend of long standing, probably about the same age as Sam. Perhaps they were schoolmates. Daisy still likes to call him "Billy." He eventually became a faculty member at the University of Pennsylvania.

University of Pennsylvania, Van Pelt Library, Rare Book and Manuscript Folder MISC MSS
Samuel Barber and Daisy Barber (Samuel's mother) to William Miller; six items

[Mill 1]   December 27, 1954, Christmas card from Barber to Miller
The card has a photograph of Capricorn on it with: "Merry Christmas from 'Capricorn' " then (handwritten) "Thanks for the kind note—I have been laughing about the sugar pills." [Whatever that means!]

[Mill 2]   October 10, 1959, postcard, Daisy Barber to Miller
Daisy says she sent his letter to Sam and he will take care of the tickets [for Barber's birthday celebration at Curtis]. She says she can't believe Sam is going to be 50 years old and adds, "he doesn't like it either."

[Mill 3]   November 14, 1959, Barber to Miller
Barber says his mother forwarded Miller's letter and says that he doesn't know exactly "what is up for that horrible occasion—my fiftieth." There will be a chamber music concert at Curtis, and Barber will send Miller tickets.

[Mill 4]   Undated, official printed invitation to the Curtis celebration
With handwritten note: please admit Wm Miller and guest.

[Mill 5]   March 19, 1960, Daisy Barber to Miller
Daisy says that she is sorry that she didn't get to see Miller and have a chat (at the birthday gala), but is glad he enjoyed it. It was also too bad he couldn't have more time with Sam. He leaves for Europe in April "so we are having a lark" in New York before he goes.

[Mill 6]   Undated note, MBB (Marguerite Barber, or Daisy)
Daisy says that it was good to hear from him and when he is in West Chester perhaps he could look her up. She is proud of having a friend at the University of Pennsylvania (Philadelphia crossed out) ("sorry"). She knows Sam will be, too. At the end she adds: "Poorly written note but the best I can do."

Eugene Ormandy

Ormandy (1899–1985), born Jenö Blau in Hungary, emigrated to the United States in 1921 and became conductor of the Philadelphia Orchestra in 1938, a position he held until his retirement in 1980. He lead the orchestra in several Barber works, beginning with the premiere of his Violin Concerto in 1941.

University of Pennsylvania, Van Pelt Library, Register: Walter H. Lemore Annenberg Rare Book and Manuscript Library: Eugene Ormandy Papers 1921–1991: Ms. Coll. 91
78 boxes and 2 map drawers; principle holdings: Mrs. Eugene Ormandy, received 1987–1998, consisting of correspondences, administration papers, and memorabilia.
I. Correspondence, 27 boxes; 26 general and 1 box interoffice correspondence; Folders in boxes arranged alphabetically by correspondent; Barber letters are in Folders 131 and 132: some are actual letters from Barber to Ormandy, others are carbon copies of letters sent from Ormandy to Barber.

Folder 131

[Orm 1]   October 8, 1959, Ormandy to Barber
Ormandy offers Barber a $5000 commission for a major work "of symphonic proportions."

[Orm 2]   October 12, 1959, telegram from Barber to Ormandy
Barber says he must decline the offer.

[Orm 3]   October 13, 1959, Ormandy to Barber
The donor is willing to extend the commission to the next three years. Ormandy asks if Barber can make the "big festival piece" a little longer [the *Toccata Festiva*].

[Orm 4]   April 18, 1960, Ormandy to Barber
Ormandy again asks Barber if he can now do the piece, and have score and parts sent by April 1, 1961.

[Orm 5]   April 25, 1960, Barber to Ormandy
Barber says that he has accepted two other commissions and "must regretfully say no." He says he will begin orchestrating *Toccata Festiva* at once. [The piece now has this final name.]

[Orm 6]   April 26, 1960, Ormandy to Barber
Ormandy says that if Barber cannot accept the commission, he will have to offer it to another composer.

[Orm 7]   October 3, 1960, Ormandy to Barber
In reference to the September 30 premiere of *Toccata Festiva,* Ormandy chastises

Barber for walking away just as he was beckoning him for a bow. Despite being a bit miffed, Ormandy still tries to offer Barber the commission he has been writing about since the year before.

[Orm 8]   October 10, 1960, Barber to Ormandy
Barber again declines the offer, mainly because he is working on a piece for the opening of Lincoln Center and a piano concerto. [These two commissions apparently became combined.] Charles Munch will conduct *Die Natali* on December 22; Barber hopes that Ormandy may do it another year. [Munch did indeed premier it on that date.]

[Orm 9]   December 12, 1967, Barber to Ormandy
Barber declines Ormandy's commission for a work for 1976. He wants to compose what he wants. He thanks him for his faith in his music, "past and future." [Heyman, p. 463.]

[Orm 10]   December 20, 1967, Ormandy to Barber
Ormandy accepts Barber's declining of the commission "with reluctance," and hopes he will continue his creativity where he left off a year ago. He feels "the best is yet to come from you." [Heyman, p. 463.]

[Orm 11]   November 10, 1969, Ormandy to Barber
Ormandy asks if Barber would be willing to compose an orchestral work (about 20–25 minutes in length) to be delivered by January of 1974. [There is evidently no record of Barber's reply, if any.]

[Orm 12]   August 31, 1972, Ormandy to Barber
Ormandy asks if he might submit Barber's name to the International Arts Committee for the Bicentennial of the United States. He has in mind a large scale work, perhaps using chorus and soloists, and "picking themes of a patriotic nature."

[Orm 13]   October 25, 1972, Ormandy to Barber
Ormandy has not yet received a reply from the previous letter and asks again if Barber can do the piece. The committee is to meet in November.

[Orm 14]   November 9, 1972, Ormandy to Barber
Mary H. Krause encloses a copy of the letter of August 31 [Orm 12] "in case you did not receive it," and hopes that he can reply soon.

[Orm 15]   November 22, 1972, Barber to Ormandy
Barber just received the second letter; the first "got stuck in Europe." He declines the commission because he is really "not good at these patriotic things." Barber is delighted that Ormandy will open next season with *Toccata Festiva*. He wonders if the pedal cadenza might be too long. [In the file is a copy of this letter with a handwritten note saying: "send to organist, ask his opinion."]

[Orm 16]   August 18, 1973, Ormandy to Barber
Ormandy again requests an orchestral work of about 25–40 minutes, which could include vocal soloists and chorus. [This is not the same as the "patriotic" commission offered earlier.]

[Orm 17]   August 23, 1973, Helen M. Franklin (Barber's secretary) to Ormandy
Franklin says that she has sent his letter from August 18 (see [Orm 16]) to Barber in Italy, where he is spending the summer. She believes he will reply soon.

Folder 132

[Orm 18]   May 25, 1976, Ormandy to Barber
Madame X [Audrey Poon] becomes a sponsor for Barber's latest work [eventually known as the *Third Essay for Orchestra*]. Ormandy states the financial requirements for performance and recording and requests that a short score be sent as soon as possible. [Complete letter in Heyman, p. 498.]

[Orm 19]   December 6, 1976, Ormandy to Barber
Ormandy states the financial terms for the commission. Mrs. Poon has the check for $40,000 ready to mail. Ormandy would like to get the orchestra programs set for all of next season. [Heyman, p. 498]

[Orm 20]   December 21, 1976, Ormandy to Barber
Ormandy mentions that Norman Carol will play Barber's Violin Concerto (with James Levine conducting) in January [the weekend of the 7th and 8th] 1977, and it would be nice if he could attend rehearsals. His Piano Concerto will be played by Ted Joselson in February [the weekend of the 18th and 19th], and Ormandy hopes that Barber can come to the performance and "take a well-deserved bow."

[Orm 21]   March 9, 1977, Ormandy to Barber
Ormandy asks about the length and instrumental requirements of Barber's new piece. Does it call for soloists or chorus? Ormandy would like to include *The Lovers* on a new recording, especially if Tom Krause is available. He tells Barber that Joselson's performance of his Piano Concerto was "fantastic." [Heyman, p. 500.]

[Orm 22]   April 6, 1977, Barber to Ormandy
Barber informs Ormandy that the Piano Concerto cannot be recorded under this commission. Krause would be ideal for *The Lovers* recording. Barber says that he will start on the new work once he gets to Italy. It will take up one side of a record and does not require soloists or extra instruments. He is pleased with RCA's re-release of "my old *Vanessa*." He is eager to have *Prayers of Kierkegaard* recorded

and tells Ormandy that he will never forget his performance of it. [This probably refers to Ormandy's Carnegie Hall performance a year earlier.] [Heyman, p. 500.]

[Orm 23]   April 12, 1977, Ormandy to Barber
Ormandy would like to see the new score [probably of the *Third Essay*]. There are tentative plans to record *The Lovers,* but there are problems in the possible recording of *Prayers of Kierkegaard.* He says it was too bad it wasn't recorded earlier.

[Orm 24]   April 18, 1977, Ormandy to Barber
There appear to be problems with Mrs. Poon's check.

[Orm 25]   October 24, 1978, Ormandy to Barber
Ormandy promises to review the score of the *Third Essay* and asks for a tape. He mentions Mrs. Poon's suicide and says "for your sake I hope she paid for the commission of your *Third Essay.*"

[Orm 26]   November 16, 1979, Barber to Ormandy
Barber tells Ormandy that he still has his wonderful performance of his concerto ringing in his ears. He is happy that Ormandy is performing *Die Natali,* but hopes that he might "doctor up" the bad places. [Heyman, p. 408.]

[Orm 27]   December 3, 1979, Ormandy to Barber
Ormandy says that he has been rehearsing *Die Natali,* and asks if Barber could attend the last rehearsal and sit with Gretel [Ormandy's wife] at one of the performances. [Heyman, p. 408.]

[Orm 28]   December 12, 1979, Ormandy to Barber
Ormandy regretfully had to remove *Die Natali* from the program. Although he realizes the problems in the score, he thinks that Barber should make any changes himself. Are there other scores to perform in future seasons?

[Orm 29]   August 5, 1980, Ormandy to Barber
Ormandy says he is sorry that Barber could not attend his birthday party last November and hopes he is feeling better; he also hopes that Barber can attend Isaac Stern's performance of the Violin Concerto on September 17.

Dorothy Slepian Packer

Packer (1923–), wife of Leo S. Packer, is a musicologist who has taught at Boston University, the State University of New York at Buffalo, and Nazareth College in Rochester, New York.

Library of Congress, Music Division: Dorothy Slepian Packer Collection

[Pack 1]   April 19, 1945
Barber tells her that the study score of his First Symphony is published by Schirmer, and the *Capricorn Concerto* will be published by the end of the

summer. A performance of the *Capricorn Concerto* will be broadcast on May 2, on CBS Radio.

Quincy Porter

Porter (1897–1966) was a composer and professor of music at Yale from 1946 to 1958.

Yale University Music Library, Archival Papers: The Quincy Porter Papers
Established by Lois Porter, 1972.
MSS 15   66 boxes, in 12 series; section I contains the correspondences with Porter and over 100 individuals, including Barber.

Box 13, Folder 167

[Porter 1]   May 7, 1962, Porter to Barber
Porter invites Barber to replace Elliott Carter for a year as visiting professor at Yale and states the teaching duties. He wishes that their "paths might cross a little more often."

Box 1, Folder 2

[Porter 2]   May 19, 1962, Barber to Porter
In reply, Barber thanks Porter for the offer but says that it does not interest him. He would prefer to "see composition students through" all four years. He also wishes that their paths might cross more often. [Heyman, p. 204.]

William Schuman

Schuman (1910–1992) was a prominent American composer, president of the Juilliard School of Music from 1945 to 1962, and a friend and colleague of Barber's beginning in the late 1930s. Schuman also succeeded Carl Engel as director of publications at G. Schirmer (which published both his and Barber's works) and later served as their special editorial consultant.

New York Public Library: Performing Arts Division: The Papers and Records of William Schuman
Letters between Barber and William Schuman
Most of Schuman's letters to Barber are typed. The letters are usually addressed "Dear Sam," but seem to end more formally, with "faithfully, William Schuman;" yet these are carbon copies retained by Schuman for his files. It is likely that the original letter ended with a handwritten signature, probably just "Bill."

Series I: JPB 87–33

Box 6, folder 3, Barber 1/11/50 to 10/6/60

[Schu 1]   Undated, but before February 11, 1947 and probably close to Jan. 1, Barber to Schuman
Barber asks Schuman if he can write to Paul Kletzki, Clarens (Monteux) Switzerland. "I'm sure he'd like to hear from you. Happy New Year."

[Schu 2]   February 11, 1947, Schuman to Barber
Schuman thanks him for sending Kletzki's address, and asks if he has met John Verrall, "our new music editor" at G. Schrimer. [Schuman was also working for Schirmer at the time.]

[Schu 3]   April 8, 1947, postcard from Barber to Schuman
Barber says that he is finishing up a new piece. [This could be *Knoxville: Summer of 1915.*] He says that Verrall seems capable and very nice.

[Schu 4]   April 29, 1947, Schuman to Barber
Schuman asks if he can come for a visit as soon as his school duties are over. [These duties are apparently teaching students at the Berkshire School; see (Kouss 56).] He mentions possible new biographies of contemporary composers and that Schirmer insists that the two of them, "the firm's stars," be the first two.

[Schu 5]   August 31, 1949, Barber to Schuman
Barber says that he will send him a copy of his Sonata [the Piano Sonata, completed a few months earlier]. He also extends his best wishes for Schuman's new ballet. [This is probably *Judith*, choreographed by Martha Graham, which later had its premiere on Jan. 4, 1950.]

[Schu 6]   January 18, 1950, Schuman to Barber
Schuman extends Barber an invitation to teach at the Julliard summer school. [Heyman, p. 204.]

[Schu 7]   January 1950, telegram from Barber to Schuman
Barber feels that he must decline Schuman's offer. [The exact date is difficult to read but must be shortly after the invitation.] [See (Schu 6)]

[Schu 8]   February 9, 1950, telegram from Barber to Schuman
Barber wishes he could be present at the performance of the Boston Symphony Orchestra. [For the premier of Schuman's Violin Concerto, scheduled for the next day. Isaac Stern was the violinist with Charles Munch conducting.]

[Schu 9]   June 12, 1951, Barber to Schuman
Barber asks Schuman to harmonize "Happy Birthday" for Mary Curtis Zimbalist (who endowed the Curtis Institute). Included in the folder is Schuman's

contribution, a chromatic version of the tune. A copy of this, with ten other contributions (but not Barber's) may be found in the Viles dissertation, "Mary
Louise Curtis Bok Zimbalist" (Item 500), appendix F, pp. 225–258.

[Schu 10]   July 30, 1951, Barber to Schuman
Barber tells him about all the various "Happy Birthday" variations. [This letter
looks like an exact copy of the one he sent to Copland on the same date. See
(Cop 3).]

[Schu 11]   August 30, 1951, Mary Curtis Zimbalist to Schuman
Mrs. Zimbalist thanks him for his contribution to her birthday gala. [See her similar letter to Virgil Thomson (Th 3).]

[Schu 12]   September 17, 1951, Schuman to Barber
Schuman is pleased that Mrs. Zimbalist's birthday greeting worked out so hand-
somely, but is a bit embarrassed by his own "modest" contribution.

[Schu 13]   November 27, 1951, postcard from Barber to Schuman
Virgil Thomson asks a group to lunch. [This looks like the same invitation as the
postcard in the Copland collection (Cop 5) postmarked the day before.]

[Schu 14]   April 1, 1952, Schuman to Barber
Schuman talks about the full-page announcement of ASCAP and suggests that it
is time for another lunch of the "Terrible Five." [The group clearly consists of
Barber, Copland, Schuman, and Thomson. Who is the fifth? Is it Menotti?]

[Schu 15]   October 27, 1953, Schuman to Barber
Schuman praises Barber's *Hermit Songs,* saying that no one has "the particular
gift that you display in these new works." [Heyman, p. 342.]

[Schu 16]   November 20, 1953, Barber to Schuman
Barber thanks Schuman for his letter [Schu 5], calling it the "nicest I've ever
received." [Heyman, p. 342.]

[Schu 17]   Undated but probably October 1956, telegram from Barber to
Schuman
Barber congratulates Schuman on the success of the festival [what is this?]. He
says that he has been confined to his studio with a "painful attack of operaitis."
[He is undoubtedly working on *Vanessa,* making the date most likely to be not
long before (Schu 5).]

[Schu 18]   November 7, 1956, Schuman to Barber
He is pleased that Barber's new opera [*Vanessa*] will be produced by the Metro-
politan Opera next year. He mentions that he never succeeded at interesting the
Met in contemporary American operas.

[Schu 19]   December 1, 1956, Barber to Schuman
He mentions that the fourth act of *Vanessa* is not yet complete. Maria Callas is not interested. [She actually came to Capricorn to sing through early stages of the score, but apparently did not like it.] [Heyman, p. 384.]

[Schu 20]   March [no exact date given], 1958, from Schuman's secretary to Barber
The recording he promised Barber is being sent. [No indication as to what recording that is.]

[Schu 21]   September 21, 1960, Schuman to Barber
Schuman promises that he won't say anything bad about Barber. [Is this for an interview; an article?]

[Schu 22]   October 3, 1960, Barber to Schuman
Barber too would say nice things about Schuman, but would prefer to say them without so many listeners.

[Schu 23]   October 6, 1960, Schuman to Barber
Schuman thanks Barber for his "lovely note" and looks forward to seeing him.

Series 2, Box 49, Folder 1   10/3/62 to 2/5/68

[Schu 24]   October 3, 1962, Barber to Schuman
Barber says he likes hearing his Piano Concerto in Lincoln Center with the "raising and lowering of clouds like Zeus." [This is an acoustical feature of Philharmonic (later Avery Fischer) Hall.] [Heyman, p. 419.]

[Schu 25]   October 8, 1962, Schuman to Barber
Barber's letter made him realize again how sorry he is that they meet so rarely, and they should do something about it.

[Schu 26]   October 18, 1963, Schuman to Barber
Schuman hears that the paper Barber prepared was "simply brilliant," and his delivery of it was "charming and most effective." He looks forward to seeing the script of it. [What paper? Where did he present it?]

[Schu 27]   March 12, 1964, Barber to Schuman
Barber says, "isn't it nice they [probably the critics] give "an occasional nod to us? You old conservative, you."

[Schu 28]   March 13, 1964, Schuman to Barber
It is silly that they so rarely meet. He says "that critic" [who?] seems to think that "quality has to do with vocabulary, or some such nonsense."

[Schu 29]   June 1, 1964, Schuman to Barber
Schuman is overjoyed that Barber will write a new opera for the new Metropolitan opera house. [This as yet untitled work, of course, will become *Antony and Cleopatra*.] [Heyman, p. 434.]y

[Schu 30]   June 13, 1964, Barber to Schuman
Barber says it is always good to have good wishes from one's friends, but Schuman's message meant particularly much to him: "Extra Special!"

[Schu 31]   September 8, 1966, Schuman to Barber
Schuman says that his heart already beats faster "on those opening chords."

[He is possibly referring to the opening chorus of *Antony and Cleopatra,* which had its debut a week later. Did Schuman attend a rehearsal and hear those chords?]

[Schu 32]   October 7, 1966, Schuman to Barber
Schuman asks Barber to send a signed picture for his studio wall. He encloses a photo taken at the opening of the new Met.

[Schu 33]   November 14, 1966, Barbara Mitchell to Schuman
Mitchell, Barber's secretary, forwards the photograph he requested and extends Barber's good wishes.

[Schu 34]   February 2, 1968, telegram from Barber to Schuman, care of the Philadelphia Orchestra
Barber says that he is sorry that he will miss Schuman's Symphony. Best wishes for its success. [The Philadelphia Orchestra performed Schuman's 7th Symphony on that day.]

[Schu 35]   February 5, 1968, Schuman to Barber
Schuman hopes that during Rudolf Serkin's tenure, Curtis will become an institute, "not just a personal vehicle." [Serkin became the director of the Curtis Institute at the beginning of 1968 after 28 years of "family" leadership by Efrem Zimbalist, Mary Curtis Bok's second husband.]

Series 3, Box 93, Folder 15   12/20/74 to 1/18/80

[Schu 36]   December 20, 1974, Schuman to Barber
Schuman encloses a clipping from *Saturday Review/World* (September 7, 1974), p. 6, in hopes that it "might at least amuse" him. [It is not included in the file, but it is a letter Schuman wrote to Irving Kolodin (from the "Letters from Readers" column) thanking him for his recent article on Barber, "Farewell to Capricorn" [see Item 274]. He commends Kolodin for his evaluation of Barber's

music and agrees that his music is "not sufficiently appreciated." He also gives his ideas on vocabulary vs. quality, somewhat like the views expressed in the letter (Schu 28).]

[Schu 37]   April 10, 1975, Barber to Schuman
Barber says his position is "hopeless" and can't be improved and thanks Schuman for his "charming note." [Is this hopeless situation a personal crisis? It might involve the sale of his and Menotti's home, Capricorn, which took place during this period.]

[Schu 38]   May 30,1979, Schuman to Barber
Schuman is emotionally moved after hearing the PBS telecast of *Vanessa* and says that the last pages are "among the finest of operatic literature." He also enjoyed *Souvenirs* and "just about anything you write." [Heyman, p. 391.]

[Schu 39]   June 2, 1979, Barber to Schuman
Barber thanks him for being "so kind to his music," and says that he could never write a crescendo like the one in Schuman's Third Symphony. [Heyman, p. 391.]

[Schu 40]   January 18, 1980, Schuman to Barber
Schuman tells Barber that he is sorry he couldn't attend last Sunday's concert. He encloses an "irreverent but affectionate nonsense" for Mrs. Belmont's 100th birthday. [Mrs. August Belmont was an important member of the Board of the Metropolitan Opera for many years.]

[Schu 41]   March 8, 1980, Barber to Schuman
Barber tells Schuman that he is sorry he cannot accept the MacDowell Colony medal (in person). He is too ill to travel to Peterborough for the ceremony, but he does appreciate the honor.

[Schu 42]   May 8, 1980, Schuman to Barber
Schuman asks if Menotti could attend the MacDowell ceremony (on August 24) and speak on Barber's behalf? Or could he send a written response which he (Schuman) might read? [Schuman was then chairman of the MacDowell Colony. Barber indeed sent him a response: the exact same anecdote about Edith Sitwell that he used to accept the Gold Medal of the American Academy and Institute of the Arts. See (Acad 6)].

Fabien Sevitzky

Sevitzky (1891–1967), whose real name was Koussevitzky, was the nephew of Serge Koussevitzky, both of whom were conductors and double bass players. Among other conducting positions, Sevitzky was leader of his own group, The Philadelphia Chamber String Sinfonietta, during the 1930s.

Library of Congress: Sevitzky Collection ML 94. S55 LM 110/18/D/2

[Sev 1]   October 24, 1938, Barber to Sevitzky
Barber apologizes for some misunderstanding about *Adagio for Strings*.
[Sevitzky evidently wanted to perform it with his Chamber String Sinfonietta.]

[Sev 2]   December 7, 1938, Sevitzky to Barber
Sevitsky says he was disturbed about what happened to *Adagio for Strings* for his
concert but is satisfied with Barber's explanation.

Harold D. Spivacke

Spivacke (1904–1977) was assistant chief librarian of the Music Division of the
Library of Congress from 1934 to 1937, while Oliver Strunk was chief librarian.
Spivacke succeeded him in that position in 1937 and stayed there until 1972.

Library of Congress, Music Division: Old Correspondence Collection

[Spiv 1]   June 20, 1943, Barber to Spivacke
Barber requests some recordings of American folksongs that are housed in the
archives at the Library of Congress. [Heyman, p. 234.]

[Spiv 2]   June 23, 1943, Spivacke to Barber
Spivacke replies that these recordings cannot be given away, but sends a catalogue listing the albums and their prices. [Heyman, p. 234.]

[Spiv 3]   July 23, 1943, Mary Jean Kempner, Associate Feature Editor of
Vogue magazine, to Spivacke
At Barber's request Kempner sends Spivacke a manuscript. [Even though the title
is not mentioned, it is the *Adagio for Strings*. There is no apparent reason why an
editor of *Vogue* magazine should have the manuscript in the first place.]

[Spiv 4]   July 27, 1943, Spivacke to Kempner
Spivacke thanks Kempner for sending the manuscript.

[Spiv 5]   July 27, 1943, Spivacke to Barber
He tells Barber that he has received the manuscript of *Adagio for Strings* [the first
time the title is used in this sequence of letters].

[Spiv 6]   July 28, 1943, Barber to Spivacke
Barber indicates that the red markings in the score are by Toscanini, who used it
for the first performance. [Heyman, p. 168.] [This letter is on microfilm, Music
1907, as a part of Item 20. The original no longer belongs to the Spivacke file but
is probably housed with the original manuscripts of Item 20.]

[Spiv 7]   November 5, 1943, Barber to Spivacke
Barber tells Spivacke that he has been assigned to compose some "serious music"

for the Air Corps and says that it is "so wonderful to be composing again." [This work eventually becomes the *Second Symphony.* The *Commando March,* the only other possibility, had already been completed the previous February.]

[Spiv 8]   June 14, 1951[2?], Mrs. Willem Willecke to Spivacke
Mrs. Willecke encloses a carbon copy of the letter sent to Samuel Barber. Invitations will be mailed out soon. [It is difficult to know what these invitations are for; a concert at the Library of Congress? It is too early for the recital of *Hermit Songs.*]

[Spiv 9]   November 21, 1951, Spivacke to Barber
Spivacke asks Barber if he has accepted membership on Executive Board of the International Music Council of UNESCO.

[Spiv 10]   November 21, 1951, telegram from Barber to Spivacke
In this somewhat confusing telegram Barber says, "Sorry no quartet; will let you know if ever."

[Spiv 11]   July 6, 1954, Spivacke to Barber
Spivacke confirms the engagement for a concert with Leontyne Price at South Mountain in Pittsfield, Mass., on July 17. [There is no mention of the *Hermit Songs.*]

[Spiv 12]   November 10, 1960, Barber to Spivacke
Barber tells him that he has just completed the score of *Die Natali.* [Heyman, p. 407.]

[Spiv 13]   November 21, 1960, Spivacke to Barber
He reminds Barber that the commission letter requires the composer to <u>donate</u> his manuscript. He asks him to consult his accountant to see if the donation can be deducted on his income tax.

[Spiv 14]   March 20, 1961, Barber to Spivacke
Barber says that he will send the original manuscript of *Die Natali* to be deposited in the Serge Koussevitzky Collection.

[Spiv 15]   April 3 1961, Spivacke to Barber
Spivacke is delighted that Barber will send him the manuscript of *Die Natali* and says that he will arrange payment. [The holograph of this manuscript is on microfilm Music 1811, Item 2, as a part of the Koussevitzsky Collection.]

Oliver Strunk

Strunk (1901–1980) was chief librarian of the music division of the Library of Congress from 1934 to 1937.

Library of Congress, Music Division: Old Correspondence Collection

[Str 1]   March 2, 1937, Miss Daniels (first name illegible), secretary to Mr. Engels, at Schirmer, to Strunk
Barber's secretary asks to whom the score and parts of the String Quartet should be sent. The parts should be ready in about a week.

[Str 2]   March 3, 1937, Strunk to Barber
Strunk is considering a performance of the String Quartet at the Library of Congress or elsewhere in Washington on April 20. [Heyman, p. 154.]

[Str 3]   March 16, 1937, Barber to Strunk
Barber sends the first two movements of his String Quartet and says he will send the third movement later. [Heyman, p.155.]

[Str 4]   c. March 19, 1937, Strunk to Barber
Strunk acknowledges the arrival of the String Quartet and says that there is no hurry for the third movement. [Heyman, p. 155.]

[Str 5]   c. April 9, 1937, Barber to Strunk
Barber is pleased that the String Quartet will be performed and lists the tempi. He also gives a list of the people who should be sent invitations. [Heyman, p. 156.]

[Str 6]   April 12, 1937, Strunk to Barber
Strunk confirms that the invitations have been sent. [Heyman, p. 156.]

Deems Taylor

Taylor (1885–1966) was a prominent American composer, critic, and writer on music. He was the president of ASCAP from 1942 to 1948 and its director from 1933 to 1966.

Yale University Music Library, Archival Papers: Deems Taylor Papers (not yet catalogued)
MSS 66

[Tay 1]   October 3, 1941, postcard from Barber to Taylor
Barber thanks Taylor for his telegram about The Overture to *The School for Scandal*. The radio reception was bad but the tempi were fine and it sounded like a good performance. He looks forward to "your newest" in Philadelphia. [What work is this?]

Virgil Thomson

Thomson (1896–1989) was a prominent American composer and music critic, working for many years at the *New York Herald Tribune*. While Thomson was somewhat critical of Barber as a composer during the 1940s, they became friends during the 1950s and remained so until Barber's death.

Yale University Music Library, Archival Papers: The Virgil Thomson papers
Established by Thomson in 1978.
MSS 29   155 boxes, in 9 series, III contains correspondence totaling over 40,000 pages, containing letters to and from important American and French cultural figures since 1920, including Barber.

[Th 1]   June 12, 1951, Barber to Thomson
Barber asks Thomson to join in the cooperative project of writing a harmonization of "happy birthday" for Mrs. Zimbalist. [See letter of the same date sent to Schuman (Schu 9)].

[Th 2]   July 30, 1951, Barber to Thomson
Barber thanks Thomson for his contribution to the Zimbalist album. He is happy with the many contributions. He sent similar letters to Copland [Cop 3] and Schuman [Schu 10].

[Th 3]   August 30, 1951, Mrs. Zimbalist to Thomson
Mrs. Zimbalist extends her thanks and appreciation for his "happy and gay" contribution. [She presumably sent similar letters to all the contributors. For example, see (Schu 11)].

[Th 4]   July 19 1953, Barber to Thomson
A diverse letter of many ideas. Barber says that he has been reading letters to Gertrude Stein. He laments the death of his uncle Sidney Homer. The U. N. meeting in Europe was awful. He comments on the news of Thomson leaving the *New York Herald Tribune*. The ballet at Cologne was danced quite well. [What ballet?] P.S. "My ASCAP check is <u>smaller</u> after all this talk." [This refers to the controversy over royalties that came to a head a year earlier. See letters to Copland (Cop 4 and Cop 6), Schuman (Schu 14), and Edith Evans Braun (Braun 3)].

[Th 5]   c. Feb 1954, postcard, Barber to Thomson
Barber prefers that Thomson not conduct the orchestral version of *Souvenirs* until after the premiere of the ballet version.

[Th 6]   No date but probably early January 1958
Not a letter but Schirmer's printed invitation to supper at the Ambassador Hotel, which honors Barber following the world premiere of his opera *Vanessa.*

[Th 7]   January 18, 1962, Barber to Thomson
Barber thanks Thomson for "the holiday cheer" he sent them (intended for "imbibing") and invites him to Capricorn for a visit that is "long overdue."

[Th 8]   January 9, 1963, Barber to Thomson
Barber says there is no pressure to join the AGAC. The purpose is to establish a "basic minimum agreement" between composer and publisher.

[Th 9]   1965[?], Barber to Thomson
A strange note about an accident six months ago. Barber says he feels "like Marat in his bath."

[Th 10]   May 4, 1970, Thomson to Barber
Thomson encloses a "fan letter for you delectation." [It is not included in the folder.]

[Th 11]   February 10, 1978, Barber to Thomson
"The Nature of Melody" has never been published. [A reply to an inquiry about a book?] There is a new discography by David Hall. Barber mentions his illness.

[Th 12]   February 9, 1981, A copy of *In Memoriam* program for Barber's service, from St. Bartholomew's Church, NY
This is presumably Thomson's own copy.

Related letters concerning Thomson and Barber in Thomson Papers

MSS 29A   Series IVA   Box 90, Folder 7
Document relating to the American Academy and Institute of the Arts and Letters.

[Th 13]   September 10, 1979, Thomson to Barber
Barber asks Thomson to second the nomination of Lee Hoiby for membership in the Institute. He was not elected the previous time. See Academy letters [Acad 28] for the original request to "second" from Mary M. Miller.

MSS 29   Series IVA   Box 98, Folder 83
This file contains a series of letters between Thomson and David J. Oppenheim, Music Director of the Masterworks Division of Columbia Records, regarding the recording of Barber works.

[Th 14]   October 19, 1950, Oppenheim to Thomson
Oppenheim asks if Thomson knows what Barber work is to be recorded, and who Barber wants to perform it.

[Th 15]   Undated, but probably late 1954 or early 1955
Barber's *Hermit Songs* are added in pencil to a printed list of pieces to be recorded in the Modern American Music Series in 1955.

[Th 16]   Undated but slightly later than [Th 15] above
This document seems to confirm the recording of *Hermit Songs* released June 6, 1955 as Col. ML 4988 (with Haieff's String Quartet No. 1). This is the recording with Leontyne Price and Barber (see Item 570).

Virgil Thomson/John Fahey correspondence about Barber

John Fahey communicated with several people when working on his dissertation about Barber's music (see Item 356). The following letters are between him and Thomson. Fahey's original letter of inquiry is not included here, but does appear in the appendix of his dissertation.

[Th 17]   November 29, 1982, Thomson to Fahey
Thomson replies to various inquiries for Fahey's thesis, but questions the validity of his text-and-music investigation. [This letter also appears in the appendix to Fahey's thesis.]

[Th 18]   December 7, 1982, Fahey to Thomson
Fahey asks Thomson about various people in Barber's life: e.g. Gama Gilbert, Dario and Susanna Cecchi, Florence Kimball, Robert Horan, and Pack Browning.

[Th 19]   December 14, 1982, Thomson to Fahey
In his reply, Thomson discussed Florence Kimball and mentions that Robert Horan teaches at UC Berkeley. He doesn't know Pat (sic) Browning.

LETTERS TO INSTITUTIONS

New York: American Academy of Arts and Letters

The National Institute of Arts and Letters was founded in 1898 and The American Academy of Arts and Letters in 1904. They merged in 1976 and became known as The American Academy and Institute of Arts and Letters. In 1993 the organization took on the single name, American Academy of Arts and Letters

The file on Samuel Barber consists of 163 items. Correspondence 1940–81 regarding membership in Institute and Academy (53 letters to Barber, 11 letters, 4 cards from Barber; 14 letters, 2 cards about Barber; 46 RSVP forms), 4 address verification forms; 2 nomination documents; 5 pages of biographical material; 25 press clippings, including the *New York Times* obituary.

The letters involve correspondences between Barber and various members of the academy including: Douglas Moore, Mark Van Doren, Glenway Wescott, and Barbara Tuchman, presidents; Felicia Geffen, assistant to the president; Mrs. Matthew Josephson, librarian; Van Wyck Brooks, Marchette Chute, and Leon Edel, secretaries.

Nomination and honors documents for Barber

[Acad 1]   June 7, 1940
A proposal to nominate Barber to the National Institute of Arts and Letters is made by Walter Damrosch and seconded by Deems Taylor and Daniel Gregory Mason.

[Acad 2]   July 1, 1958, Douglas Moore to Felicia Geffen
Douglas Moore tells Felicia Geffen that Walter Piston is the key for Barber's
nomination to the American Academy of Arts and Letters.

[Acad 3]   August 29, 1958
A proposal to nominate Barber to American Academy.

[Acad 4]   November 28, 1958, Mark Van Doren to Barber
Van Doren tells Barber that he has been elected to the Academy. The ceremony is
to be held on December 5, 1958.

[Acad 5]   December 5, 1958, note about the induction ceremony
Barber fills the thirtieth chair, vacated by Henry D. Sedgewick.

[Acad 6]   Jan. 14 1960, Geffen to Barber
Geffen sends Barber his medallion of membership.

Gold medal of the Academy

[Acad 7]   March 3, 1976, Barber to Mr. Salisbury
Barber says he is honored at being chosen to receive The Gold Medal of the Academy in Music for 1976.

[Acad 8]   April 15, 1976, Barber's secretary to Mary M. Miller
She gives a list of names (probably guests at the ceremony), including Charles
Turner and Manfred Ibel.

[Acad 9]   May 6, 1976, Miller to Barber
She asks Barber if he could send a copy of his acceptance speech for the ceremony
of May 19 and mentions that William Schuman will present him with the medal.

[Acad 10]   May 19, 1976
This is a copy of Barber's acceptance speech for the medal in which he tells of his
meeting with Dame Edith Sitwell at W. H. Auden's house.

[William Schuman's tribute is printed in Proceedings of the American Academy
and Institute of Arts and Letters, 1977, p. 26. Quoted in Heyman, p. 509, 511.
The Sitwell story is basically the same as the one read at his MacDowell award
ceremony and is told in the newspaper account in the *New York Times* (see
Item 34).]

[Acad 11]   May 8, 1979, insurance document
The insurance company asks about the value of the gold medal that Barber
received at the ceremony.

[Acad 12]   May 16, 1979, Miller to Accounting Management
Miller states that the current value of the gold medal is $1,112.

Exhibition of May–June 1959

[Acad 13]   No date, but probably the end of March 1959; Mrs. Matthew Josephson to Barber
She asks Barber if he would participate in the exhibition. It would display one of Barber's compositions in various stages: the original manuscript, a blueprint, and the published score.

[Acad 14]   April 6, 1959, Mrs. Josephson to Barber
She acknowledges the receipt of three sheets from the manuscript of *Vanessa,* insuring them for $200.

[Acad 15]   April 27, 1959, Josephson to G. Schirmer Co.
She acknowledges the receipt of the blueprint score, insuring it for $50.

[Acad 16]   June 18, 1959, Miller to G. Schrimer Co.
At the end of the exhibition, she returns the blueprint score and tells them that the first page was used.

[Acad 17]   June 19, 1959, Miller to G. Schirmer Co.
A letter confirming that she has sent the blueprint score, and asks if Schirmer has received it.

[Acad 18]   June 18, 1959, G. Schirmer Co. to American Academy
Schirmer confirms the receipt of the blueprint score. (These letters [Acad 17 and 18] show overlapping dates.)

[Acad 19]   September 14, 1959, Miller to Barber
She tells Barber that they are keeping the three sheets from *Vanessa* in the safe.

[Acad 20]   September 23, 1959, Miller to Barber
Miller tells Barber that she is returning the three sheets from *Vanessa.*

[Acad 21]   September 26, 1959, postcard Barber to Miller
Barber acknowledges the receipt of the sheets.

Barber's nominations and recommendations for others

[Acad 22]   February 6, 1948, Barber to Van Wyck Brooks
Barber recommends Robert Horan for the Institute Academic Grant.

[Acad 23]   November 9, 1949, Assistant secretary to Barber
The author admits that Richard Rodgers name was omitted from list of candidates.

[Acad 24]   April 11, 1957, [Geffen] to Barber
She asks if Barber could write a short citation for Lee Hoiby.

[Acad 25]   April 14, 1957, Barber to Geffen
Barber's response about Hoiby states: "his fresh and lyric approach conceals an intellectual strength of exceptional promise."

[Acad 26]   May 2, 1961, Geffen to Barber
Geffen asks Barber to nominate Henry Cowell for membership to the Academy. Barber returns the same letter by saying he is "happy to."

[Acad 27]   March 21, 1973, Geffen to Barber
Copland has nominated William Schuman for membership in the Academy. Geffen asks if Barber would second the nomination.

[Acad 28]   June 12, 1978, Miller to Barber
Miller asks Barber if he would second the nomination of Lee Hoiby for membership in the Institute. Barber returns the same letter saying, "very happy to second."

[Acad 29]   June 4, 1979, Miller[?] to Barber
She asks Barber if he could second the nomination of Louise Nevelson for membership in the Academy. [There is no documented reply.]

[Acad 30]   August 8, 1979, Miller to Barber
She asks Barber if he could second the nomination of Dominick Argento for nomination to the Institute. [There is no documented reply.]

Committee work

[Acad 31]   January 30, 1956, Louise Bogan to Barber
She thanks him for serving on the Departmental Committee for three years.

[Acad 32]   February 5, 1959, Glenway Wescott, president to Barber
He asks Barber to accept a three-year term on the Grants Committee, which meets once a year. [There appears to be no reply, but Barber must have accepted.] See [Acad 34] below.

[Acad 33]   January 2, 1962, Barber to Geffen
Barber says that he cannot accept a new committee assignment because he plans to be in Europe half of each of the next three years. [Heyman, p. 462.]

[Acad 34]   January 31, 1962, unsigned author, probably Marchette Chute, secretary, to Barber
Barber is off the Grants Committee, and is now appointed to the Departmental Committee.

[Acad 35]   February 2, 1962, Marchette Chute to Barber
Chute thanks Barber for serving on the Grants Committee for the last three years.

[Acad 36]   May 8, 1963, Geffen to Barber

Geffen informs Barber of the meeting on May 21. The same letter is returned with a note saying that he can't make it.

[Acad 37]   December 21, 1963, Postcard from Barber to the Institute
Barber says that he has received only envelopes, with no ballots in them.

[Acad 38]   November 24, 1964, Geffen to Barber
Geffen promises Barber that there will be a better balloting procedure next year.

[Acad 39]   February 9, 1965, Leon Edel to Barber
Edel thanks Barber for serving three years on Departmental Committee.

[Acad 40]   February 14, 1965, Geffen to Barber
Geffen tells Barber that the Grants Committee has already been selected. [Although no letters document it, it sounds as if Barber wanted to change from the Departmental Committee back to the Grants Committee.]

[Acad 41]   January 22, no year [but possibly 1967], Barber to Geffen
Barber declines service on Departmental Committee because he will be frequently in Europe during the next three years.

[Acad 42]   February 4, 1970, Geffen to Barber
Geffen tells Barber that he has been appointed to the Departmental Committee for the next three years; the letter is returned with the word "declined" written in pencil across the top.

The death of Samuel Barber

[Acad 43]   January 26, 1981, Barbara Tuchman, president to the family of Samuel Barber
The Academy extends its sympathy upon the death of Samuel Barber.
(Also included are two copies of the formal announcement of Barber's death.)

About possible tribute to Samuel Barber

(Documents in one plastic folder)

[Acad 44]   February 24, 1981, David Diamond to Academy
This is a tentative tribute to Barber from David Diamond, stating that Barber's death is a serious loss. He will do an official tribute if Menotti cannot or won't.

[Acad 45]   March 10, 1981, Miller to Menotti
Miller asks Menotti if he could write a commemorative tribute on Barber for the next luncheon meeting on December 4 [nearly nine months away].

[Acad 46]   April 2, 1981, Doris Woolfe, American Opera Center, to Miller
Menotti says that he would love to write a tribute, but cannot at this moment. He

doesn't want to do a hasty job. He suggests Mr. Wittke or Dr. Heinsheimer [both from G. Schirmer].

[Acad 47]   April 6, 1981, Miller to Woolfe
Miller still hopes that Menotti can write a tribute; it will be published as a part of the Academy proceedings.

[Acad 48]   October 16, 1981, Miller to Woolfe
Miller asks if she can announce Menotti's tribute. If he cannot attend the meeting, perhaps a colleague could read it.

[Acad 49]   November 30, 1981, Miller to Menotti
Miller tells Menotti that she is sorry he cannot have his tribute ready for the meeting on December 4, but if he can write one between December 17 and the end of the year, it still can be published in the proceedings.

[Acad 50]   December 30, 1981, Miller to Menotti
Miller asks if Menotti's tribute is ready. If so, she will delay the publication of the proceedings.

[Acad 51]   January 11, 1982, Menotti to Miller
Menotti much regrets that his tribute is not ready, but promises it will be for the next issue of the proceedings [i.e. almost a year later!].

[Acad 52]   March 17, 1982, Miller to Menotti
Miller again asks Menotti if he has completed the tribute. If he has, it can be read at the December 3 meeting.

[Acad 53]   September 23, 1982, Miller to Menotti
Miller, one last time, asks Menotti if he could send a tribute within the next month or so.
There is no evidence that Menotti ever wrote that tribute. Nothing appears in the 1982 proceedings of the Academy or in any issue after that.

Miscellaneous

[Acad 54]   February 10, 1946, Barber to Geffen [?]
Barber submits the name of Robert Horan to the Institute, calling him an "extra-ordinarily talented" poet. [Heyman, p. 217. She says Geffen is the recipient of the letter, but this seems too early.]

[Acad 55]   December 12, 1958, Geffen to Barber
Geffen asks Barber to please send her a bill for his recent travel expenses.

[Acad 56]   December 27, 1965, Geffen to Barber
Geffen tells Barber that the information in the biography of *Who's Who* is incorrect regarding his Pulitzer prizes.

[Acad 57]   December 31, 1965, Barber to Geffen
Barber tells Geffen that a mistake occurred when the Pulitzer Traveling Fellowships of 1935–36 were mistaken for actual Pulitzer prizes.

[Acad 58]   November 19, 1971, Geffen to Anita Goek [sp?], picture editor of Encyclopedia Britannica
Geffen says that the Academy has no photograph of Samuel Barber. [This is evidently in answer to a request for one.]

New York: American Academy in Rome

The Library of the Academy contains over 120,000 volumes in the fields of classical studies and the history of art and architecture. It contains a rare book room and the Arthur Ross Reading Room.

The Academy Centennial Directory contains a one-paragraph biography of Barber (p. 20), which mentions his studies, career, employment, fellowships, honors, and awards. It concludes with a list of his important works.

[Rome 1]   January 31, 1935, Application for Fellowship in Musical Composition
Barber submits two of his works: "Music for a Scene by Shelley" and a Sonata in C Minor for Cello and Piano.

[Rome 2]   September 13, 1935, a generic letter from Dr. S. Barber (Sam's father)
This letter certifies that Samuel Barber has had a vaccination for smallpox, and an inoculation for typhoid.

[Rome 3]   April 1, 1936, Barber to Roscoe Guernsey, Executive Secretary
Barber asks if he could book a passage on the *Paris,* and to please send him Randall Thompson's address.

[Rome 4]   April 2, 1936, Guernsey to French Line
Guernsey asks if Barber could book on the liner, *Paris,* at a 30 percent reduction.

[Rome 5]   April 3, 1936, Guernsey to Barber
Guernsey tells Barber that he has booked passage on the *Paris,* giving the cost and an actual diagram of cabin.

Undated. Academy in Rome Roster: a form filled out by Barber. This was not an application, but more of a report for the Damrosch Fellowship, including the chief works accomplished during this fellowship: in the first year, Symphony in One Movement; in the second year, String Quartet.

[Rome 6]   November 21, 1941, Guernsey to John Walker
This is a brief biography of Barber, listing his works and performances.

[Rome 7]   March 14, 1943, Laurence P. Roberts, Director to Barber
The Academy will pay traveling expenses ($2,500) and for services next spring. These services entail monitoring the progress of the Music Fellows and giving them criticism and technical help. Roberts tells Barber that during the remainder of the time he may do his own work and travel.

[Rome 8]   June 13, 1946, Barber's father to Academy
Barber's father presents a brief biography of his son, primarily concerning his three years in the military and his "Symphony dedicated to the Army Air Forces."

[Rome 9]   February 28, 1947, telegram from Roberts to Barber
Roberts is very anxious to see Barber about the possibility of accepting a residence at the Academy in Rome next spring.

[Rome 10]   April 6, 1947, Barber to Roberts
Barber replies that he is happy to accept the residence at the Academy next spring.

[Rome 11]   May 14, 1947, Mary T. Williams, Executive Secretary, to Barber
She asks Barber for a list of American musical works, to be included in the library in Rome.

[Rome 12]   July 17, 1947, Barber to Williams
Barber gives the requested list, "just a start-off," including: all Schirmer Study Scores, all the works of Harris, Schuman, Piston, Bloch, "and me." He also lists several recordings, including many of his own: Toscanini's *Adagio for Strings,* Ormandy's *Essay for Orchestra,* Walter's *First Symphony.*

[Rome 13]   July 29, 1947, Williams to Barber
Williams thanks Barber for the list of scores and recordings [Rome 12].

[Rome 14]   January 22, 1948, Williams to Passport Division, Department of State
This document certifies that Barber has been appointed to the staff of the American Academy in Rome for four months, beginning March 1, 1948.

[Rome 15]   January 27, 1948, Fugazy Travel Bureau to American Academy
The travel bureau presents a bill for transportation; a suite from New York to Naples, $736; a single from Naples to New York, $430.

[Rome 16]   February 3, 1948, Williams to Barber
Williams asks Barber if he couldn't get a cheaper eastbound passage.

[Rome 17]   February 11, 1948, Williams to Barber
She encloses a check for $500, the first of 5 monthly installments of his stipend.

[Rome 18]   February 12, 1948, postcard Barber to Williams
Barber asks her to send his checks to the Mount Kisco National Bank.

[Rome 19]   February 17, 1948, Williams to Barber
She asks Barber to send a deposit slip from his bank in Mount Kisco.

[Rome 20]   April 29, 1948, Mt. Kisco National Bank to Williams
The bank sends a credit statement of $500.

[Rome 21]   September 14, 1948, Laurence P. Roberts to Barber
Roberts encloses a telephone bill for 117,461 lire, which the Academy has paid. Could you please reimburse?

[Rome 22]   January 25, 1955, Vittoria Bori to Williams
Bori sends Williams five bills for Barber totaling 53,600 lire.

[Rome 23]   February 1, 1955, Williams to Barber
Williams asks Barber to send a check to Mrs. Bori for $86.45 [the 1955 equivalent of 53,600 lire].

[Rome 24]   February 2, 1955, Barber to Williams
Barber encloses the $86.45 and thanks her for the "negative information on Turner." [Is this his close companion, Charles Turner?]

INDEX OF LETTERS

The following is an alphabetical list of various people referred to in the preceding correspondence. Each name is followed by the collection number that was assigned to the letter in this chapter. A second list follows, containing various compositions by Barber that are discussed in the letters.

People

Argento, Dominick	[Acad 30]
Arnold, Gen. Matthew	[Dam 2]; [Dam 3]
Auden, W. H.	[Acad 10]; [Bid 1]
Bax, Arnold	[Cop 2]
Beethoven, Ludwig Van	[Braun 7]; [Th 3]
Belmont, Mrs.	[Schu 40]
Bernstein, Leonard	[Kous 49], [Th 8]
Bloch, Ernst	[Cop 2]; [Rome 12]
Brown, Mrs. Anne [?]	[Kous 44]
Browning, John	[Cop 16]
Browning, Pack	[Th 18]
Callas, Maria	[Schu 19]

Callaway, Paul	[Ellin 1]
Carol, Norman	[Orm 20]
Carter, Elliot	[Porter 1]
Cecchi, Dario & Sussana	[Th 18]
Chavez, Carlos	[Cop 2]
Chopin, Frédéric	Horo [1]
Clarke, Gilmore T.	Acad [3]
Coolidge, Peggy	Spiv [6]
Copland, Aaron	Acad [27]; Rome [12]; Schu [13]; Thom [8]
Cowell, Henry	Acad [26]
Dallapiccola, Luigi	Cop [2]
Damrosch, Walter	Acad [1]
Diamond, David	Acad [45]
Dohnanyi, Ernst von	Cop [2]
Gilbert, Gama	Thom [18]
Gordon, Jacques	Str [1]; Str [2];
Graham, Martha	Kous [51]; Horo [5]
Granger, F [arley?]	Cop [8]
Hall, David	Thom [11]
Harris, Roy	Cop [2]; Rome [12]
Heinsheimer, Hans	Horo [1]
Hindemith, Paul	Cop [2]; Kous [51];
Hoiby, Lee	Acad [24]; Acad [25]; Acad [28]; Thom [13]
Homer, Sidney	Braun [5], Thom [4]
Honegger, Arthur	Cop [2]
Horan, Robert	Acad [22], Thom [18], Thom [19]
Horowitz, Vladimir	Kous [38]; Kous [39];
Ibel, Manfred	Acad [8]; Cop [13]; Cop [14];
Jannsen, Werner	Engel [1]
Joselson, Tedd	Orm [20]
Kimball, Florence	Th [19]
Kletzky, Paul	Schu [1]; Schu [2]

Koussevitzky, Serge	Bid [4]; Cop [1]; Dam [2]; Burgin [1]
Krause, Tom	Orm [21] Orm [22]
La Farge, Christopher	Bid [4]
Levine, James	Orm [20]
McLeish, Archibald	Acad [3]
Martinu, Bohuslav	Cop [2]
Mason, Daniel Gregory	Acad [1]
Menotti, Gian Carlo	Acad [1]; Acad [45-54]; Bern [2]; Bern [5]; Bid [3]; Braun [1]; Braun [2]; Braun [4]; Braun [6]; Braun [7]; Braun [8]; Braun [10]; Braun [11]; Cop [4]; Cop [7]; Cop [8]; Cop [12]; Schu [42]
Meredith, Burgess	Bid [6]
Moore, Douglas	Acad [3]; Cop [4]
Münch, Charles	Burkat [3] Orm [8]
Nevelson, Louise	Acad [29]
Orlando, Orazio	Bern [6]; Cop [19]
Ormandy, Eugene	Bid [6]; Kous [38]; Rome [12]
Piston, Walter	Acad [2]; Acad [3]; Rome [12]
Poon, Audrey	Orm [18], Orm [19] Orm [24] Orm [25]
Price, Leontyne	Braun [6]; Spiv [9]
Rodgers, Richard	Acad [23];
Rodzinsky, Artur	Bid [2]
Saidenberg, Daniel	Cop [1]
Sedgewick, Henry D.	Acad [5]
Serkin, Peter	Braun [10]
Serkin, Rudolph	Schu [35]
Shaw, Robert	Braun [9]
Schuman, William	Acad [9]; Acad [27]; Rome [12]
Shostakovitch, Dimitri	Bid [6];
Sitwell, Dame Edith	Acad [10];
Steber, Eleanor	Kous [51]; Kous [54]
Stein, Gertrude	Thom [4]

Stern, Isaac	Orm [29]
Stravinsky, Igor	Braun [1]; Cop [2]
Szell, George	Kous [36]; Kous [38]
Taylor, Deems	Acad [1]; Acad [3];
Thomas, Dylan	Kous [11]
Thompson, Randall	Rome [3]; Rome [12]
Thomson, Virgil	Cop [5]
Toscanini, Arturo	Bid [4]; Bid [6]; Rome [12]; Spiv [4]
Toscanini, Mrs.	Horo [3]
Tully, Alice	Horo [5]
Turner, Charles	Acad [8]; Cop [12] Rome [24]
Verall, John	Schu [2]; Schu [3]
Von Karajan, Herbert	Burkat [3]
Walter, Bruno	Bid [3]; Bid [6]; Rome [12]
Wilder, Thornton	Kous [51]
Wood, Henry	Spiv [12]
Zimbalist, Mary Curtis;	Schu [9]; Schu [11]; Schu [12]; [Thom 1]

Barber Compositions

Adagio for Strings, Op. 11	Bid [4]; Bid [6]; Braun [7]; Kouss [1]; Kouss [2]; Kouss [3]; Kouss [49]; Rome [12]; Sev [1]; Sev [2]; Spiv [3]; Spiv [2]; Spiv [5]; Spiv [6]
Antony and Cleopatra, Op. 40	Schu [29]; Schu [31]
"Between Dark and Dark"	Bid [7]; Bid [10]
Capricorn Concerto, Op. 21	Cop [1]; Cop [17]; Kouss [36]; Kouss [49]; Rome [12]; Pack [1]
Commando March	Burgin [1] Kouss [16]; Kouss [17]; Kouss [18]
Concerto for Piano and Orchestra, Op. 38	Orm [20]; Orm [21]; Orm [22]; Schu [24]
Concerto for Violin and Orchestra, Op. 14	Bern [5]; Kouss [5]; Orm [20]; Orm [29]; Rome [12]

Concerto for Violoncello and Orchestra, Op. 22	Kouss [40]; Kouss [41]; Kouss [42]; Kouss [43]; Kouss [44]; Kouss [47]; Kouss [48];
Die Natali: Choral Preludes for Christmas, Op. 37	Braun [9]; Orm [8]; Orm [26]; Orm [27]; [27]; Orm [28]; Spiv [12]; Spiv [13]; Spiv [14]; Spiv [15]
Dover Beach, Op 3.	Coo [1]; Coo [2]; Coo [3]
Essay for Orchestra, (No. 1), Op. 12	Dam [1]; Kouss [8]; Kouss [10]; Kouss [12]; Rome [12]
Excursions, Op. 20	Kouss [38]; Kouss [39]; Rome [12]
Fadograph of a Yestern Scene, Op. 44	Braun [11]
Hermit Songs, Op. 29	Braun [6]; Schu [15]; Spiv [11]; Thom [15]; Thom [16]
Knoxville: Summer of 1915, Op. 24	Braun [9]; Kouss [54]; Kouss [57]; Kouss [58]; Kouss [59]; Kouss [60]; Kouss [61]
The Lovers, Op 43	Orm [21]; Orm [22]; Orm [23]
Medea, Op. 23	Braun [7]; Burkat [4]; Burkat [5]; Kouss [52]
Music for a Scene from Shelley, Op. 7	Dam [1]; Rome [1]
Overture to *The School of Scandal* Op. 5	Dam [1]; Kouss [4]; Kouss [7]; Kouss [12]; Taylor [1]
Prayers of Kierkegaard, Op. 30	Braun [6]; Braun [9]; Burkat [1]; Burkat [2]; Burkat [3]; Ellin [1]; Kouss [64]; Orm [22]; Orm [23]
Second Essay for Orchestra, Op. 17	Bid [4]; Bid [7]; Finney [1]; Kouss [9]; Kouss [11]; Kouss [12]; Kouss [38]
Sonata for Piano, Op. 26	Horo [1]; Horo [6] Schu [5]
Sonata for Violoncello and Piano, Op. 6	Coo [2]; Coo [3]; Coo [7]; Rome [1]
Souvenirs, Op. 28	Braun [3]; Thom [5]
A Stopwatch and an Ordnance Map, Op. 15	Bid [1]; Kouss [10]
String Quartet in B minor, Op. 11	Coo [4]; Rome [Roster]; Str [1]; Str [2]; Str [3]; Str [4]; Str [5]; Str [6]; Spiv [10]

Summer Music, Op. 31	Cop [9]; Cop [10]
Symphony No. 1, Op. 9	Dam [4]; Kouss [9]; Kouss [19]; Pack [1]; Rome [Roster]; Rome [12]
Symphony No. 2, Op. 19	Dam [2]; Dam [3]; Dam [4]; Kouss [14]; Kouss [15]; Kouss [18]; Kouss [19]; Kouss [20]; Kouss [21]; Kouss [22]; Kouss [23]; Kouss [24]; Kouss [25]; Kouss [26]; Kouss [27]; Kouss [28]; Kouss [29]; Kouss [30]; Kouss [31]; Kouss [32]; Kouss [33]; Kouss [34]; Kouss [63]; Rome [8]; Spiv [7]
Third Essay for Orchestra, Op. 47	Orm [18]; Orm [25]
Toccata Festiva, Op. 36	Cop [13]; Orm [1]; Orm [5]; Orm [7]; Orm [15]
Vanessa, Op. 32	Acad [14]; Acad [15]; Acad [16]; Acad [17]; Acad [18]; Acad [19]; Acad [20]; Acad [21]; Braun [7]; Burkat [4]; Cop [10; Cop [11]; Schu [17] Schu [18] ; Schu [19] Schu [38]; Thom [6] Orm [22]

Works of Other Composers

Berlioz [unnamed work]	Bern [9]
Britten: *Peter Grimes*	Bern [9]
Copland: *Rodeo*	Cop [1]
Dallapiccola: *Canti del prigione*	Cop [2]
Menotti: *The Consul*	Braun [1]; Braun [10]
Menotti: *Amahl and the Night Visitors*	Braun [4]
Menotti: *Help, Help, the Globolincks*	Braun [8]
Menotti: new opera c. Feb. 1942	Bid [3]
Menotti: new opera c. Aug. 1941	Bern [2]
Schuman: Third Symphony	Schu [39]
Stravinsky: *Danses Concertantes*	Cop [1]

Index of Authors

Authors are arranged alphabetically; the numbers after their names are Item numbers, not page numbers. If the names of these authors appear within a citation, those Item numbers are also included. Names appearing only within a citation (i.e. not as author) are given in a separate index.

Index of Names

ORCHESTRAS AND OTHER PERFORMING GROUPS

(e.g. chamber music, dance troupes, etc.)

Orchestras:

ALPHABETICAL LIST OF
BARBER COMPOSITIONS

OTHER COMPOSERS AND THEIR WORKS

Index of First Lines of Songs and Choral Works